JACK SIMMONS
The
RAILWAYS
OF · BRITAIN

JACK SIMMONS
The
RAILWAYS
OF · BRITAIN

M

MACMILLAN

First published 1986 by
MACMILLAN LONDON LIMITED
4 Little Essex Street London WC2R 3LF
and Basingstoke

Associated companies in Auckland, Delhi,
Dublin, Gaborone, Hamburg, Harare, Hong
Kong, Johannesburg, Kuala Lumpur, Lagos,
Manzini, Melbourne, Mexico City, Nairobi,
New York, Singapore and Tokyo

First edition (Routledge & Kegan Paul) 1961
Reprinted 1962 (with corrections) and 1965
Second edition (Macmillan) 1968
Third edition (Macmillan) 1986

Designed and produced by Sheldrake Press
Limited, 188 Cavendish Road, London
SW12 0DA

EDITOR: SIMON RIGGE
Picture Editor: Eleanor Lines
Deputy Editor: Jane Havell
Art Direction and Book Design: Ivor Claydon,
Bob Hook
Picture Researchers: Elizabeth Loving, Sally
Weatherill
Editorial Assistant: Fenella Dick

Typesetting by SX Composing Limited
Printed in Italy by Imago Publishing
Limited

British Library Cataloguing in Publication
Data
Simmons, Jack, 1915-
The railways of Britain. — 3rd ed.
1. Railroads — Great Britain — History
I. Title
385'.0941 HE3018

ISBN 0-333-40766-0

First endpaper: an electric train crosses the
Ouse Viaduct, just north of Haywards Heath,
East Sussex, on 2 May 1949. This dramatic
37-arch viaduct with its long line of pierced
piers and its groups of Italianate pavilions at
either end was designed by J. U. Rastrick and
David Mocatta and completed in 1841. It still
carries frequent and heavy trains.

Last endpaper: the driver of Stanier 4-6-0 No.
44897 reaches inside the frames of his
locomotive at Carnforth motive power depot,
Lancashire, to replace the cork of an oiling
point in March 1968.

Frontispiece: No. 4087 Cardigan Castle
approaches Saltash station with the 6.55am
Penzance to Paddington express on 23
September 1960. The new DMU in the siding
had recently replaced the steam push-and-pull
service on the Saltash to Plymouth line.

This page: numbered as if for a military
embarkation, nine excursion trains line up at
Blackpool station in 1911 ready to take the
employees of the Bass brewery back to Burton-
on-Trent after their day's outing.

CONTENTS

PREFACE

This is a new, and considerably changed, version of a book that was written 25 years ago and somewhat revised for a second edition, published in 1968.

Its original purpose was to provide a brief general history of railways in Great Britain (excluding Ireland, which lay outside its scope), together with an account of their civil and mechanical engineering and of their operation. It was a visual as well as a literary study, including four pieces of historical description called 'Railways on the Ground'. These were accounts of three journeys over railway lines built in the Victorian age as well as a detailed look at the railway system of a single county, Suffolk. The book finished with an account of the sources of knowledge of railway history and with a list of historic locomotives preserved in museums and elsewhere. All these elements except the very last remain in the new edition, though they are differently treated and arranged.

The historical narrative has been altered considerably here and there, and briefly extended to the present day. I have added a new last chapter discussing some of the changes that railways have wrought in Britain, and making a few comparisons with what they have done elsewhere.

The old chapter, 'Railways on the Ground', has been dismembered. Accounts of four journeys are now included, each standing on its own. They are interspersed throughout the book. The first and last of these are much-revised versions of two that figured in the earlier editions. I have removed the description of the journey from Derby to Manchester because most of that line has now been shut down and dismantled; and likewise my account of the railways of Suffolk, where the system has been so much reduced by the closure of secondary and branch lines that it no longer justifies separate treatment. To replace these sections I now offer accounts of fresh journeys, made from Reading to Southampton and from Manchester to Bradford.

Although sketch-maps are provided, to enable the reader to keep his bearings, the way to get the greatest interest out of the journeys is to follow them with the 1:50,000 Ordnance Survey map. The two railway atlases mentioned on p. 249 will also be useful.

In describing the objects to be seen from the train, the words 'left' and 'right' have been avoided, since they have different meanings according to the direction in which the traveller is facing. 'Up' and 'down' have therefore been used instead; and the directions to which they refer are explained at the head of each journey. It is then only necessary to bear in mind that British trains keep to the left-hand rails.

The bibliographical appendix in the earlier editions of this book has been entirely rewritten. Now called 'Sources of Knowledge', it has been shortened (largely for one reason, explained there) and brought up to 1985. The list of preserved locomotives has been dropped; they are now far too numerous to be listed one by one. In the first edition 55 were listed; in the second, 87. The number now exceeds 1,600.

The most conspicuous new element in this book is provided by the pictures. Hardly any of them appeared in the previous editions; a good many have never before been reproduced – at least in a book about railways. Their purpose is to extend and enrich the text, to indicate the wealth of interest that pictures of all kinds (not just photographs) can afford.

PREFACE

I have been generously helped by a number of people. Gordon Biddle and Peter Baughan made valuable suggestions to me on some of the new and the revised sections. I am most grateful to Simon Rigge and to all his excellent colleagues of the Sheldrake Press for their patient hard work during the production of the book. They have been mainly responsible for the illustration. In assembling the pictures we have been aided notably by Richard Riley, Gordon Biddle and Mike Pope, and by John Edgington of the National Railway Museum, from which more than a third of the pictures have come. Three other institutions have also given us particularly liberal help: the London Transport Museum, the Ironbridge Gorge Museum, and the North of England Open Air Museum at Beamish.

Leicester   J.S.
2 September 1985

A woman booking clerk in the office at Sidmouth Junction on the Southern Railway dates a ticket for a traveller in 1941. During both world wars, women occupied a good many posts which had previously always been held by men.

Navvies engaged on building the Great Central Railway at Catesby, Northamptonshire, between Willoughby and Charwelton, pose for a group portrait with their mascot in the 1890s. Employed directly by the contractors – in this case T. Oliver & Son – navvies endured very rough conditions, but were usually paid well. L. T. C. Rolt, historian of the building of this line, has written of them: 'Although the navvy of the 1890s had become a member of a comparatively civilised species which no longer terrorised the countryside, his old reputation for lawlessness and ungodliness died hard.'

THE MAKING OF THE RAILWAYS

—— ORIGINS ——

This ticket, kept as a souvenir by its purchaser, provided a ride on a demonstration steam train hauled by Richard Trevithick's locomotive, Catch Me Who Can. *The train ran on a circular track on waste ground near Euston Square in the summer of 1808 and did much to publicise the new means of propulsion by steam.*

The history of railways, as we know them today, begins in the year 1830. All the essential elements of a railway were then first combined together. But most of those elements originated very much earlier. The idea of a 'rail way' – of a track, that is, constructed especially for the accommodation of wheeled vehicles – is to be found in Babylonia, Greece and the Roman Empire. Wooden tracks, on which four-wheeled wagons ran, were in use in the mines of Germany, Alsace and Romania in the 15th century. The railway first appeared in England soon after 1564, introduced by Germans mining in the Lake District. Within forty years it had come to serve as the chief means of transporting coal from the pit-head down to navigable water. One such railway was in use at Wollaton, near Nottingham, in 1603-04;[1] there were others, dating from these years, at Broseley in Shropshire and at the mouth of the River Blyth in Northumberland. It was in Northumberland and Durham that the use of railways was developed most rapidly – so that in the 18th century they were often called 'Newcastle roads'. They were short and very simple in construction, generally taking the surface of the ground. Early in the 18th century, however, some longer and more elaborate lines were built in County Durham, which required substantial engineering works: most notably the Causey Arch (with a span of a hundred feet) and the embankment at Beckley Burn, both on the Tanfield wagon way. They are the oldest railway bridge and embankment now to be seen in the world.

On all these early railways the rails themselves were of timber, though they were sometimes protected by thin iron plates laid over the surface, to reduce the wear from the friction of the wheels. Rails wholly of iron were first made and used (mounted on top of wooden rails) at Coalbrookdale in Shropshire in 1767. This strengthened the track to bear heavier loads and endure more intensive use. The wheels of the wagons were also made of iron, with flanges of the modern form; but in certain parts of the country, such as the North Midlands and South Wales, an alternative flat wheel was in use, the flange itself being part of the track, which was then called a 'plateway'.

The wagons were moved on these lines by horses, by human power, or by the force of gravity. Although the steam engine was being developed during the 18th century, and was later applied to road and water transport, it was not until 1804 that Richard Trevithick, the Cornish engineer, produced the first locomotive designed for a railway.[2] When this was tried at Penydarren, near Merthyr Tydfil, it worked successfully but proved too heavy for the flimsy track on which it had to run. Trevithick was soon followed by other pioneers such as Blenkinsop, Hedley and George Stephenson. Through Stephenson's patient experiments at Killingworth and Hetton, the locomotive was steadily improved. In 1822 he demonstrated one of his machines to Edward Pease, who was concerned in the plan for building a railway between Stockton and Darlington, and convinced him that that railway ought to be operated, at least in part, by locomotives.

The Stockton & Darlington was the largest and most elaborate railway that had yet been projected. Its main line was nearly 27 miles long, and the company was authorised by its first Act of Parliament, passed in 1821, to raise capital of more than £100,000. Moreover, it was to carry passengers as well as goods. It was not the earliest railway to do so: that distinction seems to belong to the Oystermouth Railway, running along Swansea Bay, on which a horse-drawn passenger service began in 1807. Another was in operation on the Kilmarnock & Troon Railway in Scotland by 1818. But the Stockton & Darlington was the first to secure powers (under its second Act, of 1823) to operate traffic by locomotives.

It was opened on 27 September 1825. Although Stephenson's engine *Locomotion* hauled passenger trains on that day, it did not do so in regular service. The traction on the railway was oddly mixed: partly by horse, and partly by stationary engine. Passenger coaches ran in competition with one another; and just as on the roads they paid tolls to the turnpike trusts, so on the railway they paid tolls to the company. The receipts from the carriage of passengers, however, were of trifling importance – only 3 per cent of the total in 1826-28. The mainstay of the company's revenue was coal traffic.

The Stockton & Darlington Railway was visited by engineers and industrialists from all over Britain and from overseas. Its success, though not spectacular, was solid enough to encourage other ventures of the same kind, and some 25 new railways were authorised in the years 1826-30. One built at this time was of outstanding importance: the Liverpool & Manchester Railway, which can justifiably claim to be the first modern railway to be brought into use in the world. It was the first to convey passengers and goods entirely by mechanical traction. The traffic, moreover, was handled by the company itself, not by lessees. Here was an organism quite different from a turnpike road, and much more elaborate. The company owned bridges, tunnels, tracks, passenger vehicles, wagons, motive-power, stations and offices, and it paid and controlled staff to manage them. The capital it was authorised to raise before the opening of the line amounted to £865,000. The towns it linked were two of the most important in the country, with a combined population of 350,000. Behind Manchester, too, lay the great cotton industry of east Lancashire; whilst into the Mersey and out of it flowed a sizeable part of the whole external trade of Great Britain. The opening of the railway, on 15 September 1830, was recognised at the time as a landmark in the technical and economic development of the world. It is a landmark that has stood ever since.

When the Stockton & Darlington Railway was formally opened on 27 September 1825, John Dobbin made a detailed sketch of the scene at Darlington. Long afterwards he worked it up into this larger picture. His rendering of the engine is crudely inaccurate, but he conveys the spirit of the scene admirably. This was the first picture ever made of the opening of a railway, and was the forerunner of many others in later years, particularly those reproduced in the Illustrated London News *from 1842 onwards.*

—— THE FIRST TRUNK RAILWAYS ——

The Liverpool & Manchester Railway was successful from the start. Its expectations of passenger traffic were fulfilled. It was reckoned that, if every place in them were taken, all the coaches on the road between the two towns could accommodate a maximum of 700 passengers a day; in the three years 1831-33 the railway actually carried, in full trains and empty ones, a daily average of nearly 1,100. Unlike its predecessors, the Liverpool & Manchester was, and always remained, primarily a passenger line, but its receipts from the carriage of goods were by no means negligible. The profits from both classes of traffic were sufficient to enable the company to pay its shareholders an average dividend of 9½ per cent every year from 1831 to 1845. The operation of the traffic, too, was handled adequately by the new locomotives. Although the opening of the line was marred by a fatal accident (the President of the Board of Trade, William Huskisson, MP for Liverpool, was knocked down by a train), it carried its passengers in safety thereafter; and even if not everybody liked the new means of travel, no one had any serious reason to complain that it was dangerous or inefficient.

This being so, it may seem surprising that railways did not immediately multiply fast. Only ten new lines were sanctioned by Parliament in 1831 and 1832. Two of these were in Lancashire – one of them virtually a dependency of the Liverpool & Manchester. Three more were never made, and the combined length of the other five was under sixty miles. People were waiting to see if the Liverpool & Manchester would fulfil its early promise before they plunged into the costly and hazardous business of extending the railway system on a large scale.

Edge Hill station, Liverpool, bustles with activity as a train prepares to leave in about 1848. This lithograph by A. F. Tait shows the station just after the iron and glass roof had been constructed over the platforms and the tracks; the tunnel leading to Lime Street station is in the background. The locomotive, of the Liverpool & Manchester 'Bird' class, is heading a train bound for Manchester, with passengers' luggage being strapped on to the roofs of the carriages. The iron balcony on the right allows the company's officers to oversee the handling of business on the platforms.

That is not the whole explanation, however. The political disturbance of the country at the time must also be taken into account: the agitation for the Reform Bill, involving grave riots at Bristol and Nottingham in 1831, preoccupied the minds of the investing classes. Moreover, the passage of a Bill through Parliament was a large undertaking. Two great railways were projected at this time, but both failed at first to secure the parliamentary powers they needed. These were the London & Birmingham, joining the two towns in its name, and the Grand Junction, which proposed to build a line from Birmingham to link up with the Liverpool & Manchester at Warrington. They were opposed by a multitude of interests: canal and coach proprietors, turnpike trustees, landowners who thought either that the railway would ruin their property or that they were being insufficiently paid for it.

Both these schemes were successful when they were re-submitted in 1833; but the London & Birmingham had to pay more than £500,000 for the land it needed, and the expenses involved in obtaining its Act of Parliament amounted to a further £73,000. These two lines were quickly followed by the London & Southampton (1834) and the Great Western from London to Bristol (1835). These companies have a special place in the history of British railways, for they formed the first of the great trunk lines out of London. They were on a much bigger scale than their predecessors. The Liverpool & Manchester was thirty miles long, and the Newcastle & Carlisle (authorised in 1829) twice that length. But the four new lines made up 380 miles between them.

The launching of these trunk lines was followed in 1836 by a feverish effort to extend the railways in all directions. 'Feverish' is the right word: that year brought the first great fit of railway speculation. The country had settled down politically after the excitements of the contest over the Reform Bill. The price of government securities was rising and the interest on them falling, so that there was money lying ready to be invested in projects that could offer hope of a good profit. What could be more tempting than these new railways, with the Liverpool & Manchester paying 10 per cent in 1836 and the Stockton & Darlington raising its dividend from 11 to 14 per cent in 1837? The consequence was that 1,500 miles of new railway were authorised by Parliament in 1836-37. Together with those already established, they were designed to carry the railway eastwards to Dover and Yarmouth, westwards to Exeter, northwards to Lancaster and Gateshead. Nor were these communications limited to a series of lines radiating from London. Great cross-country railways were undertaken in the Midlands and the North, from Gloucester to Birmingham, from Birmingham to Derby and Leeds, from Manchester to Sheffield. Little was as yet attempted in Wales, but that little included the Taff Vale line from Cardiff to Merthyr, which became one of the most profitable companies in the whole of Britain. In Scotland the lines authorised in these years ran from Arbroath to Forfar and Dundee, and from Glasgow to Greenock and Ayr – with the vital 46 miles between Glasgow and Edinburgh added in 1838.

When these are all put together, the outlines of a railway system begin to emerge. Yet 'system' is a misleading word if it suggests order or plan, for there was little of either. The British railways 'were propagated blindly and wastefully like living things'.[3] They present a very strong contrast to the railways of Belgium, the only other country in Europe that developed them with anything like the same speed. In Belgium the government drew the map of the railway system, ordaining that there should be four main lines meeting at Malines, from Ostend, Antwerp, Liège and Brussels. These were all built at the expense of the state, and controlled by it. Thereafter, branch lines were constructed by private enterprise. But the circumstances in Belgium were peculiar. It was a new state (established by revolution in 1830), and the railways were designed to attract international trade at the expense of Holland. No such considerations were present in Britain. Parliament took, at first, no positive action at all, intervening only to prevent the railways from doing certain things thought to be against the public interest. It would limit maximum fares and charges; it would guard landowners from unjustifiable damage to their property and insist that compensation be paid for land that was taken; it would see that existing roads and canals were protected against physical injury where railways crossed them. But no more. The government would not put up capital for the construction of railways, and neither would it accept any responsibility whatever for their management.

Since the state, therefore, had nothing to do with the planning and laying out of the railways, they grew up haphazardly, not necessarily where there was most need for them, but where capital and leadership were most readily forthcoming, and where opposition to them was weak or negligible. Some people supposed that these early lines represented the consummation of the railway system. A well-informed economist, J. R. McCulloch, doubted whether there was much scope for building more railways. Though he gradually modified his views, he continued to believe in 1837 that 'the advantages likely to be derived from the extension of the system to other parts of the country have ... been a good deal exaggerated'.[4] Even those who hoped most of the railways were inclined to wait for the opening of the trunk lines authorised in 1833-37, and to see the results of their operation, before pressing on to extend the system further. Little more than 250 miles of new railway were sanctioned by Parliament in the six years 1838-43; in one year, 1840, not a single new company was established. On the other hand, over 1,500 miles of line were opened for traffic in these years, bringing the aggregate mileage of working railways in the country to more than 2,000 by the end of 1843.

Not all these ventures were successful. The Eastern Counties Railway, which obtained powers in 1836 to build a line of 126 miles from London to

Ipswich, Norwich and Yarmouth, took seven years to totter as far as Colchester (51 miles) and there gave up. It suffered every kind of financial misfortune, and its poor services provoked much merriment in *Punch*. The Eastern Counties was an exceptionally bad railway, but there were others little better, with perhaps less excuse for their shortcomings. The railways were still passing through the stage of experiment in every department of their work: financial, administrative, engineering, operational, commercial. What is astonishing is not that there should have been some feeble and inefficient companies, but that there were so many strong enough to survive the difficulties of establishment and growth and, in addition, to yield good returns to their shareholders.

At the opposite end of the scale to the Eastern Counties Railway stood the London & Birmingham, a steady, prudent concern with a consistent record of success from its opening. Its management showed a marked regard for economy, establishing a tradition of carefulness that endured at Euston under its successor the London & North Western. Undoubtedly, it clung too long to the use of the tiny locomotives designed for it by Edward Bury, its trains remaining slow as a result. Yet it was capable of gestures of the utmost grandeur. It spent £35,000 on Philip Hardwick's gateway at Euston, which – despite what later and baser generations did to dwarf and deface it – long remained one of the noblest public monuments in London, and ten years later it commissioned Hardwick's son to design the Great Hall of the station, a work of equally fine quality. Nor was this all. The Curzon Street station in Birmingham was a defiantly handsome building that towered over everything around it. The bridges and other engineering works on the line, though never ostentatious, reflected a quiet, assured prosperity.

By the early 1840s the railways were beginning to establish themselves as a national institution. The Post Office thought them safe enough to be used for the carriage of mails – a traffic that had begun on the Liverpool & Manchester line in 1830 and was regulated by Parliament ·in 1838. The military authorities relied on them for extensive movements of troops during the Chartist disturbances of 1839 and 1842.[5] The Queen herself made a railway journey in 1842, and used the railways as a matter of course

The construction of the front of Euston Station, London terminus of the London & Birmingham Railway, was sketched in October 1837 by J. C. Bourne. In the foreground are the bases of the Doric columns of the great portico, made of Bramley Fall sandstone brought from north-west of Leeds. The Doric arch and the two flanking pavilions were all demolished in 1962.

The Ionic gateway of Curzon Street station, Birmingham, at the northern end of the London & Birmingham Railway, was built to complement the Doric arch in London. In Bourne's drawing, the house on the right of the gateway gives some indication of the massive scale of Philip Hardwick's design.

thereafter whenever it was convenient, all over the island.

This success was reflected in the financial esteem in which the railways were held. John Francis, a well qualified contemporary observer, wrote: 'In 1843 railways, though depressed in value, were regarded as good as consols. They formed an investment for surplus capital, into which safe men entered with a conviction of their stability. It was a mode of transit tried and found true. . . . The established lines were conducted by men who could not have done a mean action had they tried, and would not have done it if they could. The monied public felt this, and purchased freely where they trusted fully.'[6] In the same passage Francis to some extent confirmed the judgments of McCulloch. The lines that had been built by 1843, he said, 'were deemed sufficient by the most imaginative schemers, who never dreamed of millions being expended on new roads to save a few miles'. Yet that is what began to happen in 1844.

—— THE MANIA AND ITS CONSEQUENCES ——

The speculation of the mid-1840s has often been spoken of as irrational frenzy: a conception reflected in the name that is usually attached to it, the Railway Mania.[7] There was indeed an element of lunacy in the business, and *Punch* laughed at the absurd companies that were floated and found subscribers fool enough to support them. Its 'John o' Groats and Land's End Junction, with branches to Ben Lomond and Battersea'[8] was hardly more ludicrous than some that really came before the public: the Great Eastern & Western Railway (from Yarmouth to Swansea), and the Southern Counties Union & Bristol Bath & Dover Direct.

Some people foresaw the course that the Mania was likely to take. They had recent precedents in the Canal Mania of 1792-93 and the previous railway boom of 1836-37. Early in 1845 Francis Mewburn, a solicitor who had helped to launch the Stockton & Darlington Railway nearly thirty years before, wrote in his diary: 'I am alarmed at the number of new lines before Parliament and continuing to be brought forward. A panic will come. That is unquestionable, but I think it will be staved off so long as we have 15 millions in the Bank of England; as soon as a bad harvest comes, then the gold will be withdrawn, accommodation at the bankers' will decrease,

Dismayed by the falling value of his shares, a railway speculator comes home and stamps on his certificate – 'a scene performing now in every town', wrote the cartoonist in this satire on the Mania of the 1840s.

In a painting of the 1820s by an unknown artist, a workman, his dogs and a draught horse cross the tracks of the Surrey Iron Railway. Opened in 1803 and operated by horses, the ten-mile railway linked Croydon with the Thames at Wandsworth, following closely the course of the River Wandle. It carried country produce into London and building materials out of it, but did not prosper and was closed in 1846.

The opening in 1830 of the Liverpool & Manchester Railway, the first in the world to be worked entirely by steam power, was commemorated by this jug portraying the famous Moorish Arch just west of Edge Hill station, Liverpool.

An unusual idea for improving communications in London was the proposal to run this 'railway street' through the heart of Westminster. The railway was to have used the atmospheric system of propulsion, tried on the South Devon line in 1847-48 (see page 95) and so would have entirely avoided the emission of steam and smoke.

This portrait by an unknown artist depicts a young railway engineer in a landscape dominated by the embankment of his railway. His identity is not known: though he was thought at one time to be George Stephenson, his dress is that of the mid-19th century, thus ruling out both George and his son Robert. But although anonymous, he lives in his portrait. With the stance of a man ready to accept any challenge, he is the very type of the junior resident engineers who bore so much of the burden of Britain's railway construction.

instalments [of payments on shares] continue to be called for, shareholders will not be able to sell, and then for the crash.'[9] That is just what took place during the next three years.

Nevertheless, it is a mistake to emphasise too heavily the speculative aspects of the Mania – they were the most obvious and dramatic but not, in the long run, the most important. Crude and wasteful though the Mania was, it reflected more serious economic impulses than the mere desire to get rich quick at someone else's expense. The argument that additional railways were an unnecessary luxury does not hold water. By the end of the year 1844, with the exception of the Chester & Holyhead Railway and a few very short local lines, Wales was still wholly without railway communication. No railways had yet been undertaken westwards from Birmingham or eastwards from Nottingham. A series of lines, actual or prospective, ran from Kilmarnock through Glasgow and Edinburgh to Berwick; but otherwise, apart from the little railways of Dundee and Arbroath, there were no Scottish railways at all. No line had yet been sanctioned to connect Scotland with England: the traveller had to make use either of a steamer from Ardrossan to Fleetwood or of a coach from Berwick to Newcastle.

These serious deficiencies had to be repaired before even the outline of an adequate railway system could be said to have emerged. Moreover, on the map two lines might appear to connect, by serving the same town or even entering the same station, but fail in fact to provide a convenient interchange of traffic. With the exception of the great trunk lines, the early companies were small concerns, fiercely individualistic, often on bad terms with their next-door neighbours or even at open war with them. One classic example is the enmity between the Midland Counties and the Birmingham & Derby Junction Railways, which met in the splendid Derby 'trijunct' station designed for them and the North Midland company by Robert Stephenson and Francis Thompson in 1839. They offered alternative routes between Derby and Rugby – a very important stretch, since almost all the traffic between the North East and London passed through Derby. The Midland Counties route was substantially shorter than the Birmingham & Derby route. But Derby station was staffed by North Midland men, who favoured the Birmingham & Derby company. 'Cut-throat competition' hardly describes the vigour of the rivalry between the two smaller railways. For three glorious years the traveller made merry at their expense as stage by stage they cut their rates, each trying to secure custom by the cheapness and alleged superior convenience of its trains. In the long run this war led to suicide. There could be only one sensible ending to it: the amalgamation of the two rivals with their northern partner, which was finally achieved in 1844 when a combined Midland Railway company was formed by Act of Parliament.

This was the first important amalgamation in the history of British railways. The idea of it came from Robert Stephenson, George's son, by this time on the way to becoming the greatest railway engineer of his time. It was not he who carried it through, however, but a very different man: George Hudson. Hudson was a tradesman of York who, by a combination of strong Tory politics and acute opportunism in business, was building up for himself a powerful position in the new railway world. He differed in two respects from most of the other people who made great fortunes and positions for themselves out of railways. First, he was interested in railways and nothing else. He had a hand in other concerns – the Sunderland Dock Company, the York Union Bank – but only because they were adjuncts to his railways; he even controlled a glass works at South Shields which roofed

George Hudson, the 'Railway King', lived from 1800 to 1871. By the age of 46 he controlled nearly half of England's railways. Lord Mayor of York and an MP, he had an astute business sense and a thorough understanding of railways that made him the first British railway tycoon. This portrait by James Andrews is not the most flattering, but is perhaps the truest – stout, tough, shrewd and uncompromising.

the stations on his lines. Second, Hudson was interested in railways solely as a financial proposition; he had no technical knowledge of how they worked, beyond what a quick layman's brain could assimilate. That was the business of other people, and he wisely left it to them. He had an eye for good men and backed them. He understood railways through and through as financial organisms. He personifies the Mania; but just as the Mania is remembered too much for its drama and violence, so Hudson is thought of too exclusively as the cheapjack 'Railway King', who reigned for a short time in hectic vulgarity and then had a spectacular fall. His financial chicanery is indefensible, and that met its proper reward. But along with it went a true vision of the weaknesses of the railways of his time and an understanding of the means to repair them. When his reign ended, no one dared quote him as an authority; yet, in one important matter at least, his practice was continued and developed. Alone among railway politicians, he understood the importance of the principle of amalgamation.

The making of the Midland company in 1844 was Hudson's first great stroke. In many ways it remained his best. Three rival amalgamations of the same kind quickly followed it, all made absolute by Parliament in 1846-47. The Liverpool & Manchester, Grand Junction, London & Birmingham and Manchester & Birmingham companies were combined into one, which was known as the London & North Western. Five companies, furnishing between them a continuous line from Manchester to Grimsby, came together under the title of the Manchester Sheffield & Lincolnshire Railway. Finally, the Lancashire & Yorkshire was formed out of the amalgamation of the Manchester & Leeds with five smaller companies.

Such unions as these were not open to the charge of attempting to set up a monopoly. 'Monopolistic' amalgamations, giving a district wholly into the charge of a single company, were looked on with general disfavour, though several such monopolies were in fact sanctioned by Parliament in later years. Hudson was interested in amalgamations of both kinds. At the height of his power in 1849 he was, with insignificant exceptions, in financial control of the whole railway system of Northumberland, Durham and north and east Yorkshire; his Midland company had a monopoly in Nottinghamshire, Leicestershire and most of Derbyshire; and the Eastern Counties, which he also controlled, dominated East Anglia. His 'kingdom' stretched from Berwick to Bristol, from Carlisle to Lowestoft and London. North of the Thames, only four major companies remained obstinately outside it: the London & North Western (with its ally the Lancaster & Carlisle), the Lancashire & Yorkshire, the Manchester Sheffield & Lincolnshire, and – an embryo still, but much the most important to Hudson – the Great Northern.

The Great Northern scheme had a history stretching back to 1825. It was really a railway version of the historic Great North Road. For the companies associated under Hudson, it was of the utmost importance that the Great Northern should be defeated: it threatened to destroy their control of the traffic from London to the North East. Its proposed route between London and York was thirty miles shorter than that via Derby; whilst, from a strategic point of view, it would cut straight through the very heart of the territory occupied by Hudson's companies.

The Great Northern's struggle to obtain its Act in 1845-46 was the greatest battle ever fought in Parliament over a single railway; the railway itself was the longest ever authorised in Britain at one stroke. The company and its allies spent £433,000 before its Act was passed in June 1846. What its opponents spent on the contest, directly and indirectly, is impossible to

1 Caledonian
2 Lancaster & Carlisle
3 North British
4 York Newcastle & Berwick
5 Stockton & Darlington
6 Clarence
7 York & North Midland
8 Leeds & Thirsk
9 Lancashire & Yorkshire
10 Chester & Holyhead
11 Chester & Birkenhead
12 Shrewsbury & Chester
13 Manchester Sheffield & Lincolnshire
14 Maryport & Carlisle
15 Newcastle & Carlisle
16 London & North Western

17 East Lincolnshire
18 Midland
19 Eastern Counties
20 Norfolk
21 Eastern Counties
22 South Eastern
23 London Brighton & South Coast
24 London & South Western
25 Great Western
26 Bristol & Exeter
27 South Devon
28 Taff Vale
29 East Anglian
30 Great Northern (under construction)

Lines controlled by
George Hudson in 1849
Other lines

calculate; but certainly the expenditure on promoting and opposing this single Act of Parliament approached £1 million. Before this is condemned as a shocking waste of money, two things should be remembered. First, the stakes were exceptionally high, and these were not great prices to pay for control of this great artery of traffic. Second, this was the method that Britain chose for developing her railway system: the method of private action, of *laissez-faire*. The true responsibility for the inefficiency and waste of the Mania lay primarily upon the British people, through their government and Parliament, which declined to assume the direction of the railway system at its critical formative stage in the authoritarian manner of the Continent.

Not everyone acquiesced, even at the time, in this abdication of responsibility. In 1838 the Duke of Wellington condemned 'the improvident manner in which the Legislature had passed the railway Bills without any guard against their monopoly and mismanagement'. As each Bill had come up for discussion in the House of Lords, he tried to secure a clause in it requiring the new company to be bound by any general measure introduced by the government within the succeeding year. But, he added with a touch of contempt, 'the government shrank from that duty, and introduced no measure at all.'[10] True, the Duke was old, and the railways new-fangled; and it was his political opponents, the Whigs, whom he was criticising. As usual, however, there was a powerful infusion of common sense in what he said. And if it was true of the lesser mania of the 1830s it was true in a more obvious and vital sense of the greater one of 1844-47.

The most important 'general measure' passed in these years was Gladstone's Act of 1844. When first presented to Parliament as a Bill, it attempted to do three things: to increase the direct control of the government over the management and working of the railways; to give it power to purchase them outright at a future date; and to compel them to provide reasonable minimum conditions of comfort for the conveyance of third-class passengers. As soon as these terms were published, the companies and their shareholders howled in protest. 'The railway plunder Bill', they called it, and they fought it line by line as it passed through Parliament. In the end the provisions of the Bill that gave the government authority to interfere in the working of the companies disappeared; and its clauses were made applicable only to new lines to be established in the future, not to those already in being. The government was authorised to purchase these new companies at any time after 21 years had elapsed. This power was never in fact exercised. Nonetheless, the Transport Act of 1947, under which the state bought the railways, was putting into practice a policy that had first been envisaged 103 years before.

The Act did, however, give effective protection to the interests of third-class passengers. They were now guaranteed at least one train a day, running at a minimum speed of 12 mph; carriages were to be furnished with seats and protected from the weather; and the passengers were to pay at the rate of not more than 1d a mile. That these conditions applied only to new railways did not matter: once they were established, the existing companies necessarily had to accept them also. Some of them still subjected third-class passengers to inconvenience. The Great Western Railway – which always regarded them with a qualified liking – had a way of forcing them to begin their journey in the small hours. For many years the only third-class train from London to the West Country set out at 6am. The company's employees referred to it as 'the Plymouth Cheap'. But discomfort and indignity did not matter much when third-class passengers could now claim, as a right, a service faster than that provided by even the most

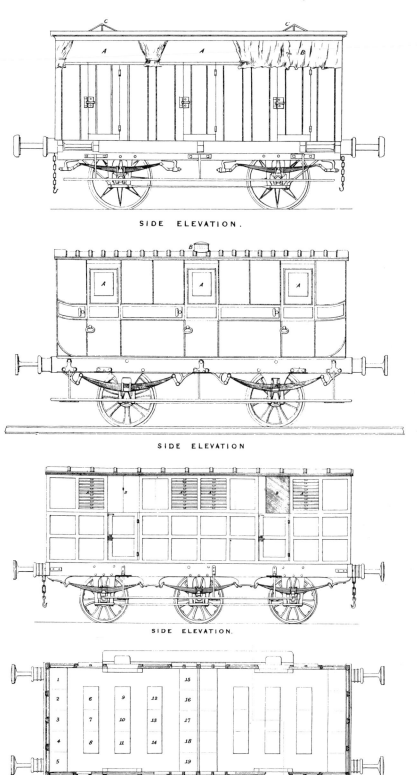

SIDE ELEVATION.

SIDE ELEVATION

SIDE ELEVATION.

PLAN

These drawings reveal the rudimentary features of carriages designed for conveying Parliamentary (penny-a-mile) passengers in 1845. The London & South Western carriage (top) seated thirty, and was equipped with leather curtains which could be pulled back along an open panel at the top of the carriage to provide ventilation. The features marked 'C' on the diagram were glass skylights. The Midland Railway carriage (second from top) was considerably more stylish, its curved side-panels reminiscent of the stage-coach. It was the most comfortable and best-lit Parliamentary carriage of the time, with glass windows (marked 'A') and an oil lamp ('B'). The Yarmouth & Norwich Railway carriage (third from top) was the biggest, designed for 38 passengers. It was a six-wheeled vehicle, with air provided by sliding shutters and light by Venetian blinds. The plan (bottom) shows how seats were arranged, with passengers sitting across the width of the carriage.

brilliant of the old mail-coaches, and at a much lower price. If the accommodation was spartan, it was a great improvement on clinging to the outside of a coach, exposed to rain and wind. Of all classes in the community, the poor clearly stood to benefit most from the railway.

In dealing with the Bills promoted by individual railway companies in these years, Parliament often seemed to act capriciously. This was not surprising, since the task of dealing carefully with the mass of railway schemes now being presented was hopeless. In November 1845, at the beginning of the great speculative boom, *The Times* stated that over six hundred new railways were already projected, at an estimated cost of £563 million – whilst another six hundred were reported to be on the way. In the three Parliamentary sessions 1845-48, some 650 railway Acts were passed, authorising the construction of nearly 9,000 miles of line, in addition to the 3,000 for which sanction had been given down to the end of 1844. Considering how suddenly this speculation sprang up and how ill equipped Parliament was to handle it, the wonder is that the task was performed without breakdown, rather than that the performance entailed some injustice and many anomalies.

By 1854 nearly all the chief main lines of the modern railway system of England had been completed or authorised. Two of the three great lines from London to the North – the western and the eastern – were finished, needing only a little improvement here and there in the course of the succeeding century. In south-eastern England, both lines to Norwich (via Colchester and via Cambridge) were complete, and London was linked with Dover, Brighton, Portsmouth and Southampton. A continuous line, though under the control of three separate companies, stretched from Ramsgate, parallel with the coast, to Dorchester. Westwards from London a great line ran, forking into two at Swindon: one arm reached to Bristol and Plymouth, the other to Gloucester, Cardiff and Carmarthen. Birmingham already had two competing routes, from Euston and from Paddington. From Crewe through Chester and along the coast of North Wales the railway stretched out to Holyhead, which had become the chief station for traffic to and from Ireland. Moreover, most of the great cross-country lines in the Midlands and the North had now been built. From Leeds it was possible to travel by train to Newcastle, Hull, Bristol and Morecambe; and there was a choice of two routes to Manchester, Liverpool and Birmingham.

Some important English lines were still to be built in the suburbs of London and in rural districts; but these were in the nature of improvements on the existing system. By 1854 the most considerable English towns not yet served by a railway were probably Luton, Devizes and Weymouth.

Things were not so far advanced elsewhere in Great Britain. The Welsh railway system was confined to the two great coastal lines already mentioned and to a few short lines in the south-eastern valleys and the north east. Otherwise, the map of Wales continued to show a total blank; nor was there much under construction. The Scottish railway system comprised a line from Berwick to Edinburgh, together with two from Carlisle to Glasgow; and they were linked with Perth, Dundee and Aberdeen. A number of short lines had been built in the 'waist' of Scotland and the Lothians, in Fife and Angus. But that was almost all.

The expansion of the railway network encountered some difficult problems. The tracks had not been constructed to a single gauge. In the early days several had been tried. The 4ft 8½in of the northern coal lines, adopted in the days of horse traction, had always been used by the Stephensons, and it ruled without question throughout the North of England and, with some exceptions, in Scotland. But as engineers began to think about railways in the 1830s, this gauge encountered its critics. That it had been found suitable, by long experience, for horses working on colliery lines did not prove its fitness for the steam locomotive. If the gauge were somewhat wider, there would be more room in the engine for its mechanism and in the vehicles it drew. There would be greater stability in running and substantial economy in operation. These arguments were advanced most forcibly by the young I. K. Brunel and were accepted by the Great Western Railway, whose line was accordingly built to the gauge of 7ft. The theory behind the adoption of this gauge was sound, though its full potential was missed through failing to provide for greater height as well as greater width between the rails. Naturally, the lines connected with the Great Western adopted the 7ft gauge. The directors of the Eastern Counties Railway also decided that their line should be built to a broad gauge. But their engineer, John Braithwaite, thought that 7ft was too much, and a compromise of 5ft was determined on. The line was built to that gauge from London to Colchester and, by an associated company, to Bishop's Stortford. When the Irish trunk railways came to be established – very much more on the initiative of the state than in Great Britain – yet another gauge of 5ft 3in was adopted; it remains standard in Ireland to this day.[11]

The inconvenience of this multiplicity of gauges passed almost unnoticed until broad- and narrow-gauge lines began to arrive at the same point, as they did at Gloucester in 1845. Passengers then complained of the annoyance of having to change trains, and traders of the damage that their goods sustained in transshipment. By this time the Great Western company and its allies were extending their lines westwards into South Wales, northwards to Birmingham, and were even threatening an invasion of Manchester. There was a serious danger of multiplication of points like Gloucester over half of England and Wales. Parliament alone could avert that nuisance, by insisting on a national uniformity of gauge.

It was already too late. All that Parliament felt able to do – after an inquiry held at the very height of the speculation – was to lay down that 4ft 8½in should be regarded as the standard gauge, to which all new railways should conform unless a different one was specifically permitted. This was

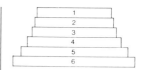

By the 1840s no fewer than five different gauges were in use in Britain, with a sixth in Ireland. Shown here in a diagram taken from Francis Whishaw's Railways of Great Britain and Ireland (1842), they are: 1. Scotch, 4ft 6in; 2. English, 4ft 8½in; 3. Blackwall & Eastern Counties, 5ft; 4. New Scotch, 5ft 6in; 5. Irish, 6ft 2in; 6. Great Western, 7ft.

Navvies at work on the Great Western Railway convert the line from the traditional 7ft gauge to the standard gauge of 4ft 8½in in May 1892. The line in the background has already been narrowed.

obviously a compromise adopted under the conflicting pressures of two powerful interests. But two things can be said in its defence. In the first place, even though the imposition of a uniform gauge was evidently desirable, that would have been asking more of Parliament than could realistically be expected: for this crisis in the railway world coincided with a much bigger crisis in politics, arising from the repeal of the Corn Laws. No stable government capable of so ruthless a policy could possibly have been formed. Second, the working out of this compromise proved better than it promised to be on paper. In effect, the spread of the broad gauge was now stopped. It advanced no further to the north or east. Even within its own kingdom some compromise was possible by the laying down of a third rail, creating a 'mixed' gauge, over which both narrow- and broad-gauge trains could be worked. In the end the Great Western company came to feel the inconvenience of its unique position.[12] The broad gauge disappeared for good in 1892.

The course of the Mania and the Battle of the Gauges shows how reluctant Parliament was to interfere with the railway companies. But there were other issues that it did not evade. It had never shrunk from regulating fares and rates. It had also inserted into the Acts authorising the construction of individual railways many clauses designed to protect the public against possible danger: it insisted upon adequate fencing of lines, regulation of level crossings and imposition of speed limits (trains on the Taff Vale Railway, for example, were forbidden to exceed 12 mph under the company's Act of 1836).

As with similar legislation governing mines and factories, a body of civil servants was needed to see that Parliament's decisions were carried out. Railways were placed under the Board of Trade, and by an Act of 1840 a 'Railway Department' of that Board was established, whose small staff included two inspectors. Among their earliest duties was that of reporting on all serious railway accidents – a function that they and their modern successors, the Inspecting Officers of the Ministry of Transport, have discharged ever since. Very quickly the Railway Department of the Board of Trade became the recognised means of communication between the government and the companies, an instrument by which it could bring pressure to bear on them to adopt technical improvements of many kinds, particularly those designed to ensure greater safety.

The British railways' freedom from state control was, therefore, not absolute. If the government did not run or manage them it supervised their working and, in one field of policy after another, it unobtrusively exercised a strong influence over them.

—— THE SYSTEM COMPLETED ——

The Mania had strikingly confirmed the power of the well established companies, all of which rode out the storm; it also left behind it a much greater number of little companies, hardly able to stand on their own and unable, on account of their poverty, to provide the kind of service that was coming to be expected. The proper answer to this problem was Hudson's answer, amalgamation. Parliament's consent was required, and so far it had been forthcoming on one tacit condition: that none of the companies sought to establish a territorial monopoly. But in 1854 this rule was broken when a private agreement between three companies (the York & North Midland, Leeds Northern and York Newcastle & Berwick) was made absolute by Act of Parliament. The three were united into one North Eastern Railway, which controlled all the important railways of Northumberland, Durham and Yorkshire north of Leeds and Selby, save two: the Stockton & Darlington and the Newcastle & Carlisle. The Bill passed into law easily, as if Parliament hardly noticed what it was doing. Admittedly, when the North Eastern company tried to amalgamate with the Newcastle & Carlisle six years later, the opposition was so strong that the Bill had to be withdrawn. But that opposition was inspired not so much by dislike of monopoly as by the hostility of neighbouring and rival companies, the London & North Western and the North British. When terms had been agreed with them, the opposition collapsed; and in 1862-63 the North Eastern was able to absorb both the older companies and thus to achieve an almost complete monopoly of a great region.

Two other similar 'monopolistic' amalgamations were sanctioned at the same time: one in 1862, which produced the Great Eastern Railway, in control of virtually the whole of East Anglia; the other in 1865-66, bringing the Scottish Central and Scottish North Eastern companies into union with the Caledonian. But there the matter ended. When other companies sought to combine in the same way – the London & North Western and the Lancashire & Yorkshire, for instance, in 1871-73; the Great Northern, Great Central and Great Eastern Railways in 1909 – they were forbidden to do so. Not until the passing of the Railways Act of 1921, in the changed conditions following the First World War, was the old principle finally abandoned.[13]

Where no monopoly was in question, Parliament usually agreed readily enough to the union of small companies, or the absorption of a smaller one by a large neighbour. In 1859 the London & North Western absorbed the Chester & Holyhead, and the Lancashire & Yorkshire combined with an old antagonist, the East Lancashire; the Great Western united in 1863 with the West Midland company (which was itself a combination of three smaller units, dating from 1860); and in 1865 the Edinburgh & Glasgow joined forces with the North British. Though hundreds of small companies remained up and down Great Britain, their number started slowly to decrease, and fewer of them were genuinely independent. They were often leased or worked by companies whose lines adjoined theirs.

Such small companies were the main instrument by which the railway system was extended in Wales and northern Scotland. The system in the interior of Wales was begun in the 1850s, and it was then extended with remarkable speed, owing much to the energy of contractors like David Davies and Thomas Savin, who found a large part of the capital required. Almost all the chief lines were opened in 1859-67. In those eight years the railway was extended from Whitchurch and Shrewsbury to Pwllheli, Aberystwyth and Swansea.

The expansion of the Scottish railway system was a larger task, and it was carried through more slowly. In 1858 Inverness was linked with Aberdeen and so – however circuitously and inconveniently – with the South. It was better served five years later when the courageous line over the Grampians was completed from Forres to Perth. Plans were already in hand by that time for extending the railway far beyond Inverness to the North. It reached Strome Ferry (for Skye) in 1870 and Wick and Thurso, at the north-eastern tip of Scotland, four years later. At the same time, further south, a line was slowly stretching out in the face of great difficulties from Perthshire into Argyll; it reached Oban on the west coast in 1880.

These railways, in remote, under-populated parts of the country, were non-competitive. Elsewhere in Britain competition was the rule: a principle highly approved by the orthodox economists and successful businessmen of the time. It was a force that could stimulate the making of elaborate and

Way up in the Scottish Highlands, the station of Dalnaspidal presents a lonely picture amidst the hills of Glen Garry. Lying 1,000ft above sea level between Blair Atholl and Aviemore, it was opened in 1863 by the Inverness & Perth Junction Railway, amalgamated two years later with the Highland Railway. The new line, driven boldly across the Grampians by its Scottish engineer Joseph Mitchell, provided a quicker route from north to south, avoiding the old circuitous journey round the coast via Aberdeen.

expensive new railways – such as, for instance, the lines from Basingstoke to Exeter and from Derby through Matlock to Manchester.

The great apostle of competition, at all times, was the Midland Railway, a company whose career of sustained aggression bears comparison with that of Prussia and Germany in European politics – save that its aggression, on the whole, paid. The original Midland company, based on Derby, was sure of a steady prosperity. Under Hudson's leadership, however, it learnt to think of more glittering prizes. It could not rest content with a provincial position. It must have access to London. True, it had always enjoyed access by way of the line to Euston, but that meant transferring all its traffic to the London & North Western company, and the arrangements for handling it were far from satisfactory. Accordingly, in 1853 the Midland promoted a new line from Leicester to Hitchin to give it alternative admission to London over the Great Northern line to King's Cross, reducing the distance for which the Midland was dependent on another company from 83 miles to 32. The new line was opened in 1857; but still the Midland hankered after an entirely independent line to London, and this it achieved in 1868 when trains began to run into its flamboyant terminus at St Pancras. The opening of that station proclaimed to London that there was now a great new route to the North.

To the Midland, moreover, 'the North' meant more than Derby, Leeds and Bradford. In the previous year the company had completed its line through Matlock and the Peak District, which gave it access to Manchester, and it was already committed to building a railway through the Pennines from Settle to Carlisle. When this was opened in 1876, there was a third route from England to Scotland.

The bustling and intemperate self-confidence of the Midland naturally irritated its rivals, above all the London & North Western – a majestic, established concern, beside which the Midland looked a *parvenu*. It threw down a challenge to all the other companies in Britain. In 1872 it suddenly stated that it proposed to admit third-class passengers to every one of its trains. The example once set, other companies had to fall gradually into step, though the Great Western and the south-eastern lines continued to reserve a few of their best trains for first- and second-class passengers only. Then two years later the Midland announced that it intended to abolish the second class altogether and to lower first-class fares to the old second-class rate of 1½d a mile. In 1875 it decided to upholster all third-class carriages. Third-class passengers now had for 1d a mile the comfort and convenience for which on other railways they had to pay half as much again.

Those other railways regarded the Midland's action as outrageous, and said so. Having tried intimidation, and failed, they stuffily intimated that nothing would induce them to follow the Midland's example. As the general manager of one of them put it some years later: 'The London & North Western company have hitherto held the belief that society in this country, for all purposes, naturally divides itself into three classes, and that the wants and tastes of the community are best served by their present practice'.[14] But the London & North Western's views of society were less accurate than the Midland's. During the forty years that had passed since the opening of the Liverpool & Manchester Railway, the population of Great Britain had risen from 16 million to 28 million. Partly owing to the spread of the railways themselves, partly to other causes – a higher standard of living, cheap postage and political emancipation, for example – working men and women were beginning to travel as they never had done before. More and more of them were growing accustomed to the idea of railway journeys to and from work: 'workmen's trains', conveying them at exceptionally cheap fares, began to run in London in the 1860s. Excursion trains were a well recognised feature of the English summer and, after bank holidays were established in 1871, a visit to the sea by train came to be an

On the Settle & Carlisle line, a southbound special train hauled by preserved London & North Eastern 4-6-2 locomotive No. 4472 Flying Scotsman *crosses a viaduct over Garsdale, seven miles north of Ribblehead. There are 23 viaducts on this line, built for the Midland Railway in the 1870s; it was one of the last main lines to be built using manual methods of construction.*

A West Cornwall 'Teetotal Gala Excursion' train toils across the wooden viaduct at Redruth in 1855, hauled by three engines. The temperance movement did much to promote such expeditions, especially under powerful organisers such as Thomas Cook and John Frame. The moral of trips like this one was dinned into Cornishmen by a poem written to hail the first of them:
'Happy Camborne, happy
*   Camborne,*
Where the railway is so near;
And the engine shows how
*   water*
Can accomplish more than
*   beer.'*

annual joyous event for tens of thousands of working-class families.[15]

The Midland's policy of deliberately fostering third-class travel was shrewdly calculated. The decision of the management did not rest only on the expected receipts from passengers. A third-class coach was cheaper to build and carried more passengers than a second or a first; and some economy in working could be achieved by providing two classes of accommodation only instead of three. In spite of the indignation expressed at the Midland's new policy, the other companies gradually fell into line with it. If second class was slow to disappear, the Midland's treatment of third-class passengers set a precedent that could not be ignored. Old-fashioned railway officials continued to grumble at this pampering; but on most lines the third class presently shared in other improvements – lavatories, corridor coaches, restaurant cars. One company even outdid the Midland in courting third-class patronage. The Great Eastern set itself quite deliberately to become 'the poor man's line',[16] and it reaped a good reward. In many ways the most unpromising of the great railway properties, with an earlier history of disastrous mismanagement, the Great Eastern made the very best of itself on these lines. Between 1880 and 1914 it was able to pay an average dividend of nearly 3 per cent.

But those who questioned the wisdom of this policy were not merely a set of backward-looking diehards. Lower fares, higher speeds, more comforts and amenities suited passengers well enough, but they appeared in a different light to managements and shareholders. These changes were necessarily expensive; and the proportion of working costs to receipts tended continually to rise. As the mid-Victorian prosperity receded in the late 1870s, the railways became much less soundly based than they had been. They still had little effective competition to meet from any other form of land transport, except from tramways in towns, which began to provide services worked by horses or steam power after 1870. But increasing costs, diminishing profits and mounting unpopularity (due largely to a shocking increase in the number of accidents) were a nasty combination to face.

Comparatively little new railway construction was undertaken towards the end of the century. The Midland completed a new line from Kettering to Nottingham in 1880 and one from Sheffield to Chinley (for Manchester) in 1894. The London & South Western gradually reached down to Plymouth and Padstow between 1876 and 1899. In Scotland, the opening of the Tay and Forth Bridges (1874-90) made possible a new and direct route up the east coast; in 1898 the Carr Bridge line on the Highland Railway sliced 26 miles off the distance between Inverness and the South; and the West Highland Railway, completed to Fort William in 1894 and to Mallaig in 1901, opened up a great new tract of country, which no railway had ever penetrated before.

The three most conspicuous new railways of this period owed their existence to competition, in different forms. The Hull & Barnsley, in-corporated in 1880, was undertaken entirely because of the dissatisfaction felt in Hull with the monopolies of the North Eastern Railway and the Hull Dock Company. The Corporation of Hull backed it strongly, sold it 126 acres of land, and put up £100,000 of the company's capital. It proved an un-fortunate venture. For a time it was in the hands of a receiver, and before 1895 the company's ordinary shareholders only once secured a dividend, of less than 1 per cent. Its position then improved somewhat, but that was partly due to a working agreement with its original antagonist, the North Eastern.

The profits to be made from the South Wales coalfield in the 1880s still looked boundless, limited only by the difficulty of getting the coal down the narrow valleys and through the docks at Newport, Cardiff and Penarth. Every important valley had its own railway – some had two; yet the pro-vision was still inadequate. Accordingly, in 1884 a company was authorised to build yet another railway and a new coal port at Barry, south west of Cardiff. It was, of course, stoutly opposed by the existing railway and dock companies. In the event, however, the Barry Railway was a great financial success. In 1898 its £100 ordinary stock was never quoted lower than 254, and even in 1914 it still bore a price of 165-178.

The third of these new lines was the most spectacular. Under the leadership of an ambitious and wrong-headed chairman, Sir Edward

The enormous complex of Barry Docks was a thriving concern up to the 1920s, for it handled a substantial proportion of all the coal brought out of the South Wales coalfields. The docks were designed and built as an integral part of a new railway scheme completed in 1889. The main line comes in on the right of the aerial photograph, and innumerable branch lines fan out from it to feed the terminals in each of the docks.

The south portal of the Sherwood Rise tunnel begins to take shape as the contractors Logan & Hemingway press ahead with the Great Central Railway in the 1890s. On the high ground just north of Nottingham, Sherwood was one of the first major tunnelling works on the Great Central. The local sandstone was so solid that, apart from short lengths near the tunnel entrances, only the roof needed to be lined with brick. The 40ft deep rock cutting in the foreground is to become Carrington station.

Watkin, the Manchester Sheffield & Lincolnshire aspired in the 1890s to do what another provincial company, the Midland, had done a generation earlier: to provide itself with a trunk line of its own to London. The Midland's operation had been successful; but it had faced only two rivals. The London extension of the Sheffield company was carried through in a less prosperous era; it had to contend for traffic with three other companies; and, although it built its own London terminus at Marylebone, it reached that only by running over forty miles of the Metropolitan Railway. The line was opened (the company having changed its title to Great Central Railway) on 15 March 1899. At once it entered into energetic competition for the business of the North and the East Midlands. But there was simply not enough of that to divide between four companies, and it was the youngest and the weakest that suffered. The old Manchester Sheffield & Lincolnshire had never been a prosperous company, though its ordinary shares had occasionally borne dividends of as much as 3 per cent. The Great Central never paid an ordinary dividend at all.

Of each of these three new lines only small fragments remain in use today. They were very expensive to build and, in the long run, the traffic they were intended to carry passed to their older rivals. The facilities they offered, in so far as they were needed at all, could have been provided much more economically in other ways. They represent a wasteful extravagance, and show the Victorian devotion to the competitive principle at its worst.

Meanwhile a very important new development appeared beneath the streets of London. The first underground railway in the world was the Metropolitan line, opened from Paddington to Farringdon Street in 1863. It took 21 years to complete the Inner Circle, chiefly because it was made up of the lines of two partners, the Metropolitan and the District Railways, and they quarrelled continually. Partly as a result of the new facilities afforded

Aldersgate Street station (now Barbican) on the Metropolitan Railway in London boasted electric lighting in 1880. It was one of the earliest stations in Britain to be so equipped, although the Gare du Nord in Paris had been electrically lighted since 1875. One of the first underground stations in the world, it was built in 1863 with a specially high arched roof to allow the escape of smoke and fumes emitted by the steam locomotives.

by the underground railways, Londoners were making four times as many journeys every year by 1884 as they had made twenty years earlier. To provide more railways of the type of the Metropolitan and the District, however, would not only be expensive but highly inconvenient: the construction of these lines, only a little below the surface, interrupted all traffic on the roads above.

Engineers were already beginning to think about building a railway in a continuous tunnel far beneath the surface of the ground. P. W. Barlow and J. H. Greathead had demonstrated the possibilities of this kind of transport by their Tower Subway, which was opened in 1870 and for a short time conveyed passengers by cable traction under the Thames in a tube 6ft 7in in diameter. Twenty years later, on 4 November 1890, the first of all tube railways, in the full sense of the word, was inaugurated by the Prince of Wales: an electrically operated line from a station near the Monument to Stockwell. The success of this City & South London Railway induced it to extend its line at both ends. Before long similar railways were undertaken in other parts of London. The Central London Railway (known, because of its flat-rate fare, as the 'Twopenny Tube') was opened in 1900; the Piccadilly, Bakerloo, and Charing Cross – Hampstead lines in 1906-07. By 1913 all these lines had been combined with the District into the Underground Electric Railways Company of London. In that year they and the Metropolitan Railway together carried 426 million passengers.

—— COMPETITION AND EXPERIMENT ——

At the beginning of the 20th century the railways found themselves faced with competition from other forms of land transport and with growing internal problems. No longer a new enterprise, they were weighed down with legislative restrictions and became as a result more defensive than

Many of the larger railway companies began to run motor buses to 'feed' passengers on to their lines early in the 20th century – novelties that were duly recorded in local picture postcards. One card from the Suffolk town of Southwold records the first Great Eastern Railway bus (right); a Milnes-Daimler 20 horsepower 36-seater, which ran between Lowestoft and Southwold from July 1904. Its livery is the manufacturer's original brown, but after its first overhaul it was repainted entirely in GER red, with white window-frames. The London & South Western bus (below) ran between Exeter and Chagford until it was replaced in 1914. It stands here outside the Royal Hotel in Crockernwell, one of the stops on its route, in 1913.

– what they needed to be – forward-looking and imaginative.

The age of railway building was largely over. The Great Central extension to London was the last new main line to appear in Britain. The only railways laid down early in the new century were some short stretches, mostly 'cut-off' lines to shorten existing routes (as on the Great Western between Castle Cary and Taunton) and some branches built under the Light Railways Act of 1896, which facilitated the construction of cheap lines in country districts. These branches included the Sheppey (opened in 1901), the Leek & Manifold (1904), the Vale of Rheidol (1902), the Welshpool & Llanfair (1903) and, in Scotland, the Wick & Lybster and Fraserburgh & St Combs (both opened on the same day, 1 July 1903) and the Maidens & Dunure (1906).

The light railway was one solution to the problem of providing transport in rural districts; but it was relatively expensive and, since it required a

GREAT NORTHERN, PICCADILLY & BROMPTON Ry. PICCADILLY CIRCUS STATION.

Passengers at Piccadilly Circus station board an underground train of the Great Northern Piccadilly & Brompton Railway, in this postcard of about 1907. They entered and left the trains by balconies at each end of the carriages, passing through iron gates under the control of a gateman. The decorative tilework containing the station name was a standard design by the architect Leslie W. Green.

John Hassall's humorous poster tells Underground travellers that even the most unsophisticated country folk can find their way easily about the system. Dated 1908, it was among the first pictorial advertisements on the London Underground and would have been put up at all the newly opened stations on the electrically run Hampstead (now part of the Northern) line, the Bakerloo and the Piccadilly.

METRO-LAND

PRICE TWO-PENCE.

J.J.Dallaway

Supported on gantries, a maze of overhead high-tension cables straddles the lines at Tulse Hill in South London. Electric traction on the London Brighton & South Coast Railway started in 1909.

track, inflexible. Another instrument for the same purpose made its appearance in these opening years of the century: the petrol-driven bus. Here was a simple machine, economical to work, using public roads instead of a special track – ideal for the purpose of 'feeding' the railway from the outlying countryside. It soon ousted the light railway in the favour of the main-line companies. The Great Western, for example, showed a good deal of interest in a project put forward in Cornwall in 1897 for extending the Helston branch by a light railway to the Lizard. Negotiations dragged on to 1902, when the Great Western lost interest in the idea. Instead, in August of the following year, it began to work over this route the first permanent motor-bus service established by a railway in Britain.[17]

Between 1903 and 1914 many railway companies came to own buses, some of them on quite a large scale. But though they were quick to take advantage of the new opportunities the bus offered, they were strangely slow to exploit them to the full. If they had been prepared to invest heavily in the new vehicles, establishing subsidiary companies to manage them and develop their use, they might, at least in country districts, have integrated bus transport with their own services. However, they did not look far enough ahead; and they paid heavily for the mistake in the 1920s and 1930s.

Such criticisms, although valid and easy enough to make now, take no account of the continuing difficulties that the railways faced in the years before the First World War. They still had little to fear then from the motor-bus, but competition from the electric tram had begun to hit them hard, especially in the suburbs of the great towns. In 1907 more people travelled by tram in Greater London than by train. The London Brighton & South Coast Railway had by this time decided to electrify its South London line; when the work was carried through in 1909, and extended to the Crystal Palace in 1911-12, some of the old traffic was won back to the railway. This emboldened the company to consider further electrification, but it had done no more by 1914.

The drift of passengers away from the railway was not confined to London; nor did the railway managements succeed in halting the attack of

A substantial house and garden on the rural outskirts of London grace the frontispiece of an advertising booklet for 'the rural Arcadia' of Metro-land. Published by the Metropolitan Railway in 1921, it described with naive hyperbole the areas in Hertfordshire, Buckinghamshire and Middlesex where the company had carried out its own intensive property development. A specially commissioned poem summed up the appeal of this 'Realm of Rest from London's weary ways . . . Where comes no echo of the City's roar'.

The Brighton, *packed here with passengers waiting to disembark at the quayside in Dieppe, was owned by the London Brighton & South Coast Railway and the Chemin de Fer de l'Ouest, who had a joint agreement for working the crossing from Newhaven. Built in 1903, she was the second turbine steamship to operate in the English Channel.*

the trams after their first great onslaught at the beginning of the century. The number of passengers booked by the Caledonian Railway at its Glasgow suburban stations declined by 30 per cent between 1913 and 1922.[18]

At the same time the railways had to contend with sharply rising costs in operation and with serious labour troubles. A general railway strike – something previously unheard of – was only just averted in 1907; it actually happened four years later. With organised labour represented in Parliament, the idea of nationalisation began to be discussed and was backed by responsible public men.[19] In the face of such threats, directors, managers and shareholders prepared to defend railway property. Though this was perfectly natural on their part – indeed, on their political and economic assumptions it was their plain duty – it meant that they were not always as quick as their predecessors had been in detecting new challenges and meeting them.

A good deal of the old enterprise remained, nevertheless. For example, the British railways had long owned substantial fleets of small steamships for coastal and cross-Channel work, and now they were among the pioneers in the use of turbine propulsion. Sir Charles Parsons's prototype *Turbinia* had made its first memorable appearance in 1897. The first commercial vessel in the world to be driven by turbines was *King Edward*, a river steamer on the Clyde, which went into service in 1901. Next year a railway ship, the South Eastern & Chatham's *Queen*, was the first turbine steamer to work in the English Channel, followed by the London Brighton & South Coast's *Brighton* in 1903. And in 1904 the Midland Railway, preparing to start its steamers from Heysham to the Isle of Man and Ireland, ordered two ships to be equipped with reciprocating engines and two with turbines, all four being otherwise generally similar, so that a careful comparison could be made between the two systems. The experiment demonstrated beyond doubt the superiority of turbines for this kind of traffic.

In locomotive development, too, the British railways were doing much vigorous experimental work. The economist W. M. Acworth noted sadly in the 1890s that foreign railway engineers no longer came to Britain to learn, as they had done in former days; the traffic, he said, was now all in the opposite direction. That was not quite true. It was a two-way movement. British manufacturers were still designing and constructing locomotives in large quantity for railways all over the world. Two celebrated Scottish locomotive types, the 'Dunalastairs' of the Caledonian company and the 'Castles' of the Highland, were built in substantial numbers for use on the Continent: 235 of the former in Belgium, 50 of the latter on the French State

At Pouparts' Junction, Battersea (above left), on the London Brighton & South Coast Railway (the junction was named after Samuel Poupart, a well-known market gardener whose farm was close by), police and soldiers guard the junction box during the railway strike of 1911, while on the line at Wandsworth (left) guardsmen stand by the signals. All critical points of the system were protected by the military to prevent violence by striking railwaymen.

Sarah Bernhardt and her entourage were photographed beside her private saloon at St Pancras in 1894; perhaps unsurprisingly, the actress is one of the few people on the platform who managed to stay still for the entire length of the exposure. From the 1890s up to the First World War, the railways were at the height of their prestige and success: all manner of celebrities, from royalty downwards, travelled by train, often in specially appointed and luxurious carriages.

Railways. Conversely, three English railway companies imported 'Mogul' goods engines of two different designs from America; the Great Western more profitably bought three express engines working on the De Glehn compound system from France. It was partly as a result of the experiments made with these French machines that the Great Western's engineer, G. J. Churchward, evolved his own mature designs of express engine in 1903-09, influencing the whole subsequent development of the steam locomotive in Britain.

For all the uncertainties and occasional gloom of these years, they represent, in some respects, the climax of the story. Great things have been done since, but taken all round the railways have never offered as good a service as they did in the years before 1914.

—— THE FIRST WORLD WAR ——

The war shattered the railways as it shattered so much else of the world to which they belonged. It did not shatter them physically: the damage they suffered from enemy action was insignificant beside what was to come in 1939-45.[20] But it exposed them to intense strain which, for some of them, became almost unbearable; and it destroyed many of the old assumptions on which their thinking had long been based.

A Railway Executive Committee, consisting of the general managers of

the leading companies, had been formed by the government in 1912. Its task, in the event of war, was to co-ordinate the services afforded by the railways, to make them as far as possible into one system in order to meet the emergency. Under the authority of an Act of 1871, the government assumed control of the railways immediately war broke out. It made no attempt to administer them directly, but worked instead through the Committee, which in its turn relied on the managements of the separate companies.

The burden that fell on the companies was, necessarily, uneven. To most it meant intensification of traffic, curtailment of supplies, the interruption of many normal services and the frequent necessity of providing abnormal ones. These were difficult conditions, especially as the war dragged on into its fourth and fifth years, but still tolerable, given ingenuity and good temper. To others the war brought something graver – not only to those in the front line of defence such as the Great Eastern and the South Eastern & Chatham but also, even more strikingly, to those that were called upon to face quite unprecedented military tasks. Two companies that suffered in this way – at opposite ends of Great Britain – were the London & South Western and the Highland.

The London & South Western had long been the pre-eminent military line, serving Aldershot and Salisbury Plain; and from 1914 onwards

Waiting at Epsom Downs, the station for the Derby Day racecourse, the royal train of 1897 is headed by Class I2 4-4-2 tank locomotive No. 15, built in 1908 and specially decorated with a magnificent royal coat of arms. This train, designed by R. J. Billinton for the London Brighton & South Coast Railway, was for the use of Edward VII when he was Prince of Wales; he valued his privacy, so there were no corridor connections between the five carriages.

Herbert Ashcombe Walker (1868-1949) was appointed general manager of the London & South Western Railway in 1912. The company's business had been adversely affected by competition from electric trams since 1905, and Walker quickly began to carry through a programme of electrification. He presided over the Railway Executive Committee during the First World War, and was knighted in 1915. At the grouping of 1923, he became general manager of the Southern Railway. His vigorous policy of electrification and steadily forceful management did much to make the company respected and successful. One of the ablest managers in British railway history, he retired in 1937.

Southampton became the chief focus of communications between Britain and the Continent. But the South Western not only controlled all the railways of Southampton, it had also owned the docks there since 1892. During the four years of war, the company carried over 20 million soldiers, and 7 million passed through Southampton docks – that is, almost 4,500 a day. The use of Southampton was facilitated by its exceptional position in the British railway system. It could be reached from South Wales, the North and the Midlands by five separate routes without touching London: by Bath and Blandford, by Salisbury, Andover, Newbury, and Basingstoke. The second and last of these were main lines, double-tracked. The rest, however, had long stretches of single line. In the course of the war these railways were used to the limit of their capacity. The South Western was alone responsible for handling the vast traffic as it converged on Southampton; its resources were stretched to the utmost, and the strain placed upon its employees was correspondingly severe. That was made severer still because two of its senior managers were seconded to hold commanding posts in the Railway Executive Committee: the South Western's general manager, Herbert Walker, presided over it, and his assistant, Gilbert Szlumper, acted as its secretary. No single railway company, large or small, made a greater contribution to winning the war.

The Highland also, in a different way, served its country well. It provided the only railway access to two of the Grand Fleet's three bases, Cromarty Firth and Scapa Flow. In 1918 the materials for the huge minefield known as the Northern Barrage, stretching from the Orkneys to the coast of Norway, were assembled at Inverness and Dalmore, near Invergordon, many of them having been brought up by train from Kyle of Lochalsh, where they had been landed from American ships. No railway could have been less well adapted to the performance of such a vital military function. The Highland main line between Perth and Inverness is mountainous, and as it moves on to Thurso it is again steeply graded and pursues a serpentine course. More than four fifths of this line of 280 miles was single, and it was inadequately furnished with sidings and loops. This reflects no discredit on the company: it ran through a poor and thinly populated country, carrying in peace-time a very sparse traffic for nine months of the year and a heavy one only during the short summer season. But what sufficed in peace was hopelessly inadequate in war. The company owned 150 locomotives. Within the first year a third of those were out of service and another third in pressing need of repair. The Railway Executive Committee arranged for the loan of twenty engines from other companies, and more followed later; but the shortage of rolling stock of all kinds – particularly goods wagons – remained acute throughout the war. Somehow, nevertheless, the traffic was kept going, though it looked more than once as if there might be a complete breakdown. It was on this thin and fragile thread that the supplying of the Grand Fleet depended – and with it the naval security of Britain in the North Sea. That the thread did not snap was owing, in large measure, to the tenacity and devotion of the railwaymen.

But even that tenacity and devotion would have been insufficient if the Highland company had not been assisted by the other railways further south. The war proved the value of such co-operation. When it ended it was clear that companies like the Highland could hardly stand on their own again. How would they ever be able to raise the capital to replace their worn-out equipment?

Under state control, in time of war, the British railway system had been unified as it had never been previously. The argument was now heard that

state control should not be abandoned; that this was the moment for the state to purchase the railways outright. But protagonists of nationalisation were fiercely opposed by those who wished to return to the old ways. A coalition government of Liberals and Conservatives could scarcely be expected to favour nationalisation, but it recognised that it was not possible merely to put the clock back: if the railways were to return to private ownership, it must be on a new basis. In 1919, for the first time, a Ministry of Transport was established, inheriting the powers and duties in this area previously held by the Board of Trade. It was headed by a tough Scot, Sir Eric Geddes, who had himself been a railwayman and who devoted much of his abounding energy to working out a new plan for the railways.

As embodied in the Railways Act of 1921, which came into effect on 1 January 1923, this plan represented a great departure from previous practice. In the past, amalgamation had been discussed by Parliament, but discussion had led to little legislative action – and that only on the companies' own initiative. Now the initiative was taken by the government, which applied a systematic, compulsory amalgamation scheme of its own. Leaving aside the underground lines of London and certain very small and insignificant provincial companies, all the railways of Great Britain were now to be combined into four 'groups', north-western, eastern, western and southern. In this way 120 companies were reduced to four. One of these derived from a single existing company, the Great Western, with the addition of the Cambrian Railways and the small, though for the most part prosperous, lines in the Welsh Valleys. The other three were composite

Troops line up after alighting from a train at Southampton during the First World War; they are about to board a ship for service overseas. The railways played a vital role during the war: as well as facilitating the widespread movement of troops, they were also responsible for the carriage of coal, weapons and ammunition all over the country.

organisations. The biggest, the London Midland & Scottish, was based on the London & North Western, the Midland, the Lancashire & Yorkshire, the Caledonian, the Glasgow & South Western and the Highland Railways. The new London & North Eastern included the three companies that had tried to amalgamate in 1909 – the Great Eastern, Great Northern and Great Central – together with the North Eastern, the North British and the Great North of Scotland. The smallest of the four groups, the Southern, comprised the London & South Western, the London Brighton & South Coast and the South Eastern & Chatham.

—— AMALGAMATION ——

Each of the four new companies had the monopoly of a large territory, but the four were very unequal in size. Competition did not disappear. It continued, for instance, between London and Exeter, London and Sheffield, Leeds and Scotland, but its force was now very much reduced. Industrial kingdoms, like Lancashire and the South Wales coalfield, became dependent for their railway services almost entirely on a single company. The inequality in size between the groups resulted in part from the principle that, since the railways remained private property, none of the old companies could be dismembered. Artificially 'equal' groups could not therefore be created; and the anomalies arising from the application of this principle had to be accepted – even when they brought a 'London & North Eastern Railway' into North Wales. But inequality of size was less important than inequality of economic power. The Southern company was not only the smallest; its constituent companies had been particularly hard hit by the war, and two of them carried a dense and increasing suburban traffic into London, which they did not handle well. The London & North Eastern company was weaker still. In the 1920s and 1930s the North East of England, its stronghold, became one of the most grimly depressed areas in the country. The company inherited a higher proportion of unremunerative secondary and branch lines than any of the other three groups. Of its large constituents, the Great Eastern was poor through no fault of its own, and the Great Central financially ramshackle. Even the Great Northern, one of the strongest partners in the new corporation, was in some ways singularly ill equipped. Whilst the other great railways had quadrupled their tracks out of London – the London & North Western for 60 miles, the Midland for 75 – the great Yorkshire coal trains and the east coast expresses had to jostle one another on two tracks when they were hardly more than ten miles out from King's Cross.[21]

The new managements faced considerable difficulties in welding the amalgamated companies together. The task was hardest of all on the London Midland & Scottish. The old London & North Western and Midland Railways had been opposed to each other not merely in an economic sense as competitors: for nearly three generations they had adopted opposite ideas and practices. Which would now prevail? After a short interlude, during which the new company took its tone in some respects from a junior partner, the Lancashire & Yorkshire, it became plain that the Midland's notions had won, that Derby had triumphed over Crewe.

The London Midland & Scottish company also had a similar difficulty to face in Scotland. The Caledonian and the Glasgow & South Western Railways had fought each other with peculiar ferocity for years, in Glasgow and Ayrshire and all over the Firth of Clyde. It was beyond the power of a mere Act of Parliament to force these two long-standing enemies to become friends – except in so far as they were willing to combine together in order to take a stand against the decrees of the new bosses in London.

Of all the big four companies, it was the smallest, the Southern, that showed the greatest enterprise, under the leadership of Sir Herbert Walker. After the war he had returned to his own company, the London & South Western, where he had been closely associated with the electrification of the suburban lines in London in 1915-16. At grouping he became general manager of the new Southern Railway, which was subjected from the first to well justified criticism of its suburban services, in the press and in Parliament. Walker had no doubt that electrification was the solution and drove through a programme that ultimately stretched far beyond the suburbs, in the old sense of the term: perhaps it would be more accurate to say that by 1939 it had made suburbs of Chatham, Brighton and Portsmouth, with two or three trains up to London every hour of the day. This gave the Southern Railway the biggest electrified suburban system in the world.

To the traveller it meant a service improved almost beyond recognition. Commuters from Croydon or Orpington benefited no less than long-distance travellers from Portsmouth, a town that, for its size and situation, had always endured the worst 'express' service in England. From the point of view of the company and its shareholders, electrification paid handsomely. It not only solved the baffling problem of conveying established passenger traffic; it created new traffic of its own, to and from the Isle of

A Southern Railway electric train set, No. 4515, leaves Peckham Rye for Holborn Viaduct in 1957. The first set of four coaches is made up of vehicles converted from steam stock and formerly owned by the London Brighton & South Coast Railway. The last four coaches, just visible, date from 1941: this modern stock was gradually superseding the converted steam carriages, which were uncommon by this time.

Wight for example. When all the three Dartford lines were electrified in 1925, the central one through Bexleyheath carried only a small traffic and the new service over it seemed extravagant. The Southern's policy, however, was right. The good train service encouraged suburban building, with the consequence that every train on the three Dartford lines came to run at its full capacity in the rush hours.

By comparison with that achievement, the timid ventures into electrification made by the other three companies were insignificant. When big schemes were drawn up, they were not implemented. The Midland company had undertaken to electrify the London Tilbury & Southend line when it absorbed it in 1912; but nothing was done either by the Midland or by the London Midland & Scottish to redeem that pledge. A government committee on main-line electrification reported in 1931 that the cost of the national scheme it had considered would be £261 million, on which the likely return, in the most favourable circumstances, would be less than 7 per cent. The current economic crisis put any such expenditure out of the question. The idea was looked at again in 1938 by the Great Western company, which considered electrifying its main line from Taunton to Penzance, but it was rejected shortly before the outbreak of war in 1939.

It would be unjust, however, to convict the three largest companies of a stolid, unimaginative conservatism. Certainly the London Midland & Scottish *ought* to have electrified the Tilbury line, and it could well have afforded to do so. But it had no other suburban problem comparable in magnitude with those that the Southern took over in 1923. Neither had the Great Western. The London & North Eastern undoubtedly had a problem in Hertfordshire and Essex, but two things deterred the company from proceeding to electrification. The first was its poverty: it would have been very difficult for the London & North Eastern to raise the necessary capital, for its credit never stood high. Second, though the suburban traffic of Liverpool Street was as dense as that of the Southern stations, it was very much more efficiently worked by steam than that of, say, London Bridge. The whole system had been ruthlessly overhauled and modernised, on American lines, in 1920. Although travelling into and out of Liverpool Street was a dirty and uncomfortable business, it was more punctual and reliable than travelling south of the Thames. The London & North Eastern management tended therefore to think that, whilst sooner or later these lines would have to be electrified, the task could wait until other jobs had been done. That time did not come until 1935; and the work had, in the end, to be completed after nationalisation.

For the two northern companies the 1920s were a time of consolidation, during which the new managements sought to bring their services and equipment back, as far as possible, to pre-war standards. But conditions had changed since 1914. Now the petrol-driven vehicle had made its way everywhere. The bus was a formidable new rival to the train; and the motor-lorry was as formidable a competitor for freight traffic. This was the critical moment: the war had shown the capabilities of petrol-driven vehicles, and thousands of those who had handled them then saw what could be done with them in peace-time. Within ten years of the end of the war the railways were losing ground fast – in the towns and on rural branch lines to the bus, and everywhere to the lorry. Their reaction was painfully slow. They interested themselves in a few bus undertakings, especially after 1928, when their legal powers to do so were enlarged; they closed a few unremunerative branches. And that was all.

Again, this ingloriously defensive attitude on the part of the railways

can be understood in the light of the past and of their current economic difficulties. Labour problems caused them increasing anxiety. Even in war-time, in 1917, there had nearly been a railway strike. There was one in fact in September 1919, and a coal strike (which, in the days of steam haulage, was almost as serious for the railways) in 1921. The General Strike of 1926 hit the railways very hard indeed; and here, as in other industries, it left behind it a legacy of ill will between management and men.

During the general strike of 1926, soldiers with a Lewis machine gun protect the railway at Newcastle Central station. The government had learnt the importance of heavy deterrent action during the railway strike of 1911.

These strikes were accompanied by a steep rise in costs. That did not hit the railways alone; but whereas other commercial concerns were free to raise prices as they saw fit and pass on the burden to the consumer, the railways were severely limited, by a hundred years of legislation, in their freedom to raise fares and rates. Both were increased, while the railways were still under the control of the government, in 1920; but no further general increase took place until 1937. The railways thus found themselves undercut by the cheaper and more flexible motor vehicle on services that were being run at a loss, and at the same time prevented from increasing rates and fares on the services in which they still enjoyed a strong position.

All this was bad enough in the 1920s. With the slump of 1929-31 it grew much worse. There was then nothing for it but defensive action of a drastic kind. That was not nearly drastic enough. Rather more than 1,200 miles of line were closed from 1923 to 1947. It was the beginning of an effort to tackle

The cover of a booklet, published in 1938 by the Railway Companies' Association, superimposes an impassioned plea on the layout of Cannon Street station. It was part of the railway companies' case for a 'square deal': the repeal of out-dated laws which restricted their operation while allowing road transport to cream off the profitable freight traffic. 'Your fuel, your food, your letters, your newspapers, your entertainments depend on railways', readers were reminded. The outbreak of war the following year cut short the campaign; but immediately after the war the railways were nationalised and most of the old restrictions were removed.

the task, but only the beginning. No vigorous drive to win back lost traffic from the roads by new methods seems seriously to have been considered.

One long-term solution to this problem was indicated by what happened in London. In 1929 the Underground group of companies and the London County Council put forward a joint scheme for the co-ordination of transport services. Though it was rejected by Parliament, another plan, with a similar end in view, was eventually embodied in an Act of 1933. This established a London Passenger Transport Board, which was entrusted with the biggest transport monopoly yet created in Britain: a complete monopoly of both road and rail passenger transport in the London area, excluding only the main-line railways. There was plenty of opposition to the idea of setting up this mammoth combine, but the measure was on the whole a wise one, conceived in the public interest.

Here was an example of the co-ordination of road and rail transport at the command of the state. But the state issued no other directives of the same kind in these years. Confronted with the fierce competition between road and rail – a competition that benefited neither the rivals nor the public – it stood aside, hesitating to intervene. It gave a little help to the railways: as in 1935, when it made available to them a loan of £30 million to enable major works of reconstruction and electrification to be undertaken. But on the main question – the relationship between road and rail in the transport system of the country as a whole – it had no lead to offer. Here was a refusal to accept responsibility quite as deplorable as that of the governments in the early days of the railways a century before. Morally, it was worse: for whereas in the 1830s and 1840s *laissez-faire* was the orthodox policy expected of governments in this country, in the 1930s that policy was clearly outmoded. In fact, the government refused to intervene not from adherence to any principle but from timidity. This was, after all, the Age of Baldwin.

In 1938 the four companies began concerted pressure on the government to give them freedom to fix their own rates and fares. As they put it in their popular campaign, they were asking for a 'square deal'. They were justified in arguing that the law was antiquated and unrealistic; justified too in pointing to the many services they had rendered to the country in the past and in claiming that their weak economic position was hampering their ability to render similar services in the future. In 1939, as war approached, with all the demands it was certain once again to make on the railways, their arguments made some progress. But the government had reached no decision in the matter when war broke out.

The story of the British railways in the inter-war years is not an entirely sombre one. Though they were on the defensive, and on some fronts fighting a losing battle, they had some fine achievements to their credit. The Southern could boast of electrification as the greatest triumph of the period, but it had other claims to distinction too. It did more than any other company in the rebuilding of stations. The architectural style it adopted involved a relentless and unimaginative use of ferro-concrete, but the new stations at Surbiton, Richmond, Ramsgate, Hastings and elsewhere offered accommodation and facilities greatly superior to the old. The Southern was almost alone in building new railways in these years: the Ramsgate and Lewisham loops, for example, the Wimbledon–Sutton line and the Chessington branch. Finally, in 1936, in collaboration with France's Chemin de Fer du Nord, it inaugurated a profitable train-ferry service between London and Paris.

The Great Western's effort was less striking, but it had started in better order and was in less urgent need of improvement. Having led the way in

The Southern Railway's 'Night Ferry' train (left) steams out of Victoria to meet the boat at Dover during the 1930s. It was a very heavy train, calling usually for two engines: here it is headed by an L1 4-4-0 as pilot to a second engine behind. The Southern Railway board had resolved to establish a train ferry service to France in 1932; after numerous difficulties – physical, technical and political – it was finally inaugurated in 1936. At Dover harbour, the twin-screw steamships Hampton Ferry and Twickenham Ferry (below) wait for the train from London. A third ship, Shepperton Ferry, was held in reserve. Specially built in 1934 for the crossing from Dover to Dunkirk, each could accommodate 12 sleeping-cars and forty wagons 25ft long, as well as motor traffic.

developing automatic train control, an extremely important safety device (see p. 200), it now extended the installation to the whole of its main lines. It was the only one of the four companies to make widespread use of diesel railcars on the Continental model, so anticipating the practice of British Railways from 1954 onwards. It effected two useful improvements in its main route to the West Country, which enabled express trains to by-pass Westbury and Frome stations. In September 1932 its up Cheltenham Spa Express was accelerated to run from Swindon to Paddington at an average speed of 71·4 mph. This was the fastest schedule in the world.

The most spectacular efforts of the London & North Eastern company were also in the realm of speed. In 1935-37 it introduced a series of stream-lined express trains that gave Newcastle, Edinburgh, Leeds and Bradford a substantially faster service to and from London than any they had known

In its garter blue livery, the London & North Eastern's A4 Pacific No. 4489 Dominion of Canada leaves King's Cross with the London – Edinburgh 'Coronation' express in 1937. This class of streamlined 4-6-2s, designed by Sir Nigel Gresley for high-speed service, covered the 393 miles of the journey to Edinburgh with eight articulated twin coaches and an observation car in six hours non-stop. Between the wars, the British railways had great success with these long-distance performances.

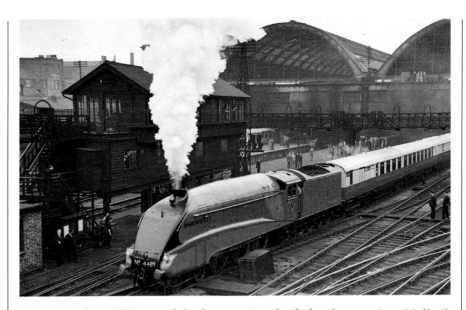

before. And in 1938 one of the locomotives built for these trains, *Mallard*, attained 126 mph, the highest authenticated speed that has ever been reached by a steam locomotive. Though the company did not feel able to tackle its worst problem, that of improving the main line out of King's Cross, it effected an important change for the better by widening the Great Eastern line from Romford to Shenfield, and it made a start on an extensive programme of electrification.

The London Midland & Scottish Railway looked, more than any of its fellows, to the USA for an example. This was proclaimed in its very terminology. On this railway, as on no other in Britain, the chairman was also 'president of the executive'. Among the vice-presidents was a distinguished man of science, Sir Harold Hartley. Under his direction the company embarked on a programme of research, with modern laboratories at Derby (opened in 1935) and a testing station for locomotives, established jointly with the London & North Eastern company, at Rugby. The London Midland & Scottish pursued very much further than either of the other composite companies the strict standardisation of its equipment, especially in signalling and locomotives. It too went in for high-speed trains, putting on an express to run between London and Glasgow in six and a half hours. The London Midland & Scottish also interested itself, to a greater extent than the other three companies, in the development of air services within the British Isles from 1934 onwards – an intelligent attempt to 'tame' a potentially dangerous competitor.

A general review of the working of the Railways Act of 1921 suggests that it proved, in practice, a failure. Like most transport legislation passed in Britain in the 20th century, it was already behind the times when it came into force. The very large new organisations it established had to be managed by railwaymen quite inexperienced in conducting their business against the fierce competition they now faced. They assumed that the railways enjoyed monopolistic powers that had in fact passed away. A new marketing policy – strong in aggression and defence – was called for. Neither the managers of the old companies nor the next generation, trained under them, were well suited to devising it. No less important, the rigid restraints that the Act still imposed on them when they tried to meet that

The railway companies' involvement in other, potentially competitive, forms of transport was not confined to the running of road vehicles. In the 1930s several companies inaugurated air services. The City of Cardiff, shown here, was a 'Rapide' twin-engined De Havilland Dragon biplane; it provided a fast link between Plymouth, Cardiff and Birmingham for the Great Western Railway from March 1934. A similar model is preserved in the Science Museum collection at Wroughton, Wiltshire. Railway air services ceased with the outbreak of the Second World War, and were not reintroduced afterwards.

competition fettered and discouraged them, making them cautious when they needed to be bold, in the tradition of the men who had created the railway system in the 19th century.[22]

It must be appreciated, however, that the managements of the four companies had to work in adverse circumstances; and the time at their disposal was short. In 1939, less than 17 years after the Act came into force, the Second World War broke out.

—— THE SECOND WORLD WAR ——

The Second World War imposed an even greater burden on the railways than the First. The special degree of strain that fell on certain companies in the first war was imposed on all the railways alike in the second, stretching their capacity to the utmost. Air raids produced far more devastation. There were 9,200 'incidents' on the railways, 247 of which put the piece of line concerned out of use for more than a week. A total of 24,000 goods wagons were destroyed or damaged, and 14,000 passenger vehicles.[23] The second of these figures is particularly striking. Even though some of these coaches sustained only slight damage, they had to be taken out of service while they were being repaired; and the total stock of passenger vehicles at the beginning of the war was only a little over 40,000.

The strain on the railways' resources was evident to the ordinary traveller. Whereas on some lines restaurant cars continued to be run throughout the first war, they were withdrawn altogether in 1944. On the trains that still ran, overcrowding became persistent and notorious. The coaches on some trains were reported to be so weighed down that their running boards fouled station platforms. Yet passenger travel increased, in spite of these discomforts and all the limitations imposed on it. In the last six months of war it was greater in volume than it had been in peace-time.[24]

What was even more important was the burden directly imposed on the railways by military operations. These reached their peak in 1944, when the invasion of France was being prepared and carried out. In that year the railways ran 178,000 special trains for the government – nearly a third of the total number run during the whole six years of war. They had the task of conveying to the south coast almost all the troops that arrived from overseas

London Transport made 79 Underground stations available as air-raid shelters during the Blitz in 1940. Only the tunnels built at the deeper levels were safe for the purpose; those nearer the surface would be damaged by the bombs. The children crowded into Highgate station (above) had some of the best conditions: when all the space on the platforms had been taken, adults used to sleep on the floor of the tunnels themselves, legs stretched out beneath the tracks. In what was perhaps the worst railway 'incident' during the Blitz, the new buildings at Sloane Square suffered a direct hit on the evening of 12 November 1940 when a train was just leaving the station (above right). There were 79 deaths, three 'missing presumed dead', and rail services were disrupted for a fortnight.

in the Clyde and the Mersey; and it was on them that the greatest responsibility fell for the continuous movement of supplies to the ports as long as the invasion of Europe continued. They did not fall down on their job. When VE Day arrived they could feel justifiably proud of the part they had taken in one of the greatest military operations in history.

The physical condition of the railways when the war ended was frankly deplorable. Almost at once, before they had had time to repair any of the damage they had suffered or to consider their position in the post-war world, they found themselves at the centre of a political storm. At the general election held immediately after the war a Labour government was returned to power. It was committed to the nationalisation of the railways.

Under the Transport Act of 1947 the railways were compulsorily purchased by the state. At midnight on 31 December the old railway companies and the London Passenger Transport Board ceased to exist, and a state system took their place on 1 January 1948, under the control of the British Transport Commission.

—— THE RAILWAYS NATIONALISED ——

The nationalisation of the railways brought many changes in their conduct and operation. The first and most obvious was the change in management. Though they were all now 'British Railways', under common ownership, they could not be run as a single unit. The nationalised railways were divided into six Regions. Three of them were based, roughly, on the arrangements adopted in 1921: the Southern and Western Regions corresponded to the systems of the Southern and Great Western companies; the new London Midland Region comprised the English and Welsh lines of the old London Midland & Scottish Railway. The London & North Eastern's English lines were divided into an Eastern and a North Eastern Region. Finally – the one part of these arrangements that could be called an innovation – Scotland became a Region of its own, with the lines of the former London Midland & Scottish and London & North Eastern companies north of the border all falling under the control of a Chief Regional Officer in Glasgow.

The new British Transport Commission's first business was to put the railways on their feet again, in both a material and a moral sense. No great duty could have been undertaken in more discouraging circumstances. The Commission was instructed that its services must pay for themselves – but that, for the moment, was an impossible ideal. The first thing was to re-equip the railways, to repair the damage they had sustained during the war, and to catch up on the arrears of maintenance. This in itself was a big job; money was scarce, prices were rising and the necessary materials were hard or even impossible to get.

But from the outset of the new regime it was clear that something more was needed than a restoration of what had gone before. The place of the railways in the economy and society of Great Britain as a whole needed reconsideration. If they were to play their proper part in the life of the country – still more, if they were ever to make ends meet – three things were essential. They must be freed of the commercial restrictions that had hampered them so severely in the past; they must be allowed to concentrate, as far as possible, on those tasks to which they were best suited; and their equipment and operation must be completely overhauled and brought up to the standards of the mid-20th century.

The Act of 1947 had not done very much to give the railways the 'square deal' the old companies had asked for in 1938. A change in this direction was attempted by the Transport Act of 1953, which allowed the railways a much increased freedom to adjust their charges. Henceforward they were obliged to publish only their maximum rates for freight traffic; below that level they were free to fix rates that competed with other forms of transport. A considerable administrative reorganisation also took place, with the object of diminishing the close central control over the Regions that was adopted in the Act of 1947. The powers of the former chief regional officers were increased to resemble those of the general managers of the old private companies.

This Act was a highly controversial measure, on which economists as well as politicians were divided. No sensible person could fail to sympathise with the management's desire to apply its resources to the work that the railways could perform best and to rid itself of the liability to maintain services that were, and were bound to remain, unremunerative. Again this was not a new policy. The old companies had closed some branch lines and in that way had effected considerable economies. The Commission carried this policy a long step further. Between 1948 and 1959 it closed 2,944 miles of railway, either to passengers or to all traffic.

At the same time a careful investigation was undertaken of every station on the whole system, considered as a commercial asset; and this led to the closing of a large number, on lines that otherwise remained open. Such thinning-out of wayside stations effected a double economy: it eliminated the costs of running the stations themselves and it assisted the movement of through traffic, no longer impeded by stopping trains. The London & North Eastern Railway had set an example before the war by closing all the intermediate stations on the 21 miles between York and Malton. In 1956 the British Transport Commission closed to passengers, at a single stroke, no fewer than 27 stations on the old Caledonian main line between Glasgow and Aberdeen. All the villages served by them were also on bus routes; and buses can usually offer a more economical and effective service to passengers in country districts than trains.

This negative policy, of ridding the British railways of unprofitable commitments, was part of something positive: a policy of improving, at every point, the services they could offer with best effect. The Commission

The panel signal box at Birmingham New Street, introduced in connection with the electrification of the Euston – Manchester and Liverpool line in 1966, was one of 19 new boxes built to replace two hundred old mechanical boxes. It alone served the whole of the reconstructed station, replacing 55 old boxes.

carried through the London & North Eastern's plans of electrification, including the line from Manchester to Sheffield, which involved the boring of an entirely new tunnel at Woodhead. In East Anglia, the introduction of the *Britannia* locomotives made possible an express service between London, Ipswich and Norwich of a quality that under earlier managements would have been quite unattainable.

Much bigger ideas were then being worked out. At the beginning of 1955 the Commission announced a plan of long-term development. It began by admitting that 'British Railways today are not working at full efficiency', and attributed this shortcoming chiefly to 'their past inability to attract enough capital investment to keep their physical equipment fully up to date'. Starting from this premise, the Commission set out the case for undertaking an expenditure of £1,200 million on 'modernisation and re-equipment'. It pointed out that, in any event, nearly half this sum would have to be found in order to maintain the existing services and the plant they demanded. Rightly arguing that it was out of the question to undertake such expenditure for so limited a purpose, it put forward a scheme of planned development under four main heads: improvement of track and signalling; replacement of steam by electric or diesel traction; modernising of passenger rolling-stock and station facilities; and – the biggest item of all, estimated to cost £365 million – the recasting of freight services, especially through the fitting of continuous brakes to all wagons (see p. 188). The result of these changes, the Commission predicted, would be 'a transformation of virtually all the forms of service now offered by British Railways'.[25]

—— MODERNISATION ——

The Modernisation Plan seems in retrospect to represent the most conspicuous achievement of the British Transport Commission in its direction of the railways. The plan set out clear objectives and indicated the means of reaching them; it aimed at a realistic estimate of expenditure, together with the revenue and economies that might be expected to accrue from implementing its proposals. When it appeared it met, on the whole, with a very favourable reception. The Conservative government promptly undertook to guarantee the necessary loan. Improvements, already begun rather tentatively, were speeded up and soon became noticeable to the railways' customers. A number of stations were rebuilt. Banbury, then an important junction, which had been a plague-spot on the system for years, was completed in 1958; Potters Bar and Broxbourne in Hertfordshire were rebuilt from 1955 to 1960. The electrification of all the Kent coast lines was finished a year ahead of time in 1962. The Glasgow suburban system also went over to electric traction in 1960-62.

The much bigger electrification of the lines from London to Birmingham, Manchester and Liverpool was completed in stages between 1960 and 1967. This required large alterations in the existing system, much of which had proved adequate, with remarkably few changes, since it was first opened in 1837-42.[26] The rebuilding of Euston station was a very complicated task. Although the Doric Arch and the Great Hall were lost, something efficient took their place. Something similar happened at Birmingham New Street, which was refashioned to become the sole central station in the city. The original New Street, though it lay below ground, had had to be provided with openings to allow the smoke of the engines to escape. As steam engines had ceased to run on the lines converging there, its successor could be entirely closed in. It was designed with a high and immensely heavy block of shops and offices above it and remains, alas, a monument of the spirit of 'brutalism' that was the architectural vogue at the time it was built. But some of its gloom and the insufficiency of its platform accommodation could be rectified at no large expense. This New Street station constituted something never seen before, and evidently desirable since the railway system first became complex in the 1850s: a great junction at the very centre of England for the passenger services of the whole country. Through trains now radiate out from it every weekday to all the largest towns and to every densely populated district in Britain, except East Lancashire and Kent. There is nothing like that anywhere on the Continent save in Belgium, with its much smaller system converging on Brussels. The making of this new junction was a national achievement, and only a national railway administration could have carried it through.

The electrified express passenger service was far better than anything offered on these lines before. From London to Manchester, it was superior to any other in Europe: twelve trains a day at 70 mph. On the route between Paris and Brussels, the same speed was maintained over a similar distance, but the frequency of the British service was greater by half, and second-class passengers were conveyed on ten of the Manchester trains whereas on those between Paris and Brussels they were admitted to only five.

Looked at in these simple terms, the Modernisation Plan might seem to have opened a new and more hopeful era for the nationalised railways. But the improvements it brought took place against a background of fearful economic disorder and of quite new competition.

The disorder was plain enough. In 1952 the railways struggled out of their war-time difficulties to reach an operating surplus of £79 million. Four years later, when the Modernisation Plan was beginning to be implemented, the surplus had turned into a deficit of £17 million. By 1961 the deficit had become £87 million; the year after it was £17 million more still. No government could allow such enormous losses to continue.

The losses arose for various reasons. Some fumbling and very expensive policies had been adopted. Too many experimental types of diesel locomotives were introduced, and the purchase of private owners' wagons, a most necessary measure, was achieved at an unjustifiably high price.[27] The reason for these questionable decisions lay partly in the Act of 1947, which had established a divided control: the British Transport Commission had the overall financial responsibility, while management – the running of

Three years after its closure in 1952, the platform of Abbotsbury station in Dorset serves as a temporary store for a farmer's hayricks. The Abbotsbury Railway, a branch line six miles long from Upwey Junction on the Great Western line to Weymouth, was opened in 1885; the company was merged with the Great Western in 1896. In all the years it operated, the line was never profitable.

the services – was in the hands of the Railway Executive.

Another much more serious cause of loss, well understood by many railwaymen, now came to public notice: the system inherited by the new administration was much too large. Even though 4,000 miles of line had been closed to passengers between 1923 and 1959, many more remained that were notoriously unremunerative. But the procedure for securing permission to close a line was cumbersome and slow, and the easing of the financial burden that these loss-making services represented was correspondingly delayed.

Just when the railways were running deeper and deeper into debt, they were confronted with formidable new competitors. Internal air services were beginning to erode the first-class rail traffic on the main business routes between large cities two hundred miles or more apart. That was disturbing, but the railways had some quick answers, especially in improving their overnight sleeper services, which could move steadily even in bad weather when air services had to be delayed or cancelled. The new competition from the roads was much more serious. In 1958 the first stretch of motorway in Britain, the Preston by-pass, was opened. Next year came the first section of the M1, running from outer London to Rugby, with a branch turning off towards Birmingham. In earlier days, when ownership of fast cars was relatively uncommon, this development might have syphoned off only the railways' richer passengers. But at the very same time the British Motor Corporation began to produce its Mini: a cheap car, small and easily manoeuvrable in cities, yet also capable of running down long stretches of open motorway at 60 mph – that is, as fast as nearly all the best express trains.

In 1955 the railways had seemed to be set on a new and hopeful course. By 1960 the outlook for them was becoming very grim indeed.

The Conservative government passed a new Transport Act in 1962, abolishing the British Transport Commission and dividing its tasks between a number of boards, including one wholly responsible for railways and another for London Transport. That resolved the dichotomy between the Commission and the Railway Executive. The new British Railways Board was to be responsible both for finance and for management.

The Act relieved the railways of the payment of interest on £1,175 million of accumulated debt. It gave them much greater freedom to fix their own charges than they had ever had before. But its main objective was perfectly clear: the new Railways Board was to move as fast as possible into solvency, by concentrating its attention on the services it could provide with profit. That meant a quick and large reduction in all the unprofitable mileage. There too the Act gave the Board some help, by simplifying the procedure for closing down the lines that ran at a loss.

Which were those lines, and how much was each of them losing? No full attempt had yet been made to answer those questions. This was clearly one of the first tasks awaiting the chairman of the new Railways Board, Dr Richard Beeching, and his officers. Their findings appeared in two reports. Disproportionate public attention was given to the first, *The Reshaping of British Railways* (1963), which is still commonly referred to as 'the Beeching Report', as if there had been only one. But it ought to be read in conjunction with the second, *The Development of the Major Railway Trunk Routes* (1965). Taken together, they represent an analysis of the profitability of the various parts of the system and a forward view of the way in which its most remunerative operations could be encouraged and developed.

The first report applied strict tests of profitability to the railway system and exposed relentlessly those parts of it that made a loss. It revealed that half the passenger stations together produced only 2 per cent of the total passenger revenue; that half the freight stations, similarly, contributed only 3 per cent; and that the least-used stations cost the railways £9 million a year. The report did not ignore the human problems that would be raised by drastic cutting back. It discussed the reduction and redeployment of staff that would be necessary, and the means of softening the impact of such measures. It recognised explicitly the hardship that might be caused in some places, and the need to weigh the economic advantages of closure in the scales of 'overall social benefit'. The British Transport Commission had been acidly criticised by the government in 1960 for taking account of social needs when its business should have been exclusively with balancing its books.[28] The new Board was not going to expose itself to any such attack. It proposed that 'Total Social Benefit Studies' should be undertaken jointly by the Ministry of Transport and the railways, and that state subsidies should be paid to maintain services that were unremunerative but judged to be socially necessary.

The publication of this report was greeted with a very loud outcry. That came, naturally, from those who used the services now under threat of withdrawal; from railwaymen who foresaw an end to their livelihood; from opponents of the Conservative government, who charged it with respon-sibility for the report; and from many other people who wished to see the existing system maintained for a variety of reasons. But the report had been well prepared, and much of its argument was unanswerable. It identified the railways' real position, and expressed it clearly. That was a service equally important to the country and to the railways themselves.

The second Beeching report was more in the nature of a discussion paper. The British railway system had emerged with numerous competitive trunk lines that duplicated one another. Competition had now ended, and there was little room for duplicates. Which route should be preferred, and consequently attract investment? The report gave an answer in each case, projecting its thought forward twenty years into the future. It is interesting today, when those twenty years have elapsed, to see how accurate its predictions were. A few of the recommendations were ignored: for in-stance, the line from Manchester to Leeds via Halifax and Bradford was

Lines open in 1914

British Rail lines
open to passenger
traffic in 1985

passed over in favour of the alternative route via Huddersfield, and the Sheffield—Manchester line via Woodhead has been closed down. But most of the routes chosen in the report were adopted.

The Labour victories in the elections of 1964 and 1966 produced a shift of government policy towards the railways. Beeching left the Board in 1965. He was made a peer – a courteous gesture from an administration that disagreed with his policies. But that could not compensate him for the scandalous personal vilification to which he had been subjected. He had done his duty well by the country and the railways, and had been rewarded with abuse.

The new Minister of Transport, Barbara Castle, set herself with determination to tackle some of the railways' problems. Her policies were embodied in the Transport Act of 1968, which separated passenger services regarded as commercially viable from those that were not, but were yet deemed to be necessary for social reasons. The 'social' services were in future to be aided by government grants. The Act also relieved the railways of the unprofitable task of dealing with small consignments of goods, turning that over to a new National Freight Corporation.

Many of the Beeching proposals for a reduction in the system had already been implemented. The route mileage fell by 30 per cent between 1961 and 1968. Under Barbara Castle these reductions were almost halted, and they have never been resumed since on such a scale – between 1969 and 1983 they amounted to only 15 per cent. A large number of unprofitable services remained, but they were now paid for by the state.

The slimming of the system, and other changes associated with it, called inevitably for a large reduction in the number of staff employed. At nationalisation it had been 543,000; by 1972 it was 197,000; by 1983, 155,000. Every measure that involved the dismissal or transfer of staff met with resistance, and this repeatedly delayed the introduction of new services and equipment – of liner trains, for example, and of electric trains between Bedford and London. No one could be surprised or could fail to sympathise with the men who were affected, but in most cases the result of their action was to damage the railways' business severely. In 1982 the Railways Board ended up with a deficit of £109 million.

The story of the British railways in the 1960s is pretty sombre; and the gloom has been lightened no more than fitfully since.[29] In part at least, their difficulties reflect the difficulties of the nation. But there are achievements to be recorded also, and it is right to salute them: for this book is concerned with achievements, from first to last.

The changeover from steam to diesel and electric traction was completed quickly once it got under way. British Railways ran their last steam trains (other than those on the narrow-gauge Vale of Rheidol line in Wales) in 1968. When the best types of diesel locomotives had proved themselves (see p. 161), they took over satisfactorily and allowed a general acceleration of services. The electrification of the West Coast main line was extended to Glasgow in 1974. By 1985 work was in hand on the conversion of the line to Norwich, and on the East Coast main line northwards to Leeds and New-castle. On that line, too, a completely new stretch of railway was built, the Selby diversion, 14 miles long, which was needed to avoid a coalfield. This was completed in 1983, the first substantial piece of new main railway built in Britain since 1910.

The acceleration of express services was taken a long way further with the introduction of the diesel-powered High Speed Trains from London to Bristol and Swansea in 1976, and to Edinburgh two years later. As they

Class 9 2-10-0, No. 92063, gathers steam as it climbs the Pennines on the way to Consett steel works in 1965, pulling a very heavy train made up of iron ore freight wagons.

entered service on all the chief lines that had not been electrified, they produced startling reductions in the times of long-distance journeys (see p. 228), and presently of some short journeys too: from London to Peterborough, for example, now takes 49 minutes (at 93·4 mph) instead of 64 minutes in 1976. Although the Advanced Passenger Train was not successful in regular service (p. 158), it pointed the way to higher speeds still. 'Fastest Through Crowded Britain' was better than most slogans the railways have adopted: for it was true.

This great acceleration was not brought about by new motive-power alone. Before these trains were introduced, the track on each line had to be overhauled, and here and there re-aligned. New safety precautions were also required. The old signalling system was quite inadequate for the control of such trains when they came to be extended to their maximum speeds. To the student of railways it was very interesting to watch the gradual elimination of semaphore signals on the first-class main lines, which roughly kept pace with the introduction of the High Speed Trains on to them. The last section of main line of that sort in England to be converted formed part of the old Midland system, running northwards from Irchester (just south of Wellingborough) to Loughborough. There the regular traveller could observe the semaphores being dismantled and removed one by one, as the whole of these fifty miles came to be controlled by electrically operated colour-light signalling, all done from one new box at Leicester: one box replacing 22.[30]

By the early 1980s the railways had to accept that their most profitable business was in the carriage of passengers, not, as it had been over most of their history, of freight. Freight traffic, although freed from most of the restrictions and burdens it had laboured under in the past, had steadily declined, from 169 million tonnes in 1979 to 145 million in 1983. The raising of the permitted lorry weight on the roads to 38 tonnes in 1983 naturally aided the competition. The railways, nevertheless, continued to battle for freight traffic, carrying large quantities of minerals, building materials and bulk liquids, and containers to and from Freightliner terminals and docks.

One expedient designed to help to balance the accounts was adopted in the 1980s. The railways divested themselves of some parts of their under-taking that were either unprofitable or produced on average only a negli-gible revenue: particularly the hotels and the ships to and from Ireland and the Continent, which were sold off from 1982 to 1984. Done at the behest of government, this was essentially a piece of Conservative 'privatisation'. The hotels and ships were large capital assets, and anyone looking at the Railways Board's accounts will see what a poor figure they cut there. All the same, it was sad to see the railways part with them, severing a link that went back more than 150 years.

Some of the most interesting developments in passenger transport occurred in the big cities, in London, on Merseyside and Tyneside. They began with the opening of the underground Victoria Line in 1968-71. Long desired and long delayed, it was the first new underground line built in central London since 1912. It proved a winner: the most valuable new aid to movement in the city since the Second World War. The extension of the Piccadilly Line to Heathrow followed in 1977, one of the earliest schemes to link airports with urban underground railways.

By 1970 the London Underground had passed into the hands of the Greater London Council. In a similar way the new urban railways in the provinces became the responsibility of regional Passenger Transport Executives, established under the Act of 1968. The Merseyside system was completed in 1978, the Tyne & Wear Metro in 1984. Both made use of existing lines originally worked by steam, with new extensions and linking sections. The Tyne & Wear Metro is 34 miles long, with 41 stations, and more planned. It is a light railway, with lightweight trains running at limited speeds, and that appears in its bridges and other structures. The

A High Speed Train (HST) Inter-City 125 leaves Plymouth station in 1985. HSTs were pioneered on the Western Region, which began trial runs in 1975. The idea behind them was simple, but novel in Britain: two streamlined locomotives or power cars that are attached to either end of the train, thereby cutting out the need for shunting the locomotives to change their direction. Pulling double-glazed and air-conditioned carriages, these engines, which can reach speeds of 125mph, are the modern successors to the pioneering designs of the 19th-century engineers.

An electric lightweight train arrives at Haymarket station on the Tyne & Wear Metro in the centre of Newcastle. Opened in stages from 1980 onwards, the new underground system now extends to South Shields and, north of the Tyne, to Whitley Bay and across to Bank Foot.

seven-mile section from Newcastle to North Shields, first opened in 1839, was the earliest railway built for suburban passenger traffic in any provincial city in Europe. The passenger travelling along it today can observe the grafting of the new railway on to the old. A system in many ways similar is the Docklands Light Railway, designed to convey passengers through seven and a half miles of London hitherto ill served by public transport. It too makes use of some older railway structures (see p. 66).

In the 1970s and 1980s British Rail continued and improved its building of new stations. Euston was the most important of them all, but there were some notable lesser ones too: Stevenage, for example, which displays very well the revival of good brickwork. It also paid a great deal of attention to the restoration and improvement of its old buildings. The remodelling of the entrance to York station, very important for its services to thousands of tourists, could scarcely have been bettered. At Leicester the accommodation for passengers on the platforms has been improved beyond recognition. Some repair work, for example at Hebden Bridge (see p. 167), was undertaken in collaboration with local authorities or other interested people, and much of it was aided by grants from public funds. In Scotland the effects of this policy present a truly heartening contrast to the glumness that so often made railway travel there depressing in the past. Notable Victorian monuments have been well cared for – Great Malvern and Stamford stations, for instance – along with others less intrinsically striking, even quite ordinary, such as Whitchurch in Hampshire, Chesterfield (always admirably kept) and, again in Scotland, Dumfries.

All this work belongs to a time when many people have found a new pleasure in railways, which is most evident in the strength of the preservation movement. The passing of the steam-worked railway was to many people a real grief. To the elderly it might mean the removal of a familiar element in their lives, even something like the loss of a friend. Many younger people felt its disappearance too, from a vague curiosity about what it had been, or a positive nostalgia for the Victorian past. And there were others – some much younger still, with little of that kind of curiosity and touched by no nostalgia – who were willing, even eager, to become acquainted with the steam railway.

The opportunity for all these people started in 1950 with the establishment of the Talyllyn Railway Preservation Society, soon followed by a second undertaking on another North Wales railway, more ancient and remarkable, the Festiniog. Neither of these lines had ever been closed, though both needed much repair work to track, locomotives and carriages before a satisfactory passenger service could be run over them. Both were laid to a very narrow gauge. And in 1960 part of a standard-gauge branch line of British Rail, long known as the Bluebell line, which had been closed to passengers, was reopened, first on lease and then through purchase by a private society.

From such small beginnings a considerable range of private steam railways sprang up, from the Highland Region of Scotland to Devon and Kent. Some of them are quite large – the Isle of Man Railway, the Severn Valley, the West Somerset, the Dart Valley, for example. Others have continued as they originally were, like the Bluebell Railway, which remains just five miles long. All have had considerable difficulties to face, financial as well as of other kinds. Contrary to the prediction of many amused scoffers, almost all of them have kept going.

L. T. C. Rolt, the leader in the movement to keep the Talyllyn alive, was the first to discern the importance of these ventures to the youngest group of interested people, to whom they offer novel and unfamiliar opportunities. Their appeal has grown greater as unemployment has blighted the lives of so many of the young, and made them welcome any new opportunity of using their hands and minds.

By comparison with British Rail these undertakings are very small beer indeed. Yet they take their place properly here, in a study of British railways of all sorts. One of the functions of the railways has been to give pleasure. They have given that abundantly over the past 150 years: to crowds going on vast excursions like Bass's (see p. 226), to families and friends travelling on their own account, to solitary individuals studying them with minute attention at home. It is one of the main purposes of this book to display a wide range of the pleasures railways continue to offer, and to suggest to enthusiasts where they may be looked for.

On the Welshpool & Llanfair Railway in Mid-Wales, locomotive No. 1, The Earl, crosses the River Banwy with a train of restored coaches in 1969. Laid out in 1903 to the very narrow gauge of 2ft 6in, the railway was closed in 1956, but reopened by a preservation company in 1963. The viaduct, severely damaged by floods in 1964, was reconstructed partly by volunteers and partly by the Royal Engineers as a training exercise.

FENCHURCH STREET · TILBURY · GRAVESEND · CHATHAM

('Down' = Fenchurch Street – Chatham;
'Up' = Chatham – Fenchurch Street. The names of stations
now open for passenger traffic are printed in small capitals.)

No one wishing to travel from London to Chatham would normally think of beginning his journey at FENCHURCH STREET. Few people, indeed, except those who commute from South Essex, think of Fenchurch Street at all, for it is among the obscurest and most inconvenient of London terminal stations. Yet to anyone interested in the history of railways the trip offers a long, rewarding afternoon.

The obscurity of Fenchurch Street is beyond dispute. Passengers arriving at the nearest Underground station have to walk on a zig-zag course and climb the platforms up very steep stairs. All the other London termini except Broad Street were either built on a level with the road, like King's Cross and Victoria, or approached by gently sloping ramps, like Liverpool Street and Paddington. There is no room for anything of that kind at Fenchurch

Street, either at the sides or the front. The building is wedged tightly between its neighbours and has a ludicrously small forecourt that cannot easily accommodate three vehicles, let alone a ramp.

Some of the station's inconvenience to passengers may be overcome by British Rail's extensive reconstruction works, but there is little that can be done to improve its operational weakness. The station has four narrow platforms only, and to work 230 services into and out of it in the course of the fourteen hours during which it is open each day represents a distinct feat of precise operation, even with electrically hauled trains.

Fenchurch Street was originally built as the terminus of the London &

Fenchurch Street station, 1954: façade, as built in 1854. The Great Eastern's standard saw-tooth awning was added later. Reconstruction behind the façade started in 1984.

Fenchurch Street station, 1984: interior before latest reconstruction.

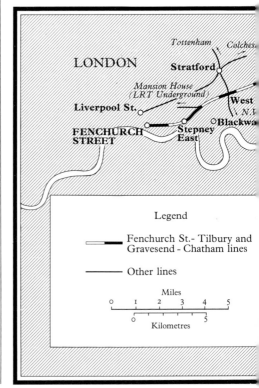

Legend

━━━ Fenchurch St.- Tilbury and Gravesend - Chatham lines

── Other lines

Blackwall Railway, a line that ran to the East India Docks, enabling passengers to reach the heart of London very much more quickly than they could if they continued their steamer journey by Greenwich Reach and the Pool.

When the railway was opened, in 1840, it ran only to a terminus at the Minories. In the following year it was carried further west, to Fenchurch Street. Although this extension was only a quarter of a mile long, that was an important quarter of a mile: for it brought a railway, for the first time, within the limits of the City of London – to the disgust of many citizens, who opposed it on social as well as on economic grounds. The first Fenchurch Street station was rebuilt in 1853-54 to the design of the engineer George Berkeley; since then it has been modified extensively.[1]

The London & Blackwall line was a curiosity among railways. At first it was operated by cable traction[2] and had no connection with any other line. Then, after cable working had been abandoned in 1849, it gradually became involved with the affairs of a new company, promoted jointly by itself

and the Eastern Counties (later Great Eastern) Railway: the London Tilbury & Southend. That company never owned a London terminus. When its line was opened as far as Tilbury in 1854, its trains ran both from Bishopsgate (the predecessor of Liverpool Street) and from Fenchurch Street; but from 1858 Fenchurch Street became its main terminus.[3]

The guest company soon became far more important than its host. In the 20th century the electric tram and the motor-bus killed the Blackwall traffic, and the eastern part of the line was closed entirely in 1926. By contrast the Tilbury and Southend business grew, at first steadily and then mightily, with the growth of Southend as a seaside resort and a dormitory for London, the building of Tilbury docks (begun in 1882), the gigantic industrial development of South Essex since the First World War and the immigration that accompanied it.

When in 1912 the big Midland company absorbed the London Tilbury & Southend, it undertook to electrify the line; but neither it nor its successor the London Midland & Scottish

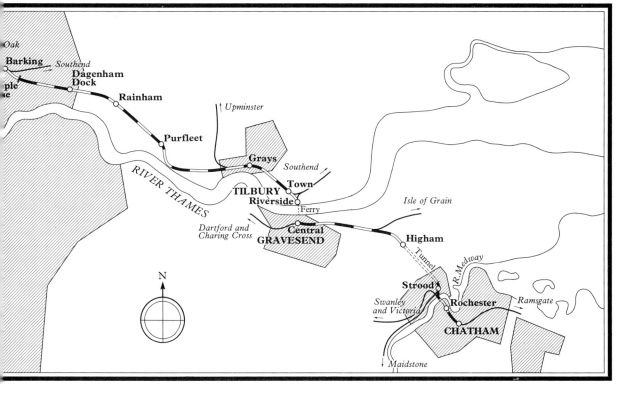

District electric locomotive hauling London Tilbury & Southend rolling stock, 1925. From 1910 onwards, through trains of this kind were run from Ealing Broadway over the District Railway and the Whitechapel & Bow to the Southend line. From Barking on to Southend they were hauled by Tilbury steam engines. The service was withdrawn in 1939.

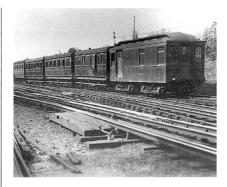

The complicated approach to Barking is indicated in this photograph, taken from Tanner Street footbridge a quarter of a mile west of the station. A London Underground line crosses the down Southend line on a flyover, to join the others beside it on the right. The line to Walthamstow and Tottenham is on the left. The car sheds are behind the photographer's back. This and all subsequent photographs on the journey were taken in March and April 1985.

honoured that promise, and it was left to British Railways to carry out the task. Its completion in 1962 ended a pressure on the steam services that had become almost intolerable.

The line runs out of Fenchurch Street above the rooftops of the East End houses, passing the sites of two closed stations, Leman Street and Shadwell. On the up side the building of the new Docklands Light Rapid Transit System is adding a new element to the line from Shadwell to STEPNEY EAST. Behind this station in former days the Blackwall line diverged, also on the up side. The district line of the London Underground system comes in one and a half miles beyond to run parallel with this one on the down side. This was originally the Whitechapel & Bow Railway, opened in 1902, a joint undertaking of the London Tilbury & Southend and District (Underground) companies. It proved valuable to the Tilbury as a means of diverting some of the passengers from its own services running into the overcrowded Fenchurch Street station. Now only Underground trains serve the five original stations from Bromley-by-Bow eastwards. At West Ham the former Great Eastern Railway line from Stratford to North Woolwich runs at a right angle underneath this line, with a new British Rail station visible on it from the up side.

At BARKING the Tilbury and District lines were joined by another line coming in from the north west to link the Midland and the Tilbury railway systems. Completed in 1894, it carried long-distance freight traffic to and from Tilbury Docks and provided a passenger service from a great arc of northern suburban stations stretching

from St Pancras to Tottenham and Walthamstow. The service is maintained now every half-hour from Gospel Oak to Barking six days a week and, in the summer, on Sundays too.

The convergence of this new line made Barking into a complex junction, with freight trains to and from the Midland system crossing the London Tilbury & Southend line on the level. A big scheme of reconstruction was undertaken here by the nationalised railways in the 1950s and 1960s. This was long overdue, and it was rendered imperative by the electrification of the

old Tilbury company's system. The main car sheds provided at the London end of the Tilbury & Southend line for accommodating and servicing passenger trains were erected here, west of the station, and the station itself, with its eight platforms, was largely rebuilt.

Immediately beyond Barking station the two arms of the Tilbury company's system diverge. The original line followed exactly the course described in its title, running to Southend by way of a long loop via Tilbury. In the 1880s the traffic to and from Southend and its adjoining communities grew more valuable. The Great Eastern company sought powers to build a branch down from its main line at Shenfield to compete for it. The Tilbury company's riposte was to project a shortening of its route by construction of a new line eastwards from Barking. These plans were both authorised in 1883. The Tilbury company's line was completed in 1888, the Great Eastern one the following year. Southend now had two competing services to London, and the two railways continued to battle for traffic until their rivalry was ended by nationalisation in 1947. The

Tilbury company's route was the shorter by six miles; but there was now enough traffic for both. The resident population of Southend multiplied five times between 1891 and 1911, mainly through the increase in commuting. The value of the traffic was attested by the electrification of both lines – the old Great Eastern one in 1956, this one six years later.

Having left the junction at Barking, the train quickly reaches another piece of new railway construction, the big Ripple Lane freight yard, built under the Modernisation Plan of 1955. One main reason for siting the yard here soon becomes apparent. At its eastern end is the passenger station of DAGENHAM DOCK (opened in 1908). The line is entering the empire of the Ford motor car company, its presence insistently plain with massed industrial buildings. On the down side is the Becontree estate, the largest of all the housing estates laid out by the London County Council. It was started in 1921, and building continued for over forty years, by which time it had come to accommodate more than 100,000 people.

On the up side is flat marshland, mostly unreclaimed, stretching down to the Thames. No sharper contrast between old and new can be imagined than what one sees here: the old villages, like RAINHAM and Wennington, survive (down side), built to the edge of the high ground; only ten or 15ft below them the marshes are given up partly to sheep and partly to immense firing ranges. John Rhode has an ingenious story, *The Elusive Bullet*, in which a traveller on the railway is killed by a stray shot as the train is passing this point.

At PURFLEET the line begins again to serve industry. The large chalk pits have been worked for centuries past; and one of the earliest railways in the south of England was in operation here, with horse-power only, before 1807. Two and a half miles further on, a branch line comes in on the down side, connecting with Upminster on the Southend main line. The junction station is GRAYS, where the up-side building is a simple structure of the 1950s, pleasant and well kept.

The train is now approaching Tilbury. A little beyond Grays additional lines appear on the up side, originally built by the Port of London Authority, which had its own railway system.[4] Tilbury was never an independent port, always an integral part of the Port of London, and its docks fell within the London system even though they lay 26 miles downstream from London Bridge.

The history of modern Tilbury is curious. When the railway arrived in 1854, there was nothing there except a farmhouse and, half a mile to the east, close to the river, Tilbury Fort. This was still very much a military stronghold, and it was extensively reconstructed in 1868. Its maintenance and improvement were justified because it guarded Gravesend Reach, the last narrow stretch of the Thames before the river opens out into its broad estuary. From a little pier a ferry crossed to Gravesend. The service, which had begun in 1850, was taken over and worked under Parliamentary powers by the newly arrived railway company. Its main business at that time was pleasure traffic crossing the river to Rosherville Gardens, a much-frequented resort just west of Gravesend.

Apart from military work at the Fort, nothing new disturbed this tract of marshland until the East & West

Purfleet station, looking south, with electric multiple-unit train for Pitsea.

Rainham station, looking east, with the Thames marshes and electricity pylons behind.

Tilbury Riverside station: booking hall.

Tilbury landing-stage, with a Soviet ship. The photograph is taken from the ferry, crossing the Thames.

India Docks Company secured powers in 1882 to buy 450 acres of it and to turn 75 of them into deep-water docks and a tidal basin.[5] The preliminary moves towards this purchase, made in strict secrecy, were concerted with the London Tilbury & Southend Railway's very able general manager, A. L. Stride. His company agreed to serve all the docks with its railways. Eventually there were fifty miles of track. This was the most completely rail-served dock system in Britain; when first built, there was no road access at all to the ships. In addition, the railway company agreed to provide a new passenger station adjoining the docks, from which a half-hourly service would be put on to London; and in London itself to build a goods depot for the Tilbury traffic at Whitechapel. The docks were opened in 1886 and quickly proved a financial disaster – disastrous to the associated undertakings nearer London and to their competitors as well, for they all ruined themselves by a war of rate-cutting. That was not ended until 1908, when the government imposed a merger on them, under a new Port of London Authority. Grave industrial troubles followed, and the ambitious and forward-looking achievement at Tilbury had hardly begun to display its full value before the outbreak of the First World War in 1914.

Meanwhile, some kind of settlement had grown up near the docks. It would have been hard to find a bleaker place anywhere in England than this one, laid out on a bitterly cold, treeless marsh. The station built by the docks is now called TILBURY TOWN, but that is a misnomer, for Tilbury has never grown into a true town at all.

Running beside the docks, the train comes to a junction, where the Southend line curves away to the east, and then abruptly enters a second station, now called TILBURY RIVERSIDE. This stands on the site of the original one, but its two pleasant neo-Georgian buildings, each with a small cupola, date entirely from 1925-30. They were designed by the architect Sir Edwin Cooper to accommodate passenger services to Europe (they ran to Dunkirk, for instance, and later to Gothenburg), the ships berthing at a large landing-stage in the open river. They provide an

ample booking hall, waiting rooms, and spaces for baggage and customs inspection. The services to the Continent have now ceased, and the once-busy station is now empty; but an occasional Soviet ship may still be seen here, sailing to Leningrad.

There is still a ferry across the river. It leaves from the same landing-stage as the large ships and runs to Gravesend. At one time seven little ships were required to maintain it.[6] Now one suffices, keeping up a half-hourly service, with another standing by spare. The passage lasts five minutes (fare £1), not enough time to take in all the interesting sights to be seen on it: Sir Edwin Cooper's buildings with ships in Tilbury docks behind them, the Fort with its big gateway of 1668, the traffic up and down the river, the low skyline of Gravesend ahead. It is a pity that the ferry does not run to the Town Pier, an elegant little structure of the 1830s that has now fallen into decrepitude; instead the ferry passengers scuttle through a grim and grubby shed erected nearby.

The old town of Gravesend, an important calling point for ships going to and from London, can never have been a beautiful place, but it had its hour of excitement in the 1830s with pleasure traffic by steamers from London, which made it for a little while into a holiday resort. A good deal of seemly building of that time remains.

The town came to have two stations, belonging to the London Chatham & Dover and the South Eastern Railways, whose idiotic competition damaged Victorian Kent. Only the South Eastern one remains in use today, GRAVESEND CENTRAL, half a mile

inland from the ferry. Its main building, on the far (up) side of the line, is delightful, with a Doric colonnade at its entrance and a charming big bow window giving on to the platform; all refurbished very well indeed by British Rail. It was designed by Samuel Beazley, one of the very few architects well known in general practice who undertook work for a railway company.[7]

This station was opened in 1849. The line from London was continued eastwards by a stretch of track almost unique in Britain: a railway laid through a canal tunnel.[8] Gravesend was separated from the River Medway, eight miles off, by a ridge of low hills. The Thames & Medway Canal, opened in 1824, had provided a direct route between them by means of a tunnel two and a quarter miles long, then the second longest in Britain. Presently the shrewd directors determined to convert the canal into the Gravesend & Rochester Railway, its line running through the tunnel on the towing-path, widened by a timber framework cantilevered out over the water. The construction of this makeshift railway, to the plans of J. U. Rastrick, is well described by the contractor's engineer, Francis Conder, who also gives a vivacious account of its inspection by

the intrepid General Pasley, on behalf of the Board of Trade.[9] It was completed in 1845. Then the company sold itself, at a comfortable profit, to the South Eastern Railway, which presently relaid the line through the tunnel with a double track on the bed of the now disused canal.

A half-hourly service is offered today from Gravesend to Chatham. The line runs through the eastern part of Gravesend in a shallow cutting, crossed by half a dozen bridges in quick succession, each carrying a street already in existence before the railway arrived. The clouds of smoke emitted by the

Gravesend station: entrance building (up side).

Leaving Gravesend, the railway burrows beneath the eastern streets of the town; they had been laid out shortly before it arrived.

locomotives must have made life very disagreeable for the residents. Clear of the town, the railway runs straight across marshland towards the hills and the tunnel.

At Hoo Junction (where there are short platforms, at which trains often stop for railwaymen working in the marshalling yard) a branch diverges on the down side, running to the Isle of Grain, which now has a large oil refinery. The branch was opened in 1882, to a pier dignified by the name of Port Victoria. The South Eastern Railway chairman, Edward Watkin, crazily imagined that this might become a packet station for steamship services to the Continent. But no regular service of that kind was ever established there.

Port Victoria and its branch line proved to have only one use – curious, special and infrequent. As the most secluded landing-place anywhere on the south-eastern coast of England that could accommodate a steamship and was also served by railway, it was sometimes found convenient for the coming and going of royalty. There was no mayor here to be presented, no population to be kept behind barriers as the ship or the train came in. Everything could be done quickly and quietly, to the satisfaction no doubt of weary royal persons as well as of those responsible for their journeys. The arrival of the King and Queen of Norway in October 1913 was the last such event at Port Victoria, almost the last flicker of its life. The failure of the place was so complete that even its name has now been erased from the map.[10]

Passing through HIGHAM station

Higham station, looking east towards the Gravesend & Rochester tunnel. The train is electric multiple unit 4 EPB No. 5017.

the train enters the long canal tunnel. To make a convenient passing-place for barges the canal engineer had provided a space open to the sky in the middle, and the train's passage through the tunnel is made memorable by this large patch of daylight.

As the train emerges from the tunnel, the line turns away on a sharp curve southward. On the down side is the old Frindsbury basin: the terminus of the canal, where it joined the Medway. The train now stops at STROOD, a junction from which one line runs to Maidstone whilst another swings east over the river. Immediately south of the station another line appears overhead from the

west. This is the old main line of the London Chatham & Dover Railway.

The history of the line into Rochester is complicated, demonstrating the almost incredible absurdities that railway competition could lead to in Britain. The East Kent company was given powers in 1853-55 to build a railway from the South Eastern at Strood across the Medway to Chatham, Canterbury and Dover. By the time it was completed in 1861 the East Kent had transformed itself into the London Chatham & Dover Railway, had quarrelled bitterly with the South Eastern, and had acquired with pertinacious ingenuity a route of its own to Victoria station in London. Henceforward for nearly forty years the two companies indulged in fatuous warfare all over Kent.

With its independent access to London, the Chatham company no longer had any need to pass its traffic to and from the South Eastern. Instead it ran its trains straight from London to a station on the west bank of the river, which it called for a time 'Rochester and Strood', though it was convenient for neither. The original spur from the Medway bridge to the South Eastern Railway now carried nothing but a single goods train a day. In 1876 a public-spirited Mayor of Rochester, Mr Toomer, took legal action to force the companies to provide a passenger service over it. He was successful; and this short piece of line became known as the Toomer Loop.

But that was not the end of the story. In 1881-88 the South Eastern secured powers to build its own line from Strood into Chatham, crossing the Medway by a second bridge only a few yards north of the existing one. The new line reached Rochester in 1891 and a station was erected in the following year called Chatham Central (it was not near the centre of Chatham; the name was just a common swindle). The only good effect of this superfluous railway was that it forced the London Chatham & Dover into constructing a station on its own line within the little city of ROCHESTER.

In 1899 the two companies – at last – formed a 'working union'. They then reconsidered the competing lines they had built. In 1911 the South Eastern

branch to Chatham Central was closed. In 1927 the old London Chatham & Dover railway was realigned, straighter than before, to run on to the newer South Eastern bridge, and its own bridge was abandoned until 1942 when it was overhauled and strengthened, to serve as a substitute for the railway or the road bridge in case either should be put out of action by bombing. It was not, in the event, ever used for that purpose. At last, in 1968, it was replaced by an additional road bridge.[11]

The passage of the railway onwards from Rochester raised difficulties of another kind. Chatham was a key point in the southern defences of Britain. It was heavily fortified, and a railway seeking to enter it had to satisfy stringent requirements on the part of the military authorities. The steep hill east of Rochester was crowned by Fort Pitt. The railway at first proposed to slice into it with cuttings and burrow through it in a very short tunnel; but the cuttings were held to weaken the fortifications and the tunnel had to be trebled in length, to 428 yards, in order to shorten the open excavations. CHATHAM station was placed between this tunnel and another, immediately beyond it to the west – not an uncommon expedient (found also, for instance, at Edinburgh, Greenock,

Birmingham and Tunbridge Wells) but particularly awkward here where the intervening space was very small. The station was always meagre and gloomy. In spite of some improvement, it is not a cheerful place now.

Still, it makes an interesting terminus to a journey that displays a wide range of the railways' services to the community. The lines between Fenchurch Street and Chatham have done much for suburban living, for the large-scale carriage of freight and for overseas trade. They have made a substantial contribution to the country's pleasure; they even at one point evoke shadowy royalties making their journeys to and from London. They fought their own dogged battle through the Second World War and suffered severely. But they are still in use and still needed. Such lines as these are the workhorses of the railway system.

The Medway crossing: above left, the South Eastern bridge, looking west; above, the view looking towards Rochester from above the east end of the canal tunnel. On the left is the empty Frindsbury basin, terminus of the old canal, to the right Strood station with the spire of Rochester cathedral across the river beyond.

Chatham station, looking east towards one of the two tunnels between which the building is sandwiched.

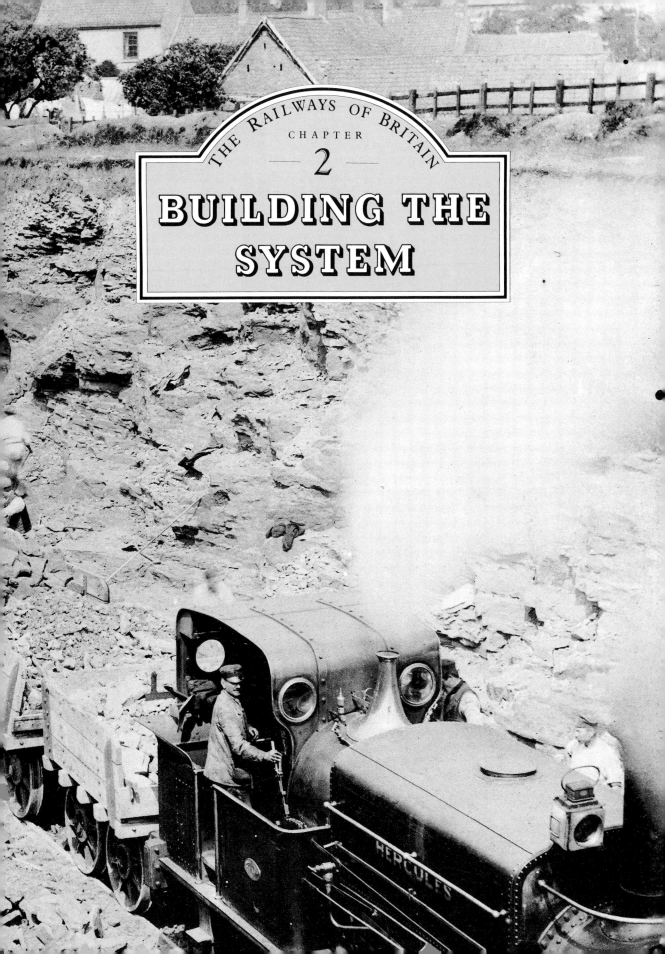

CHAPTER

2

BUILDING THE SYSTEM

—— THE LAYING DOWN OF A RAILWAY ——

What is it that determines the route a railway takes? The origin of a railway must be sought first in the decision taken by a group of people that a line ought to be built from A and B and that it was needed so much that they would either find the capital themselves or raise it from others who might be interested. It then became necessary to settle the best route for the line to follow; and that was determined, in the first place, by the physical configuration of the land it had to cross. If a high hill stood between A and B, it was important to decide whether the line should scale it, pierce it by a tunnel, or make a detour to avoid it. That decision, in turn, was affected by the geological structure of the hill itself. How easy would it be to bore a tunnel through it? The surveyor could also advise the promoters which route could be most easily – and therefore most cheaply – constructed. But other things would need to be taken into account as well: the attitude of the landowners, for example, whose property the line would cross; the desirability of making detours to serve other towns and villages or to connect with other lines of railway en route. When at last, having weighed up all these considerations, the promoters presented their scheme in the form of a private Bill, they might find themselves forced to alter the route in order to meet criticisms passed on the measure during its passage through Parliament. Even when it was sanctioned, difficulties might arise in the actual construction of the line – physical obstacles, perhaps, unknown to the original surveyor and engineer – requiring alterations to be made in order to surmount them. And at any time after the line was opened and in use for traffic, the owning company might decide to change its course, to link it up with another line, or to abandon altogether any part of it that was unprofitable – though the last of those courses was seldom taken before 1914.

A piece of railway in use today is therefore the product of a long series of decisions reached on many different grounds, at different times. Any intelligent study of it must take all of them into account: not merely the physical, geographical factors, which influenced but could never alone determine the decisions taken; nor yet just the historical factors, for the railway had always to be laid out and operated on the ground, and that necessarily produced problems of its own.

Here is a specific example. The Great Western Railway company issued its first prospectus, explaining its plans for the line between London and Bristol and soliciting financial support, in August 1833. It expressed the hope that, at some time in the future, Gloucester might be served by a branch from the main railway. That autumn a number of people in Gloucester and the neighbouring town of Cheltenham determined to carry out such a scheme themselves. As soon as the Great Western Railway Bill was passed by Parliament, a 'Cheltenham & Great Western Union Railway Company' was formed to build a line from Swindon to Cheltenham, with a branch to Cirencester. I. K. Brunel, the Great Western's young engineer, had surveyed the route and estimated, with characteristic optimism, that the railway could be built for £750,000. The line he chose was not a direct one. It never could have been since, in order to attract support from Gloucester and from the important cloth-manufacturing district around Stroud, the promoters had undertaken that the line should serve both those towns; and between Stroud and Swindon stood the barrier of the Cotswolds. How was it to be crossed? Brunel's answer was similar to that given by the engineer of the Thames & Severn Canal fifty years earlier: to tunnel through the hills in the parish of Sapperton, at the head of the 'Golden Valley'. The railway

Previous page: navvies hard at work in July 1897 dig out a cutting on the Lancashire Derbyshire & East Coast Railway. The 'Hercules' engine in the foreground, pulling a long train of wagons filled with excavated soil and rock, was one of 94 quaintly assorted locomotives used by the contractors in constructing the line.

could then have a fairly direct run south eastwards to Swindon. The line Brunel recommended was 44 miles long, although the distance between Cheltenham and Swindon as the crow flies is only 25 miles. A Bill was promoted for the construction of a railway along this route in 1836.

Meanwhile, a rival concern had been formed. It too proposed to give Cheltenham railway communication with London, but by the Cotswolds and Chilterns to Tring, where it would join the London & Birmingham Railway, at that time under construction. This scheme was in fact got up largely by the London & Birmingham company – just as its rival owed much to the support of the Great Western. The fight between the two bodies before Parliament was not really a local one: it was a contest between two established companies, each anxious to extend its power into a territory not yet occupied by railways.

The Cheltenham & Great Western Union scheme triumphed, but at the price of expensive concessions. Its Bill was strenuously opposed, for example, by Robert Gordon of Kemble House, whose land the railway would cross. He secured £7,500 as compensation for damage to his amenities, as well as an undertaking, made binding by clauses in the Act, that the line should be carried through his grounds in a tunnel (to hide it from view) and that no public station should be erected on his property. From an engineer's standpoint, the tunnel was entirely superfluous; a cutting would have sufficed.

The directors of the company found it difficult to raise the money that was needed, and it was not until 1838 that work on the line began. The Swindon – Cirencester section was ready for opening, at last, in January 1841; but the long embankment carrying the line out of Swindon gave so much trouble from landslips that it was not passed as fit for public traffic by the Board of Trade's inspector until the end of May. Even then the embankment continued to slip, on its eastern side, so that traffic could be kept going only on a single line. After piles had been tried and failed, a retaining wall of rubble, 12ft thick and 10ft high, had to be built, and this eventually rendered the embankment firm.

Such great and unforeseen expenses made the company's position much more difficult, and in 1843 its shareholders thankfully sold the concern to the Great Western. The price they got gave them back less than half of what they had originally invested.[1]

The problems faced by the promoters and engineers of the Cheltenham line were by no means exceptional. In dealing with Mr Gordon, troublesome though he was, the company was more fortunate than some of its fellows. The attitude of landowners to the early railways was very often hostile, and it is not difficult to understand why. A railway built across an estate might mean an increase in its value; but it might also involve a genuine destruction of amenities. It was reasonable that landowners should look to Parliament (which, as a class, they still dominated) for protection against damage of that kind, or at least for compensation for it. A landowner might well feel, however, that he was entitled to more than a jury would give him; and since every railway had to get its Bill through Parliament it is not surprising that landowners often bargained privately with railway companies, throwing their political support or opposition into the scales to secure a better price for their property. Sometimes this amounted, quite blatantly, to extortion. Much more often it resolved itself into an argument between the lawyers on both sides, with the landowner enjoying the advantage that the railway needed his property, needed it quickly, and was anxious to secure it with as little fuss as possible.

This contemporary lithograph by R. Martin shows very clearly the effect a new railway might have on the landscape. Here, the Leeds & Selby Railway, opened on 22 September 1834, runs right across the view from the windows of Mr Walker's country house on the left, slicing straight through the hill in the centre of the picture. The white masonry of the bridges, very conspicuous when works were new, shows up clearly. The old method of transport is represented by two stage-coaches, travelling along the main road in the foreground; while in the distance on the right the factory chimneys send their smoke into the air. The Leeds & Selby Railway became part of the North Eastern Railway in the 1850s. It now forms a section of the inter-city rail link between the Mersey and the Humber.

One detailed examination has been made of the expense incurred by the early railway companies in obtaining their land, and it leads to the conclusion that 'while individual landowners may have done well out of the sale of land to railway companies – and may even have "blackmailed" the companies on occasion – the latter nevertheless spent the bulk of their money on the more legitimate side of their business. British railway companies would have gained if land had been cheaper; but this would not appreciably have reduced their difficulties'.[2]

Some landowners used their influence not against railways, but in their favour – a landowner occasionally gave some of the land required free of charge.[3] When the promoters of the Great Grimsby & Sheffield Junction Railway were engaged in mustering all the support they could before Parliament in 1845, they received material help from a series of petitions in favour of their line from North Lincolnshire. Many of the signatories were tenants of Lord Yarborough, the greatest landowner in that neighbourhood, and a letter from his agent to the solicitors acting for the company shows how directly they were influenced: 'In case of applying to any tenants of Lord Yarborough for signatures to the petitions you may mention that it is the wish of both Lord Yarborough and Lord Worsley [his son] to give the utmost support in their power to these railways, and there is at present no better way of serving them than by joining in these petitions'.[4]

The task confronting the engineers who made the railways was to lay out the best line possible, taking all these elements – both of hindrance and of help – into account. They were not attempting something wholly unprecedented. Some of the problems they had to solve were the same as, or very similar to, those that had been tackled by the canal engineers from the middle of the 18th century onwards, though the scale of the railway builders' operations was greater, and they generally had to work at a higher speed. From its very nature, a canal had to be laid out on a line as nearly level as possible. If it had to climb hills, locks were needed, and they were doubly objectionable: first because they were expensive, second because they impeded the movement of traffic. The canal engineer therefore did his best to keep the number of locks as small as he could. They could seldom be wholly avoided, however: sometimes the canal was obliged to mount a sharp incline, and a 'staircase' of locks was necessary, such as the remarkable series of 18 that are to be seen on the north side of the railway line

Chirk Viaduct on the Shrewsbury & Chester Railway was designed by Henry Robertson and completed in 1848. It was severely criticised by some for detracting from the beauty of Thomas Telford's aqueduct of 1801. The aqueduct's ten stone arches rising seventy feet above the River Ceiriog had long been admired for enhancing the landscape, and the new railway viaduct was aligned right beside it, thirty feet higher.

from Leamington to Birmingham, between Warwick and Hatton. But the canal builders were well experienced in the avoidance of such difficulties, through carrying their lines across valleys on the level by great aqueducts, like Telford's at Pontcysyllte and Chirk in North Wales and John Rennie's Lune aqueduct at Lancaster. These were the predecessors of the railway viaducts that altered the face of so many valleys from the 1830s onwards. The canal engineers were equally skilled in tunnelling, with the same purpose of producing a level line. Brindley had bored a great tunnel for the Trent & Mersey Canal at Harecastle, completed in 1777. The canal tunnel at Standedge was over three miles long, those at Sapperton and Strood (see pp. 74, 69) over two. When the railway engineers began tunnelling certain new problems were produced that had to be carefully considered; but they did not arise because tunnelling itself was a new art.

The railway engineers made use of metal in place of timber, stone, or brick – both for things peculiar to the railway, such as the track, and for its buildings and equipment. They did not begin this practice. Cast iron was already being used extensively before mechanically operated railways appeared. The first bridge built entirely of cast iron was thrown across the Severn in 1779; the wonder of the achievement is expressed in the name the place has borne ever since – Ironbridge. A bigger iron bridge spanned the Wear at Sunderland in 1796. And in the early years of the 19th century Telford built a series of such bridges to carry his roads over rivers; they have never been surpassed for grace in Britain. The finest of them were perhaps those in Wales and Scotland: the Waterloo Bridge at Bettws-y-Coed, Craigellachie Bridge over the Spey.

When the railways came to be built, all these earlier precedents were valuable to them. There were also new problems to be solved, and they were solved by new men. Few of the great canal or road engineers ever undertook any important railway work. But the achievement of the new men was founded on the experience they inherited from their predecessors; and it must be seen in perspective, related to the development of civil engineering in the days before large-scale railway building began.

The earliest of the great main railway lines were laid out with the principles of canal and road construction still plainly uppermost in the engineers' minds. They included a few steep inclines. Where they were inevitable, as at Euston, Liverpool and Glasgow (see p. 214), they were short

In this watercolour of 1838, J. Absolon records the building of the London & Southampton Railway through the deep cutting at Weybridge, designed to keep the line as level as possible. The brick bridge with its stone dressings is complete; the contractor's engine passes underneath, its steam flying up on the other side. To the left are the 'runs' of wooden planks, which the navvies used to haul up excavated soil from the trench.

and intended to be worked by stationary engines. In this, as in so many other ways, the Liverpool & Manchester Railway set the pattern in miniature for its greater successors; and the magnificent lines out of Euston, Waterloo and Paddington were the result. It is noticeable that many of these early railways followed existing lines of communication: the Eastern Counties seldom departed more than a mile or two from the great road to Colchester and Ipswich (most of it Roman in origin).

Not all railways built in the 1830s could take so favourable a course. If there was to be a railway from Manchester to Leeds it had to scale the Pennines, and even if it tunnelled, there were bound to be stiff climbs up to the tunnel and steep descents down from it on the other side. Before the end of the decade, engineers had enough confidence in the increasing power of the new machines to include gradients as steep as 1 in 38 (as on the Lickey incline south of Birmingham) which were to be worked not by stationary engines but by locomotives; and in the 1840s some of the most famous of all railway inclines were laid out, such as those over Shap Fell and up to Beattock in Dumfriesshire. In this way the expense of tunnelling was altogether avoided. During the period of intensest activity in railway construction (1845-52), therefore, engineers could contemplate steep gradients without undue anxiety.

Indeed, they came to make too little of them. In the 1850s the cost of building railways increased, and engineers were easily persuaded to save expense by going up and down hills rather than through them. A classic example of this is the Midland line between Leicester and Bedford, built in 1853-57. Something similar may also be said of the Salisbury – Exeter line, laid out in 1856-60 – though here the nature of the country itself is considerably more difficult.

When, in 1861, Joseph Mitchell came to tackle one of the stiffest problems of railway engineering that still remained, the crossing of the Grampians between Perth and Inverness, he felt justified in providing for an ascent from Blair Athol to the Druimuachdar Pass that was more formidable, in combined length and steepness, than any incline previously laid out in Britain. The Highland Railway stands as Britain's first great monument of mountain railway building. There have been a few others: the

A contractor's train, hauled by a 'coffee-pot' locomotive, stands in an excavated trench at Kingussie, in the Highlands of Scotland, in 1863. The line under construction was the Inverness & Perth Junction Railway, superbly engineered by Joseph Mitchell. It opened in September 1863 and two years later was amalgamated with the Inverness & Aberdeen Junction Railway to become the Highland Railway.

railway from Derby to Manchester, though that is on a smaller scale;[5] the Settle & Carlisle line; parts of the extension of the Highland Railway through Sutherland; its Carr Bridge line, with the fearsome ascent out of Inverness (22 miles, half of them at 1 in 60), and the Oban and Fort William lines in the western Highlands.

These long inclines were often mitigated by short 'breathers' – stretches of relatively level line to assist the locomotive on the ascent. There were good examples in the West Country: on the climb up through the Glynn Valley in Cornwall, for example, from Lostwithiel to Doublebois; and on the Somerset & Dorset line between Radstock and Masbury, where each station was placed on an easy gradient, for convenience in starting. Joseph Mitchell followed the same practice on the Highland: at most stations the gradient was kept down to 1 in 300.

In the railways built at the turn of the century, a considerable difference appeared. The routes the later lines took tended to be more direct; their layout was much more spacious, even grand. They displayed all the self-assurance that comes from complete mastery of technique. There were not many of these lines, but they are of great interest from this point of view. The biggest of them was the Great Central's London extension, from Annesley to Quainton Road (now almost entirely closed). The Great Western Railway undertook a number of smaller works between 1897 and 1912, mostly as 'cut-offs' to remove the ancient reproach that the company's initials denoted 'Great Way Round': one example is the line from Wootton Bassett to Stoke Gifford, another the links that together created a new and shorter main line to the West Country, by way of Castle Cary.

The Great Central line south of Nottingham presented the best example, made clearer by contrast both with the Midland line over similar country and with the Metropolitan line, which it joined at Quainton Road. To begin with, the Great Central made a pretty straight run from Nottingham to Leicester, but on gradients gentle enough to permit fast running. From Leicester to Quainton Road the line was a switchback – that is in the nature of the terrain; but it was a switchback regulated to a fixed ruling gradient of 1 in 176. For nearly two thirds of the distance the train was travelling up or down at exactly this inclination, and never at any point more steeply. South of Quainton Road, however, the Metropolitan line (completed in 1885-92) was a quite different proposition: five miles at 1 in 117 up from Aylesbury, four miles at 1 in 105 down from Amersham. You could sense the grandeur of the Great Central's engineering from the train, especially on the northbound journey: in the great cuttings between Brackley and Woodford, the long steady descent from the Catesby Tunnel towards Rugby, and the gradual right-hand curve of the line as it dropped down from Ashby Magna to Whetstone, south of Leicester. 'Gradual' is the important word here: whereas on the corresponding Midland line, built in the 1850s, there were four sharp curves (two of them involving permanent speed restrictions), on this line there was not a single one.

Railway building in these last years before 1914 included some great works of widening and improvement: the changes on the London & South Western main line, culminating in the huge task of rebuilding Waterloo station; the even more complex alterations by the London & North Western at Camden and Crewe; the North Eastern's great work at Newcastle, in-

The new express route from Paddington, London, to Birmingham, opened in 1905-10, benefited from this deep chalk cutting north of High Wycombe. The route was partly new, and partly a remodelling of an older line: on this stretch, the old line was awkwardly laid out for express traffic, with a steep gradient. A second line was therefore built, two miles long, on an easier course, to be used by trains going in the uphill direction.

In the days of steam locomotion, ventilation shafts in tunnels were essential to allow steam and fumes to escape. This is one of the six shafts considered necessary in the Chipping Sodbury tunnel on the Wootton Bassett to Patchway line on the Great Western Railway. Just over two miles long, the tunnel was completed in 1903 as part of the new direct line from London to South Wales.

cluding the construction of the King Edward VII Bridge, which for the first time enabled trains for Scotland from the south to use the station without reversing. Some of the widenings from two tracks to four undertaken in these years are of interest because they gave the new engineers an opportunity to improve on the work of the old: most notably on the Midland line between Bedford and Wellingborough, where a fresh set of levels was adopted for the new freight lines, and even at one point a fresh path. Whilst passenger trains today still toil up to Sharnbrook summit, freight trains burrow through a tunnel – you can see its ventilating shafts from the train, great cylinders of blue brick on the east side of the line. The layout of these two sets of lines is a visible demonstration that the Midland company commanded greater wealth and better engineering techniques in the 1880s than thirty years earlier.

Although no construction of major new railways has taken place in Britain since 1914, valuable improvements of detail have been effected. Some of these arose from the needs of traffic in time of war: new junctions, for example, between hitherto separate systems, to quicken the movement of troops and supplies.[6] Although the Modernisation Plan of 1955 did not involve the construction of any new railway routes, one substantial new work has been required since: the 14-mile Selby diversion on the Eastern Region main line between Doncaster and York, which was brought into use in 1983 (see p. 59). Important new construction has also been undertaken for some urban railways (not part of British Rail): the Victoria Line and the extension to Heathrow Airport in London, the Tyne & Wear and Merseyside metros in the North (see p. 61).

—— RAILWAYS IN THE LANDSCAPE ——

The railways have done much to change the face of the landscape. Consider, as a simple example, the building of the great embankments that appear in the prints of Bourne, and the changes they wrought in the undulating country that they strode over. When the railways were being built in the 1830s and 1840s, many people attacked them for the destruction they were wreaking in the countryside – a great part of England was then a planned landscape in a sense in which it will never be again. Both in country and in town, these were the years in which England attained its greatest physical beauty. By 1830 the work of the 18th-century landscape artists had had time to come to maturity: the trees they had planted had grown, and all the changes they had made had mellowed. Millions of pounds had been invested, altogether, in this improvement. We cannot be surprised, therefore, that the cutting of railways through a landscape so recently brought to perfection was vigorously opposed.

There had been similar opposition to the building of the canals, but it had been much less fierce. Canals undeniably disturbed the landscape, but when they were completed they settled into it very well in time, appearing in the distance as no more than ribbons of placid water. The railways were different. They were operated by steam locomotives, which were bound to be prominent in the landscape at all times; they emitted foul smoke and made a noise that was alarming to animals and disagreeable to human beings; their fixed equipment was conspicuous; there were more of them, and they occupied more room than the canals, often in good agricultural land. Above all they were the instrument of the urban, the commercial, part of the community, the symbol of its successful and continuing assault on the ancient dominance of the landed interest. One cannot be surprised that many landowners resisted them. Squire Gordon of Kemble was a small

Trentham station on the North Staffordshire Railway was designed with shallow-sloping, pantiled roofs by Sir Charles Barry, so that it would harmonise with the great house nearby.

man; but he may stand here as their principal representative.

On the other hand, it soon became clear that such opposition would be vain. The most sensible thing for the landowners to do was to come to terms with the railways, not to defy them. When the London & Birmingham Railway encountered opposition to its original plan for a line by way of Uxbridge and Aylesbury, the Countess of Bridgwater suggested that it should take the line by the Grand Junction Canal instead, through her property at Berkhamsted and Tring. She argued that the land was 'already *gashed* by the Canal', and that a railway built beside it would make very little further difference.[7] She was a shrewd old lady; and as time went on more and more landowners followed her example.

Where there was co-operation a good deal was done to mitigate the harsh effects of the railways' invasion of the countryside. Embankments could be planted with trees, as they were on the main lines of the London & South Western Railway. Bridges and tunnel-mouths could be made ornamental, like the portals of the tunnel through Shugborough Park near Stafford. Stations might be built to harmonise with a great house or the buildings on its estate. Trentham station south of Stoke, also in Stafford-shire, was a stone building in the Italian style matching the Duke of Sutherland's house nearby, and was considerably more expensive to put up than the red-brick stations elsewhere on the same line.

Before long the rawness of the new works began to wear off, the railways were absorbed into the landscape and even admired as an enlivening feature of it. In 1842 a local antiquary, looking down from Long Cliff above Loughborough, noted that 'the trains of the Midland Counties Railway may be observed, almost uninterruptedly, from Sileby to Derby, and form a pleasing object darting across the grand panorama'.[8] Today we accept trains without thinking. Even in a wild country – up Strath Helmsdale for instance, and then over the high moorland of Caithness, which one Victorian writer called 'one of the dreariest tracts of country in Scotland'[9] – the railway has been assimilated into the countryside through which it runs so that, as a modern student of the landscape has put it, 'we take the railway earthworks and monuments as much for granted as we do the hedges and fields of the enclosure commissioners or the churches of our medieval forefathers'.[10]

In the towns the railways have often remained very much more conspicuous – disagreeably so in some places. They marred fine streets, like Friargate in Derby and Foregate Street in Worcester; their stinking presence depopulated genteel neighbourhoods; they would cut off one part of a town from another, as at Cullen in Banffshire. Again, some railways made an effort to play the chameleon, to disguise themselves as much as possible. Look, for instance, at the architectural treatment of the Great Western line entering Bath from the east, the bridges and the elegant curved retaining-walls in the cuttings, all built of dressed Bath stone – ignobly patched here and there with blue brick in later days. Or consider the trouble that was taken by the Edinburgh & Glasgow Railway to hide itself from the proprietors of Princes Street (see p. 219). Yet, in this last case, the effort was not sustained: so that many of those who regarded railways with affection were still bound to deplore the mess they wrought in the valley between the Old and New Towns of Edinburgh, perhaps the most splendid townscape in the whole of Great Britain.

It was seldom that there was in any town an individual or a body of people strong enough to stand up to the railway and dictate terms to it after the fashion of a landowner. The Corporation might have the power in

A photograph taken in about 1905 of Ludgate Hill shows how the appearance of city streets was irrevocably altered when railways were routed through and across them. Here, the heavy iron bridge of the London Chatham & Dover Railway's Metropolitan extension north from Blackfriars crosses Ludgate Hill directly below St Paul's. This piece of vandalism caused no uproar until a late stage in the passage of the Bill through Parliament in 1860, when an unsuccessful plea was made for a tunnel instead. When the bridge was complete, tricked out with the arms of the City and the company, there were loud protests: 'That viaduct', wrote one candid critic, 'has utterly spoiled one of the finest street scenes in the metropolis and is one of the most unsightly objects ever constructed in any such situation, anywhere in the world.'

theory; but it rarely exercised it in practice. Corporations sometimes concerned themselves with the general issue whether or not to encourage the entry of a railway into a town. There are striking cases of discouragement, with important consequences for the towns concerned: Abingdon, for instance, and the City of London.[11] Most towns, however, did nothing to hinder the arrival of the railway; some, like Exeter and Newcastle, actively encouraged it.[12] The line the railway took through the town was a commercial matter for the railway to settle with the owners of the land it wished to cross. When the Manchester & Birmingham Railway determined to stride across the centre of Stockport on a vast brick viaduct a quarter of a mile long, no active body of citizens appeared to question the propriety of allowing the whole town to be dominated by this viaduct, as it has been ever since. Again, when the railways built their bridges across the Thames in London in the 1860s, no one made any effective protest against their unredeemed ugliness – though Ruskin poured out a proper ridicule upon the inept decoration of the bridge at Blackfriars. 'The entire invention of the de-

The High Level Bridge at Newcastle, completed under Robert Stephenson in 1850, provides an example of the change in urban life and landscape that the railways could bring. Unique for its time, the bridge was designed for road as well as rail traffic. It made a convenient link between Newcastle and Gateshead over the Tyne and was an element in the creation of the modern concept of 'Tyneside'. The railway used the top track, while road vehicles were conveyed on the lower one. The swing bridge in front dates from 1876.

signer', he wrote, 'seems to have exhausted itself in exaggerating to an enormous size a weak form of iron nut, and in conveying the information upon it, in large letters, that it belongs to the London Chatham & Dover Railway Company.'[13]

Not all these changes were for the worse. Some of the great bridges were themselves things of beauty, an enhancement of the townscape: the viaduct at a dizzy height on the west side of Durham; the Dean Street Arch at Newcastle, and the High Level Bridge which emphasised most accurately, when it was the only high-level bridge there, the steepness of the gorge of the Tyne.

—— TUNNELS ——

Some of the greatest works of railway engineering remained largely hidden from view under the ground. The earliest railway tunnels of importance were those on the Canterbury & Whitstable, Liverpool & Manchester, and Leicester & Swannington Railways. On the early trunk lines out of London there were two much longer ones, at Kilsby and Box. Kilsby Tunnel, on the London & Birmingham Railway south of Rugby, proved especially difficult to construct. Not long after the work began a hidden spring was found, which was mastered only after eight months of continuous pumping, day and night, at 2,000 gallons a minute. The estimate for building the tunnel was £99,000; it cost in fact £300,000. It also cost the lives of 26 of the men working on it.

Box Tunnel is the earliest important example of a type of tunnel that acquired a deservedly evil reputation in later years: a long tunnel on a steep incline – fine enough when the train is running downhill, but unpleasant for the passengers and at times almost intolerable for the engine crews on the slow, suffocating ascent. When the Great Western Bill was under consideration in Parliament, much expert evidence was adduced by its opponents to prove how dangerous this tunnel would be. The evidence has been ridiculed since – perhaps a little too freely; for the tunnel has been a cause of danger in the past and it remains an inconvenience in working.

The next great tunnels to be built both pierced the Pennines: the Summit Tunnel of the Manchester & Leeds Railway at Littleborough (see p. 165) and the Woodhead Tunnel of the Sheffield Ashton & Manchester. At the time of its completion in 1845 Woodhead Tunnel was easily the longest that had yet been built for a railway – just over three miles. Like Box Tunnel it was all on a gradient; and though the gradient was only half as severe, the operation of trains through it was an even more unpleasant task for the enginemen, since it was built for a single line only and the smoke and gases were therefore confined within a much smaller space. It is probably true to say that, of all the great tunnels in Britain, this was the most physically trying to work. When the line was doubled, a second single-line tunnel was built beside the first. In the 1930s it was decided to electrify the line from Manchester to Sheffield. When the work was carried out, a wholly new double-line tunnel was built, and the two old tunnels became disused.

The building of the first tunnel, through one of the wildest tracts of England, was a formidable task. Very inadequate provision was made for the welfare of the men working on it, some thirty of whom died in the course of its construction. Reports of the evil condition of the men up on those high moors percolated slowly down to Manchester. They led, in the end, to a Parliamentary inquiry into the employment of railway labourers (1846). Even when the second tunnel came to be built, in 1847-52, there were 28 deaths from cholera within a few weeks in 1849.[14]

Much tunnelling was undertaken, of necessity, in the course of the great period of railway construction in the 1840s and 1850s, using the experience gained through the building of these early works and improving on it. A third long tunnel was driven through the Pennines at Standedge on

The London Chatham & Dover Railway embellished a number of its structures with coats of arms and other ornaments. This decoration on Blackfriars Bridge, designed by Joseph Cubitt, incurred the wrath of John Ruskin. The bridge has been demolished, but these decorations are preserved.

This photograph of Woodhead station, taken in about 1910, shows the entrance to the twin tunnels, the right-hand one completed in 1845 and the left-hand one added when the line was doubled in 1848-52. A ventilation shaft may be seen on the hillside beyond. These two tunnels, monuments to railway construction in the most difficult conditions, became disused in 1954 when the line was electrified and a new double-line tunnel was opened. The entire line east of Hadfield was closed in 1981.

the London & North Western line from Manchester to Leeds, surpassing the Woodhead Tunnel by some forty yards and remaining for forty years the longest railway tunnel in Britain. From the 1850s the amount of tunnelling was reduced, often in favour of a detour or a steeper climb. Most of the railway system of Wales and Scotland was built, not in the heroic 1830s and 1840s, but in the more careful 1850s and 1860s. And so, although they are both mountainous countries, we find that there were only six tunnels over a mile long in Wales and only one in the whole of Scotland. In England, on the other hand, there were 49.

One more historic main-line railway tunnel had yet to be built. Projected to run under the Severn, it was first sketched out by Charles Richardson in 1865, taken up by the Great Western company in 1872, and completed in 1886 at a cost of more than £1,500,000. It was different from all the previous tunnels: it was built under water. The works were flooded out twice – on the second occasion, in 1883, by a tidal wave that put them back into the state they had been in three years earlier. But the engineers, Sir John Hawkshaw and Richardson, and the contractor, T. A. Walker,[15] doggedly persevered. The tunnel is 4 miles 606 yards long, and is still the longest main-line tunnel in the country.

The remaining developments in tunnelling in Britain have all occurred in London, where the first underground railway began to work in 1863, and the first modern tube railway, the City & South London, in 1890. Its tunnels were driven under the Thames by a new method, invented by P. W. Barlow and J. H. Greathead, employing the 'Greathead shield'. In many ways the tubes are the most remarkable tunnels in Britain. If you travel on the Northern line from East Finchley to Morden by way of Bank you pass through the longest continuous tunnel in the world (17¼ miles), and from a point near London Bridge to Stockwell you are running over the original City & South London Railway. An equally interesting journey is that on the East London line from Wapping to Rotherhithe, which takes you through a pre-railway tunnel under the river – the Thames Tunnel, built by I. K. Brunel's father in 1825-43, used at first for pedestrian traffic only and turned over to the railway in 1865.

Nearly half a million passenger journeys are made through the tunnels of the London underground railways every day. Few of those who make them are aware of the magnitude or the complexity of the operations they take for granted, or of the influence that these London railways have exercised elsewhere in the world. Many other great cities now have underground railways of their own. Yet London's was the first; and it taught lessons that were learnt and applied abroad – in Paris, Berlin, Moscow, Washington, Mexico City and Caracas.

In addition to the tunnels that were built, there were also great dreams that never materialised. The most important of these is the Channel Tunnel, first projected for stage-coaches in 1802 and taken up seriously as a railway project in the 1860s. Two Channel Tunnel companies were incorporated, one in England in 1872, the other in France three years later; and in 1880-83 shafts were sunk and a total of two and a half miles of tunnel driven from Shakespeare Cliff, near Dover, and from Sangatte in the Pas de Calais. Then the work stopped. There was opposition to it on the English side, on both economic and military grounds; but the project has often been revived since, and may yet be realised. If it is, it will eclipse all its predecessors in magnitude. But the scientific and engineering skill that it will require will be derived from the long experience accumulated since Brindley tunnelled at Harecastle and the Stephensons at Liverpool and Glenfield.

During construction of the Severn tunnel on 17 October 1883 a tidal wave poured down the excavation shaft and trapped 83 men in the workings. In this contemporary engraving, the small rescue boat that was launched on the flood water approaches the navvies, who have retreated to the top of the wooden staging.

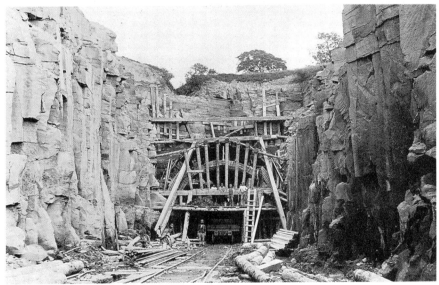

Centring shores up the entrance to the Bolsover tunnel during its construction for the Lancashire Derbyshire & East Coast Railway. Completed in 1897, the tunnel frequently gave trouble, which was one of the reasons that the line, between Chesterfield and Langwith Junction, was closed down in 1951.

—— BRIDGES AND VIADUCTS ——

The most spectacular achievement of the railways has always been represented by their viaducts and bridges, in endless variety of form and material. The earliest of the long viaducts carried the Liverpool & Manchester Railway across the Sankey Brook, immediately west of Newton-le-Willows: it was built of brick clad in stone, and was carried on nine arches nearly 70ft high. The first main lines out of London could all show fine works of this kind: the grandest of them perhaps the viaduct by which the Great Western still crosses the River Brent at Hanwell. Built in 1837 of London stock brick, it rests on coupled piers which taper slightly up to their bold stone capitals. The company named the viaduct officially after Lord Wharncliffe, who had been chairman of the Lords' Committee that considered its Bill, and his arms are carved on the south face. When the viaduct had to be widened, forty years after it was erected, to accommodate four

tracks, great pains were taken not to impair the original structure.

The London & Greenwich Railway boasted the longest viaduct. Running the whole of the railway's course, it had no architectural pretensions. It was a single series of 878 plain arches of yellow-grey Kentish brick, three and three quarter miles long, begun in 1834 and completed in 1838. The company anticipated a great revenue from the letting of these arches as warehouses, shops and private dwellings. It was disappointed.

Five viaducts may be mentioned as examples of bold work executed in the most intensive phase of railway-building in the 1840s and 1850s. The first crosses the Ouse on the London – Brighton line between Balcombe and Hayward's Heath. Though the credit for this great work belongs primarily to J. U. Rastrick, the company's engineer, its embellishment was due to David Mocatta, the architect of the stations on the line. The Ouse Viaduct is the most striking example surviving of the application to railways of the Italianate style favoured for a brief time by the early Victorians. The decoration is entirely without fussiness. Eight little pavilions serve admirably to punctuate the ends of the viaduct. It is interesting and impressive from any viewpoint – whether from below, from the train running across it, or from the air.

The other four were all completed in a single year, 1850. Length is the distinguishing feature of two of them: Digswell Viaduct on the Great Northern main line, near Welwyn, and the viaduct that carries the railway from Blackburn to Hellifield over the River Calder at Whalley. Both are perfectly plain brick structures, but they make a powerful effect by the repeated rhythm of their arches, stretching away in a countless series into the distance. The third is a work of a different kind: Robert Stephenson's Royal Border Bridge, from which the traveller between London and Edinburgh gets his view – unforgettable in the evening light – of the town of Berwick and the estuary of the Tweed. The bridge is built partly on a curve; and seen from the streets of Tweedmouth below it has a loftiness to inspire awe. Can anything illustrate better the change in the value of money during the past century than the knowledge that this stupendous viaduct was built for £120,000?

The last of these works is again different, something unique indeed in Britain: this is the Ballochmyle Viaduct, spanning the deep valley of the River Ayr just south of Mauchline on the Glasgow & South Western line. It has seven arches, two sets of three that are ordinary enough, flanking a huge central arch 181ft wide and 163ft high. This is easily the widest stone railway arch in Britain, and for half a century it remained the widest in Europe, until it was outdone by one in Austria. Here is emphatically a bridge that must be seen not from the train but from beside and below. It lies close to the main road from Kilmarnock to Dumfries (A76), and it is well worth an effort to get there. Ballochmyle Viaduct is one of the works of the Scotsman John Miller, who ought to be more widely recognised as one of the great British railway engineers.

One other viaduct, built of brick a generation later, deserves mention for its exceptional length. This is Harringworth Viaduct, carrying the Midland line across the Welland out of Northamptonshire into Rutland. Like most of the Midland's engineering works of the 1860s and 1870s, it is executed in brick of a singularly pungent red. Unhappily blue bricks from Staffordshire have been used subsequently to patch it, at some points disagreeably mottling the surface. There are 82 arches, and the whole bridge is three quarters of a mile long.

All these striking viaducts are of masonry or brick. Those were natural materials for the railway engineers to use, as they had been used by their predecessors on the roads and canals. But other materials were pressed into service also, and from an early date. Timber, for example – a material cheap and easy to transport, whose properties were well understood. As it was not at first thought likely to be able to bear the weight of locomotives, it was used in the early days chiefly for over-bridges. On the Whitby & Pickering Railway, however, which employed horses only, there were nine wooden under-bridges over the River Esk in five miles. An interesting wooden lift bridge was designed by Robert Stephenson for the Leicester & Swannington Railway's branch at Soar Lane, Leicester; it was completed in 1834.

Another remarkable experiment was the use of laminated timber in bridges built on the Newcastle & North Shields Railway in 1837-39 to the design of John and Benjamin Green, and in the Etherow and Dinting Vale Viaducts at Mottram on the Sheffield Ashton & Manchester line. One of those in the town of North Shields lasted until 1937; part of its framework is in the National Railway Museum at York. As a result of these early trials, greater use was made of timber by railway engineers in the 1840s and 1850s. On the Great Northern 'loop line' from Peterborough to Lincoln, opened in 1848, there was a series including two large bridges at Boston and Bardney.

The most famous timber bridges were those designed by I. K. Brunel on the Great Western. The first was an over-bridge in Sonning Cutting (replaced in 1893). Brunel substituted timber for masonry in the Somerset Bridge on the Bristol & Exeter line in 1843, and at the same time he built two new wooden bridges over the Thames on the Oxford branch and nine timber viaducts in the Golden Valley in Gloucestershire. These were followed by the famous series in the South West: five on the South Devon Railway between Brent and Plymouth (1848); nine on the West Cornwall Railway (1852); 42 on the Cornwall Railway between Plymouth and Falmouth (1859-63); six on the Tavistock branch (1859), and two between Churston and Kingswear (1864). The longest of all these was at Truro (443yd), and the highest at St Pinnock in the Glynn Valley (151ft). Of the

This timber viaduct at St Austell, 115ft high, was one of 42 designed by I. K. Brunel for the Cornwall Railway between Plymouth and Falmouth. The photograph was probably taken not long before the viaduct was reconstructed in steel and brick in 1898. The small projecting bays beside the track provided shelter for the platelayers when trains were passing.

total number of 64, no fewer than 42 survived until the conversion of the gauge in 1892. Thereafter they were gradually rebuilt, to accommodate two narrow-gauge tracks. They survived longest on the Falmouth branch because it was never doubled. The last of them – College Wood Viaduct at Penryn – was not replaced until 1934.

The method used in rebuilding was frequently to erect a new masonry bridge beside the old timber one. The stone piers on which the wooden superstructure rested were then left intact, and some of them can still be seen from the train today – for example, on the down side at Ivybridge. A few, such as St Pinnock Viaduct, were rebuilt by heightening the original stone piers and laying a steel girder frame across them. So there are still some fragments of the 'spider bridges' that once notably enlivened the landscape of South Devon and Cornwall. Two of Brunel's timber bridges on the Vale of Neath Railway near Aberdare survived until 1947.[16]

In 1824-25 George Stephenson erected a four-arched iron bridge with curved girders to carry the Stockton & Darlington line over the River Gaunless near West Auckland. When this historic bridge came to be dismantled it was treated with proper respect: the essential parts of the framework were removed for preservation. The whole now stands boldly outside the National Railway Museum at York.

The Stockton & Darlington also commissioned the first iron suspension bridge for a railway, on its Middlesbrough branch near Stockton. This proved unable to carry in safety the loads for which it had been designed, and even the light traffic that did pass over it bent and twisted the whole structure. The failure not only discredited the designer Samuel Brown (several of his other bridges failed too); it seemed to show that the suspension principle was unsuited to railways altogether, and it has not in fact been much applied to them in Britain, even where the span to be covered is broad. It was discarded by Robert Stephenson when he was planning the Britannia Bridge to take the Chester & Holyhead Railway across the Menai Strait. Instead he used two tubes, rectangular in section, to carry the tracks. The plan worked perfectly, and his noble bridge stood for 120 years without alteration. It is only a mile away from Telford's famous suspension bridge, carrying the Holyhead road.

By the middle of the century iron was being used for the construction of railway bridges everywhere in Britain. Some of these fine early works survive. At King's Langley and Blisworth, for example, two splendid iron skew-bridges of Robert Stephenson's design still span the Grand Junction Canal, both dating from 1838. Great engineer though he was, however, Robert Stephenson was not invariably successful. In 1847 a girder in his bridge over the Dee at Chester collapsed under the weight of a train, precipitating its coaches into the river nearly forty feet below. Five people were killed, and every single surviving passenger injured. The accident caused great alarm and raised doubts about the reliability of cast iron as a material for railway bridges. Stephenson was already at this time engaged with William Fairbairn on research into the strength of wrought iron, and he used that material for the tubes in his Conway and Britannia Bridges.

Brunel was meanwhile engaged on one of his less famous works, the South Wales Railway from Gloucester to Swansea. This included a series of timber viaducts, like those under construction at the same time on the South Devon Railway; but when one of these, at Newport, was destroyed in a fire in 1848 its central span was rebuilt in wrought iron. The most for-midable work was the bridge over the Wye at Chepstow (completed in 1852), where Brunel evolved a characteristically original solution to the special problems presented by the site. On one side of the river was a limestone cliff 120ft high, on the other low ground, liable to flooding and always full of water. The bridge was of a modified suspension type, the chains hanging from the ends of a horizontal circular tube 9ft in diameter. The great iron framework stopped abruptly two thirds of the way across the river, the remainder consisting simply of girders resting on iron columns. The bridge was reconstructed in 1948.[17]

A year before its opening in 1850, the Britannia Bridge over the Menai Strait in North Wales acquires recognisable form in a lithograph by G. Hawkins. The two openings for the rectangular tubes through which the trains were to pass may be seen already completed in the left-hand tower. The bridge was designed by Robert Stephenson, with the important assistance of William Fairbairn for the ironwork; architectural details were contributed by Francis Thompson, and the sculptured lions guarding the entrances were by John Thomas. The great iron tubes served until May 1970, when their strength was destroyed by fire. The bridge, retaining its great towers, was reopened in a new form in 1972; in 1980 a top deck was added to accommodate road traffic.

When the bridge over the Dee at Chester failed on 24 May 1847, it precipitated a train into the river with the loss of five lives. At the inquest the jury came near to returning a verdict of manslaughter against Robert Stephenson, who was responsible for the design of the bridge for the Chester & Holyhead Railway, and a special enquiry was made by the government into the properties of cast-iron in structures of this kind.

This photograph of about 1900, with its fishing boats in the foreground and the town of Saltash on the far bank, gives an idea of the scale of Brunel's Royal Albert Bridge, completed in 1859. Spanning the River Tamar between Devon and Cornwall, it was once the dominant feature of the landscape, but is now rivalled by a recent road bridge built alongside it.

The Chepstow Bridge is of interest in its own right, but more interesting still as a trial run for the much greater Royal Albert Bridge at Saltash, which carries the railway from Plymouth into Cornwall. The building of this bridge was spread over six years (1853-59), largely owing to the poverty of the Cornwall Railway company. Again, the design provided for tubes that held suspension chains running aloft between the piers, though this time the tubes were oval in section and curved in the form of a bowstring. This was the first great bridge on which compressed air was used in sinking the foundations in midstream – a method that was subsequently adopted all over the world. The Saltash Bridge remains unique. It had one smaller forerunner and no successor. The anxiety incidental to its construction helped to strain its author to breaking point, and he died only four months after it was opened.

Two years earlier another great iron bridge had been completed: Crumlin Viaduct four miles west of Pontypool, carrying the line to Aberdare over Ebbw Vale. Though it was a perfectly plain structure, with no

The grandeur of the Ballochmyle Viaduct, on the main line from Glasgow to Carlisle just south of Mauchline, is caught here in a painting by David Octavius Hill. Ballochmyle was completed in 1848 to the plans of the distinguished engineer, John Miller: a work of outstanding boldness, with a central arch of 181ft span, it was the widest masonry bridge in the world at the time, and for fifty years afterwards. It is still in use today.

The railway artist H. Geach depicted this 4-4-0 saddle tank engine heading a variety of carriages over Brunel's Gover Viaduct in the 1880s. The viaduct, west of St Austell, was one of 42 timber bridges built between Plymouth and Falmouth.

In this watercolour by an unknown artist, a Daniel Gooch 8ft single-driver speeds down the Great Western Railway towards Reading, heading a broad-gauge train of the 1870s. The track has been converted by the addition of a third rail to allow both standard and broad-gauge trains to run on it. This period of 'mixed gauge' heralded the decline of the broad gauge, which eventually disappeared in 1892. In the background is a train on the standard-gauge line of the South Eastern Railway, coming in from Wokingham.

This plate of about 1846 from a book of watercolour drawings of the South Devon Atmospheric Railway by William Dawson shows the stretch of line 'from the parish of Kings Teignton to the Newton station in Wolborough' – i.e. Newton Abbot. The engine house and pumping station, with its tall tower for the water tank, is on the left. In the atmospheric system, trains were connected by plates passing under a continuous leather flap to pistons in an iron pipe laid between the rails. Pumping engines, placed at intervals along the line, created a vacuum inside the pipe, drawing along the pistons and so moving the attached train. The system, planned to extend from Exeter to Totnes, was in operation as far as Newton Abbot from September 1847, but was discontinued after one year because of difficulties in working. The line was then converted to run with steam locomotives, but the towers of Brunel's Italianate pumping stations still survive at Starcross and Totnes.

ornament at all, its height and the open latticework of the piers on which it rested gave it an exceptional grace. One does not usually turn to after-dinner oratory for convincing simile, but one of the directors of the Newport Abergavenny & Hereford Railway, speaking on the opening day, observed that 'they had the great Britannia Bridge, the finest specimen of massive grandeur in the kingdom, and they would all say that Mr Kennard [who designed the new bridge and was contractor for it] had provided a most fitting wife for him in the Crumlin Viaduct: she was all elegance and beauty'.[18] That was a happy thought. The bridge ceased to carry traffic and was dismantled in 1966; it was a sad loss.

The success of the Britannia and Saltash bridges led engineers to consider the crossing of even wider spaces of water. In 1864 a company was formed to build a line across the Solway on a viaduct just over a mile long. It was opened for goods traffic in 1869, and for passengers in the following summer. But the line never prospered, either in independence or after it had been taken over by the Caledonian company in 1895; and the viaduct was closed in 1921. It has now been demolished.

Ten years later, in 1879, the Severn was spanned at Sharpness by a bridge three quarters of a mile long, which included a section at one end that opened over the Gloucester & Berkeley Ship Canal. This bridge, too, was a commercial failure. It survived nevertheless, partly because it came to fulfil a function that was never originally contemplated: it provided an alternative route to the Severn Tunnel, shorter than the detour by Gloucester. On Sundays in winter, when the tunnel was closed for inspection, it carried three or four passenger trains in each direction between Bristol and Cardiff. Two heavy barges crashed into one of its piers, however, in 1960, and it was taken down seven years later.

While the Solway and the Severn were being bridged, plans went forward for taking railways over the two greater estuaries of the Tay and the Forth. The Act authorising the Tay Bridge was passed in 1870, and the work entrusted to Thomas Bouch. He had long been interested in the problem presented to railways by the crossing of these two Firths. As early as 1849 he had played a part in the establishment of the first train-ferry in the world, used on the Forth. He had had valuable experience as a designer of lofty bridges. Those he built in Westmoreland and County Durham were all successful: Hownes Gill Viaduct just south of Consett, and the Tees, Deepdale and Belah viaducts between Barnard Castle and Kirkby Stephen, which were built of iron, the last of them rising to the dizzy height of 196ft. There was every reason, therefore, for people to feel confidence in Bouch's skill and experience.

The bridge he set out to build over the Tay was to be the longest in the world, and it was obviously a formidable undertaking. Yet in one important respect Bouch underestimated the magnitude of his task. Neither he nor anyone else knew, by carefully observed experiment, what allowance ought to be made for the force of gales in a structure of this kind. The limited knowledge of such matters is indicated by the continued use, in the 1870s, of calculations that had been adopted by John Smeaton in a paper read to the Royal Society in 1759.[19] These were in any case inapplicable to the Tay Bridge: it was built of iron, a material Smeaton never used for this purpose, and it was of a length and height much greater than any he had ever contemplated. Bouch stated afterwards that no special precautions had been taken against unusual wind pressures. The problem seems never to have disturbed him.

The bridge was opened for traffic on 1 June 1878, an imposing structure

Stockport Viaduct, built in 1842 for the Manchester & Birmingham Railway, dominates the town with its 27 red brick arches 110ft high. It was greeted by Francis Whishaw, writing in the year it was built, as 'most imposing', both in its design and its 'exquisite workmanship'. It completely changed the appearance of its environment. It is shown here in a postcard dating from 1910.

A full-page engraving in the Illustrated London News *commemorates Queen Victoria's crossing of the year-old Tay Bridge by train on 20 June 1879. The day after this journey, she conferred a knighthood on the bridge's designer and engineer, Thomas Bouch. Six months later, the bridge collapsed in a furious gale: there were almost eighty people in the train that went down with it, and not one survived.*

almost two miles long, curving away from Dundee to the south. Eighteen months later, on a stormy Sunday evening, the central section was blown away and a train plunged into the river. In the subsequent inquiry it emerged that the design and the workmanship of the bridge were both at fault, and the disaster was attributed entirely to these defects. (Except by Sabbatarians, who had a different explanation: to them it was the direct action of God, expressing his displeasure at the running of Sunday trains.) A new bridge was presently undertaken, in which some of the materials of the old were re-used. It was completed in 1887 and is still in use, running closely beside the line of the old one, the stumps of whose piers are still visible above the water on the eastern side.

When the disaster occurred, Bouch was already at work on another great railway bridge, over the Forth. He had campaigned for it with quiet pertinacity for twenty years before the foundation stone was laid in 1878.[20] One pier of it was erected on Inch Garvie; and that was all. The disastrous failure of the Tay Bridge completely discredited him, and he died less than a year afterwards. When the plan for the Forth Bridge was taken up again, a completely new set of designs was adopted by Benjamin Baker and John Fowler. They were new in two vital respects: where Bouch had proposed to build a suspension bridge, Baker and Fowler chose the cantilever principle; and where he was going to continue to use wrought iron, they used steel.

Of the many successful bridges that should be set to Thomas Bouch's credit, the lattice-girder and trestle Belah Viaduct on the South Durham & Lancashire Union Railway across the Pennines was one of the most dramatic. Rising 196ft high with 16 supporting iron spans, it was made from prefabricated iron parts, using timber only for the deck. The line was built primarily to convey iron ore from Furness to the iron works of Cleveland, and to take Durham coke back again. The bridge was demolished in 1962.

The lofty approach to the Forth Bridge dwarfs the houses on the banks of the river. More than one and a half miles long and built on the cantilever principle, the bridge took 5,000 men, working in shifts around the clock, seven years to build. It was opened in 1890, having cost about £3 million. It was the first large bridge in the world to be built entirely of steel.

The bridge they completed in 1890 has retained its place as one of the great engineering works of the world. The choice of steel as a material – which still represented a courageous experiment – proved wholly successful, with the result that the Forth Bridge was the parent of a number of others overseas, for example at Quebec and Calcutta. It was paid for by a group of four railway companies. The largest subscriber, oddly enough, was not the North British, which was most immediately interested in its construction, but the Midland company in England.

The Forth Bridge forms a noble climax to the story of bridge-building in Britain. The railway bridges erected in the succeeding seventy years have not been very numerous. In a technical sense, none of them has represented an innovation of decisive importance, while aesthetically, it is sad to say, most of them are best forgotten.

A fine start was made with the use of concrete on the Mallaig extension of the West Highland Railway, built in 1897-1901. The shapely Glenfinnan Viaduct stands as a lasting example of what can be done in that ungrateful

The Glenfinnan Viaduct, opened in 1901, was the first successful British bridge to be made substantially of concrete. Built for the Mallaig extension of the West Highland Railway, its 21 plain arches, without capitals, make an austere but graceful addition to the landscape at the head of Loch Shiel.

material if the design has a chaste simplicity, though even that is now much disfigured by the staining to which concrete is usually vulnerable. Calstock Viaduct in Cornwall, built of concrete blocks in 1908, equals Glenfinnan in elegance. More recent concrete railway structures have been dreary, some hideous. The British railways lost few major bridges through enemy action in the last war, which was fortunate from every point of view. There is little indication that if they had had to provide new ones they would have done so with the skilful grace shown in the great reconstruction of the railways of Italy and France.[21]

—— THE TRACK ——

The track of a railway, if less visually striking than the bridges, viaducts and tunnels which carry it under, over, or through the natural obstacles in its path, nevertheless has an interesting history of its own.

Though the earliest railways were of stone or timber,[22] the track of the modern railway has always been made of solid metal, for nothing else proved strong enough to bear the weight of the locomotive and the heavily-loaded vehicles it drew.[23] It was usual at first to spike the iron rails directly on to stone supports. In 1797, however, Thomas Barnes built a line from the Lawson Main colliery at Walker to the River Tyne, the track of which was held in 'chairs'; and this became the accepted practice in Britain for almost the next century and a half. A series of experiments made in Scotland and Cumberland led on to the next important change: the use of wrought iron, which could safely be made into rails of much greater length. It remained the standard material for railway track throughout the first great period of construction. Gradually the rails grew heavier, to support the increasing weights put upon them: from 17lb to the yard when the Bedlington line was built in 1821, to about 40lb in the late 1830s and 80lb by the middle of the century.[24] Stone blocks continued to be employed by most engineers, though not to the complete exclusion of timber. The track of George Stephenson's Leicester & Swannington Railway, for example, was laid on wooden sleepers in open sections and across embankments, and on stone blocks, set diagonally 3ft apart, in cuttings.[25] But timber was found to give smoother riding and better service, and stone sleepers were gradually displaced.

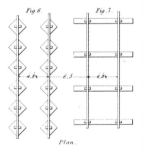

George Stephenson's method of laying track appears here as drawn in Whishaw's Railways of Great Britain and Ireland. On the right is the conventional system of wooden sleepers; on the left, the diamond-shaped blocks of stone he used in cuttings, on the ground that it was better than timber at resisting the rain-water that poured down the sides of cuttings and accumulated at the bottom.

The Belvoir Castle Railway was built in 1815 by the Butterley Iron Company of Derbyshire; it was just two miles long, and ran from the Nottingham & Grantham canal to the castle (seen in the distance). Its purpose was to convey coal to the Duke of Rutland's cellars. It was laid out to a narrow gauge, 4ft 4½in, with fish-bellied iron rails mounted on stone blocks. Though the line ceased to be used in 1918 and most of it was dismantled in 1941, some sections of it remain in the castle grounds. They are among the oldest pieces of iron railway now surviving anywhere in the world.

In considering the track, as in considering all other parts of the railway, I. K. Brunel worked out his own solutions. His track was eccentric not only for its 7ft gauge but also for its form. It was supported on continuous longitudinal timbers, knit together by transoms at intervals of 15ft and held down by piles of beechwood driven into the ground.[26] This elaborate and costly method of construction was a failure, producing a 'pitching or see-saw motion' through the sagging of the timber between the piles; and the piles were quickly abandoned. Longitudinal timbers continued, however, to be used for most of the broad-gauge track until it was finally abandoned for the narrow gauge in 1892.

As locomotives and rolling stock grew heavier and traffic more intense, greater and greater strains were imposed on the track, which was not always able to withstand them. A fair number of accidents in the 1850s and 1860s were to be attributed to this cause: for example, those at Creech St Michael on the Bristol & Exeter Railway in 1852 and at Raynes Park (then called Epsom Junction) on the London & South Western nine years later. When an accident occurred on the Newcastle & Carlisle Railway near Haltwhistle in 1851, it emerged that rails of six different weights, ranging from 42 to 82lb, were in use, and that the lighter rails were so much punished by the engines when running fast that much of the platelayers' time had to be devoted to straightening them.[27]

In the 1850s the track was strengthened by the use of the fishplate, for securing one rail to the next, in accordance with a patent taken out by W. B.

These plans show Brunel's controversial system of laying his broad-gauge track on longitudinal sleepers, supported on piles driven into the ground. Though the piles were a failure and were abandoned, the sleepers continued to be laid longitudinally on much of the Great Western until its conversion to the standard gauge.

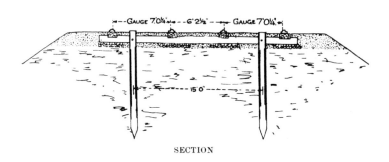

SECTION

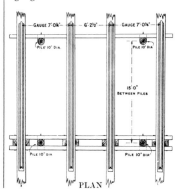

PLAN

Adams and R. Richardson in 1847. The greatest advance in this direction, however, came with the substitution of steel for wrought iron in the making of the rails themselves.

Until 1856 any such change was unthinkable, since steel was made only in small quantities, chiefly for cutlery and tools, and cost at least £50 a ton. But in that year Henry Bessemer published the details of his process of making steel cheaply, and it won its first great commercial success in its application to railway track. Bessemer's original process was modified by R. F. Mushet, who used manganese to de-oxidise and re-carbonise the steel before it was cast into moulds, and early in 1857 the first rail made in this way was sent to Derby. There it was laid down at the north end of the station, at a point where the traffic was so heavy that iron rails had had to be replaced every six months. The new rail remained in service there for 16 years. It was then removed by the Midland company and thrown away unthinkingly to scrap – a sad end for one of the most truly historic pieces of worked metal produced in the modern world.

In spite of the successful demonstration at Derby, the railways were at first cautious in turning over to the steel rail,[28] with some reason. The initial cost of steel rails was still substantially higher than wrought iron, and it was at first supposed that they would be valueless as scrap metal, whereas wrought iron could always be re-forged. However, in 1861-62 they were installed by the London & North Western Railway at Crewe and Camden. Many experiments were made to find a compromise between the older process and the new. T. W. Dodds patented a 'steeling' process for the hardening of iron rails, which was applied to a hundred miles of track on the North Eastern main line; at Crewe, rails were produced of wrought iron with steel heads. None of these devices was wholly successful, however, and in the later 1860s and 1870s steel rails gradually replaced iron. By 1878, for instance, four fifths of those used on the Great Western main lines were of steel, and the use of iron for the purpose had been virtually abandoned.[29]

At the same time other experiments were taking place, with the same object – to reduce the very heavy cost of manufacturing and maintaining the track. Extensive trials of sleepers made of iron and steel instead of timber took place on the London & North Western (to one of F. W. Webb's numerous patents) and on the Metropolitan extensions to Harrow and Rickmansworth, opened in 1880-87.[30] They were unsuccessful, and timber remained the standard material for sleepers until it began to be generally replaced, in recent years, by concrete.

The standard British form of railway track had now emerged, and it continued unchanged in design from the 1870s to the 1940s. It was an artefact no less beautiful than the locomotives and trains that sped across it, the rails resting in chairs on wooden sleepers, packed with a ballast of stone-chippings that was weeded as carefully as a bowling-green; the unseen bed sound and perfectly drained. Within this formula the track was constantly strengthened as the pressure on it increased, with heavier trains travelling at higher speeds. By the beginning of the 20th century the weight of rails on most first-class main lines was close on 100lb to the yard.

Rails were growing not only heavier but also longer. The 30ft standard length had been extended to 45ft. Some 60ft lengths had been laid down, mainly on bridges, by the London & North Western in the 1880s;[31] by 1914 that had become the accepted length on most main lines.

As the length of the rail increases, so the number of rail-joints diminishes, and the sound made by the wheels in crossing them is correspondingly reduced in frequency. Since this is the main component of noise in a

moving train, it is a matter that most obviously concerns the passenger's comfort. The ideal solution would be to do away with rail-joints altogether; and experiments in this direction, by the use of welding processes, were made in many parts of the world in the 20th century. In Britain lengths of a mile or more, made up by welding 60ft lengths together, came to be laid down in rapidly increasing numbers after 1960, as long stretches of main-line track needed renewal.

In two other respects the railways after nationalisation modified the earlier standard construction of track, though the decision was based on experiments carried out under the old regime between the wars. In 1948 the historic British practice of supporting the rail on chairs was abandoned, in favour of using a flat-bottomed rail spiked to a base plate on the sleeper, in the Continental and American manner. After the war, too, the Baltic timber that had been found by long experience to be the best material for sleepers became unobtainable, and the Douglas fir imported from Canada and elsewhere proved an inferior substitute. Concrete sleepers were therefore adopted extensively, on the welded sections of first-class line and on many lines of secondary importance.

For those who can remember it, the most perfectly smooth riding on any railway in the world was probably to be found on the line out of Euston between, say, 1910 and 1930: a classic work of engineering, its track perfectly built and maintained, its rolling-stock faultless in balance and springing, the 'Prince' or 'Claughton' locomotive hauling its train with a rock-like steadiness at 55-60 mph across county after county through the dead centre of England. The railways now have to meet new conditions: a demand for higher speeds (which are not always easy to reconcile with comfort), a deterioration in the quality of materials and equipment. Yet it would be wrong to look back with nostalgia to the past and see nothing but a falling off. There has been gain as well as loss. The tired passenger, sleeping fitfully in the train at night, soon learnt to welcome the reduction of noise as he ran on to a stretch of the new welded track by Langport or Wellingborough or Tring. Now, anyone willing to hear the old sounds must seek them with care, but they are still to be found on some long stretches, even on main lines, in the remoter parts of Britain. The journey from Perth to Inverness, for example, is not only a gripping visual pleasure as one passes through Birnam Wood and the Pass of Killiecrankie and over the Druimuachdar Summit; those who have a feeling for the old 'clickety-click' will rejoice to hear it there, for miles and miles on end.

The gradual change from timber to concrete sleepers which began in the 1950s is visible (above left) on a section of track in transition. At the same time the old 60ft rails were giving way to long welded rail, laid usually in lengths of 600ft (above). Transported on low wagons, the lengths are secured to the ground by a wire hawser looped through an eye at one end and, as the train draws slowly away, they are fed over rollers and guided into position on the sleepers by gangers. The remaining joints are welded on site.

READING · BASINGSTOKE · SOUTHAMPTON

*('Down' = Reading – Southampton; 'Up' = Southampton – Reading.
The names of stations now open for passenger traffic are printed in
small capitals.)*

This is an interesting journey on several counts. The first section of it, from Reading to Basingstoke, was originally a country branch, built by the Berks & Hants Railway, a subsidiary of the Great Western, and laid out under Brunel to the 7ft gauge. The remainder formed part of one of the early trunk lines, the London & Southampton (later London & South Western), and was built to the standard gauge of 4ft 8½in, with two engineers successively responsible for it, Francis Giles and Joseph Locke.

The passage of the line over the north Hampshire chalk land from Basingstoke to Winchester is one of the classical pieces of English railway engineering, its design and construction (almost completely unaltered) allowing the traveller still to experience something of the triumph that was shared by the engineers and their assistants, the contractors, and all the men engaged in this work, which is of a quite Roman magnificence.

And finally, the entry of the railway into Southampton, and the part it came to play in the life of that port, are worth looking at on their own. Few English towns battled with a railway company more bitterly; few came in the end to owe theirs so much.

The southern part of the line, from Basingstoke to Southampton, was opened first, in 1839-40; the northern part from Reading to Basingstoke in 1848. READING itself was on the Great Western main line, which arrived from Paddington in 1840 and was opened throughout to Bristol in the following year. Nothing is now left of the station of that time. Its entrance building, facing the town, dates from the 1870s. It is surmounted by a good Italianate glass lantern bearing a clock. The accommodation for trains was gradually remodelled down to 1899, when it assumed almost its present form, with four main through platforms and seven short bays for local traffic.[1]

'Britannia' Pacific No. 70020 Mercury heading a down special train on the Western Region main line, beneath the A4 road bridge near Reading West, 1964.

Reading is one of the very few large junctions in Britain that still makes use of all the platforms provided for it more than eighty years ago. It has taken in (at two additional bay platforms) the business of a second station built by the South Eastern Railway, accommodating trains to Guildford and Tonbridge as well as to Waterloo. All the Great Western services radiating out from the minor platforms continue. Long-distance through trains now reach as far as Glasgow, Newcastle, Liverpool and Penzance; and more than sixty trains run up to London each weekday without stopping, the majority of them at 70 mph and more.

The Basingstoke branch leaves the original Great Western line immediately outside Reading station. The first station on it, READING WEST (three quarters of a mile from the main one), was opened in 1906 to serve the suburbs and to provide a calling point for trains from the north that came down from Oxford by a western curve from the main line.

Here the railway crosses the Oxford Road. The company fulfilled the requirement in its Act that the bridge should be 'of handsome elevation', with an elliptical arch at least 40ft wide. Similar conditions were followed for the high bridge spanning the line half a mile further on to carry the Bath Road above (today the A4). Directly beyond it

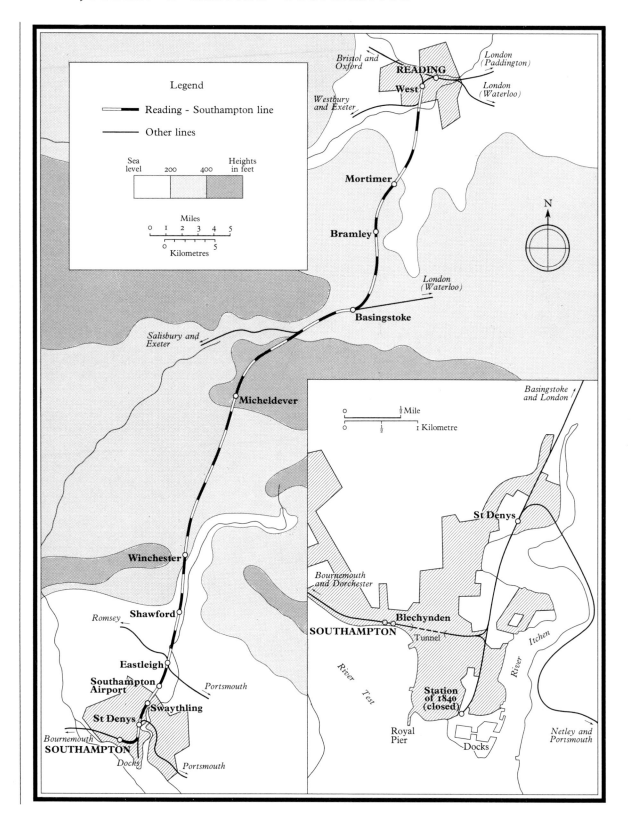

Legend

Reading - Southampton line

Other lines

Sea level 200 400 Heights in feet

Miles
0 1 2 3 4 5
0 5
Kilometres

READING

West

Bristol and Oxford

London (Paddington)

London (Waterloo)

Westbury and Exeter

MORTIMER

BRAMLEY

London (Waterloo)

Basingstoke

Salisbury and Exeter

Micheldever

0 ½ Mile
0 ½ 1 Kilometre

Basingstoke and London

St Denys

Bournemouth and Dorchester

Winchester

Romsey **Shawford**

SOUTHAMPTON **Blechynden**

Tunnel

River Test

River Itchen

Eastleigh

Southampton Airport

Portsmouth

Station of 1840 (closed)

Royal Pier

Swaythling

St Denys

Bournemouth **SOUTHAMPTON**

Docks

Portsmouth

Docks

Netley and Portsmouth

N

a line went off on the down side leading to the town's central goods station, opened in 1908 and now disused. At Southcote Junction another arm of the Berks & Hants line diverges on the up side to Newbury, today forming part of the chief route to the West of England.

The Basingstoke line runs through .one of the most extensive tracts of undisturbed agricultural country now left anywhere south of the Thames within forty miles of London. On its 15 miles it has only two stations, at Mortimer and Bramley.

There might well have been none. The Duke of Wellington, who did not care much for railways, secured a clause in the Berks & Hants company's Act that forbade the opening of any station within five miles of his seat, Stratfield-saye, except with his consent. The Duke was old and rather crotchety, but he was kind-hearted, and when some of his neighbours asked him to accept a station at Stratfield Mortimer, only two miles away from his house in a direct line, he agreed. The company promised that the building should be as 'commodious as His Grace may think fit to require'. He approved the plans for a quite modest station, opened as MORTIMER with the rest of the line on 1 November 1848. It was the sole intermediate station. People at Bramley, further south, also strove for one, but fruitlessly. Though a small siding was put in for receiving coal and other freight, the Great Western company did not open a passenger station there until 1895.[2]

At Mortimer, Brunel's Italianate

structure in red and yellow brick survives complete, 'commodious' on the up side, matched by a small shelter on the down platform. Both buildings have been excellently cleaned in recent years. BRAMLEY station is a character-

istic Great Western piece of the 1890s in sombre red and blue brick, its tiny shelter on the down side now clad with a little ivy. A good many of the original red-brick over-bridges on this line are still in use, some of them with arches, open or blind, in the supporting walls.

The line approaches Basingstoke on a sharp curve through a cutting, as it comes in to join the main line from Waterloo to Southampton. BASING-STOKE was one of the frontier posts

in the 'Battle of the Gauges' from 1848 until 1856, when a 300yd link between the Great Western and South Western lines was opened on the 'mixed' gauge – i.e. with a third rail, allowing trains on both gauges to use it. The western curve at Reading was constructed at the same time, completing a continuous route for standard-gauge trains from Southampton to Birmingham. For many years they were freight trains only, but after 1900 they came to include some long-distance expresses from Bournemouth and Southampton to the North. The number of passenger trains on this quiet line today has much increased. In 1939 there were 18 each way, only two of which had come from north of Oxford; today there are 28, the long-distance trains numbering five.

The buildings of the Great Western station at Basingstoke have been removed, and the site of its goods yard is now a car park. Beyond that, however, there is still a Great Western Hotel, which seems to date from the 1850s. If one is to believe a prominent inscription on one of its outbuildings, it continues to offer 'livery and bait stables'. The hotel must have done some business in the Victorian age with travellers to and from the deep country north and north west towards Kingsclere, for that small town never had a railway.[3]

An important branch was opened from the London & South Western line

Basingstoke station: refreshment room on up platform, 1856.

Mortimer station, about 1900. The gauge has been converted from broad to standard (hence the wide gap between the tracks), but the down (right-hand) line is still laid on the old longitudinal sleepers.

in 1854 to Andover. It was the first stage of an extension to Exeter, which was completed in 1860 and allowed the company to compete with the Great Western over a route twenty miles shorter.

The town of Basingstoke now grew steadily, drawing ahead of its neighbours Odiham and Kingsclere. Between 1871 and 1901 its population increased astonishingly by almost 20 per cent every ten years; the other two towns both had fewer people in 1901 than seventy years before.

How much of this growth was due to the railways? That question cannot be answered at all precisely.[4] But some indicators can be given. For many years every train stopped at Basingstoke; as late as 1887 only one ran through. That meant good business for the licensees of the refreshment room and those they employed. A large locomotive depot and a goods yard provided additional employment. The town was also the terminus of the London & South Western company's outer suburban service, and the frequency of trains to and from London no doubt encouraged the growth of residential districts. By 1887 there were twenty trains on weekdays in each direction; fifty years later they numbered thirty; after 1967, when the line was electrified, they increased to nearly sixty.

Since the Second World War the place has grown beyond recognition, from a compact market town of 14,000 people to the far-spreading Borough of Basingstoke and Deane with 133,000. It has become above all a centre of industrial distribution, but chiefly with the aid of the M3 motorway; the commercial buildings that have sprung up have no rail connections.

At the turn of the century the line from London was quadrupled. Basingstoke station was rebuilt in 1903. It is worth going outside to look at the tall facade, which has been cleaned. The deep plum-red bricks now show up very well and a new travel centre and booking office have been deftly incorporated. The work could not have been done with more tact.

To the west of the station two small branches used formerly to leave the main line: on the down side the Basingstoke & Alton Light Railway, opened in

1901 and closed in 1936; and on the up side the branch to the Park Prewett Hospital, one and a third miles long, used from 1914 to 1950 mainly for freight traffic.

The Southampton and Exeter lines separate two and a half miles west of Basingstoke at Worting Junction, where the up Southampton line is carried across on a bridge.[5] The four tracks now come down to two. The passage of the line on to Winchester is splendidly direct, riding over high embankments, through deep cuttings and four short tunnels, descending for 16½ of the 24 miles from Worting to Eastleigh at a steady gradient of 1 in 252.

The main credit for this grand work is commonly given to Joseph Locke, but that is not quite just. The London & Southampton company's first engineer was Francis Giles, who surveyed its line, authorised in 1834. He was a canal engineer who had worked for the Rennies and had been engineer to the Newcastle & Carlisle Railway, which had called on him for some major works. But two such undertakings, 350 miles apart, proved more than he could manage, and he threw up his earlier post in 1833 in favour of the Southampton Railway.

The work went ahead slowly and Giles was blamed, in particular for his practice of dividing the line into small sections, each in the hands of a different contractor. This was a canal engineer's practice, but it did not serve well when adopted for railways.[6] Giles was obliged to resign in January 1837. He was replaced by Locke, who reorganised the work and drove it through with dauntless persistence to its completion in 1840.

Looking north towards Worting Junction, 1985. The left-hand (up) line moves away to cross the Salisbury line on a bridge.

So the line was laid out under Giles, but for most of its length built under Locke. The ultimate test of an engineer resides in his ability to get his work done, and there Locke was always a master, far above Giles; but Giles's part in the original plan should not be ignored.

Locke replaced a number of the contractors responsible for small lengths. He entrusted the whole section from Basingstoke to Winchester to Thomas Brassey. Brassey, then aged 32, had just completed his first railway contract, on the Grand Junction line. Locke, who was also engineer to that undertaking, was so pleased with what he had done there that he invited him straight to Hampshire to carry through this contract. Nearly 19 miles long, it was one of the most exacting works, other than the great tunnels, then in progress anywhere in England. There were exceptional difficulties to be faced here, especially in the winter of 1839-40, which was one of the wettest that anyone could remember, but Brassey and his men overcame them triumphantly.

It was this work that established Brassey's national – indeed his international – reputation. By 1844 he was involved in the construction of nearly five hundred miles of railway in France.[7] Locke's merits included an almost unerring capacity to pick good collaborators and assistants. He never made a better choice than Brassey.

Here again the railway crosses a tract of very empty country. The train seems to skim over the chalk, with a farm or two here and there, and very occasionally a village (like Steventon, Jane Austen's birthplace) seen at some distance.

The railway does not reveal all its majesty either to a passenger or to anyone looking at it from the fields below, for its embankments are shrouded in a thick tangle of vegetation. It was a common practice to plant them in this way, usually adopted in order to screen them and their smoky trains from sight. When new and raw these works were extremely prominent – the high embankments most of all. Sometimes a neighbouring landowner would manage to get such planting made obligatory, where the line crossed his property, by private agreement[8] or under the company's Act.[9] But the planting might also be strictly functional, the roots of the trees helping to bind the whole structure together where the ground was loose, as it was apt to be when crossing chalk.

The bridges on this line are all of plain red brick. There was no good building stone locally; and the cost of conveying stone from a distance, especially into these uplands where there was no water transport, was prohibitive.

Three short tunnels (Litchfield, Popham number 1 and Popham number 2) now come together. The Popham pair were a substitute for one that would have been much longer, but was opened out in the middle. The sides of the cutting between them are almost vertical.

Directly beyond the second tunnel the train enters what appears, on the down side, to be a vast basin in the chalk. This was a quarry used by the railway company to provide material for new construction – for example at Brookwood, near Woking, when the embankments there had to be widened to take four tracks – and, above all, to supply filling for new docks at Southampton, built by the Southern Railway about 1930. Oil tanks were installed underground during the Second World War. There were large sidings too, used until recently to hold rolling stock in transit to Eastleigh for repair or scrapping.

The station here is of particular interest: the only one there has ever been on the 18¾ miles between Basingstoke and Winchester. It began in 1840 as Andover Road – the station for Andover, more than ten miles away to the west. When Andover got a station of its own in 1854 this name became confusing and it was soon altered to

Micheldever station, looking north from the island platform which now serves passengers, 1985.

MICHELDEVER, after a village three miles to the south.

The original building survives on the (disused) up platform: plain, four-square, still keeping its simple canopy supported on iron columns. It is a fine example of the use of local materials in a station building. The walls are faced with the flint that abounds in chalk, with windows dressed in pale yellow brick. The flint is not left kidney-shaped, which would have been serviceable, but coarse and liable to harbour dirt; it is knapped – i.e. the flints have been fractured, squared and dressed smooth.[10] This produces an excellent surface, precise, glistening, totally durable. The architect, William Tite, must have had his way here, for flintwork of this quality cannot have been cheap.

On now over more high embankments. The two tracks were made four for one and a half miles in 1902, that on the up side serving as a loop for slow freight trains ascending the long gradient, in order to allow passenger trains to overtake. Waller's Ash tunnel, 501yd long, follows. On 2 April 1842, soon after the line had opened, a portion of the brickwork in it collapsed, killing four workmen and injuring others.[11]

Not far beyond the southern end of the cutting the remains of two derelict lines appear, at what used to be called King's Worthy Junction. One comes in on the down side, the Mid-Hants Railway from Alton, closed in 1972. The other was the Didcot Newbury & Southampton, a railway that looked for support to the Great Western. This part of it was opened in 1885, running here underneath the main line and reaching as far as Winchester, where the company had its own station. It never got to Southampton. Instead it was continued six years later to a junction near Shawford, whence its trains ran forward by means of running powers over the South Western main line.

The Didcot railway's ordinary business was negligible, but it acquired a special importance in both world wars as a carrier of military traffic from the North. In 1943 a link was put in to allow trains to join the main line at King's Worthy rather than at Shawford further on; traces of it are still to be seen. The

Looking southwards along the platforms of Winchester station to the dramatic series of high bridges over the cutting beyond, 1985.

whole railway was closed in 1966.

The city of WINCHESTER lies at the bottom of the steep valley of the Itchen. The South Western station stands high up on its western side. Tite's plain building of 1840 is still in existence, with the platforms behind it reconstructed. Looking down the line from here the traveller has an impressive view through a tall narrow cutting crossed by lofty bridges. Beyond

Bulleid 'Merchant Navy' class Pacific No. 35012 United States Lines heading a down Bournemouth express past Shawford Junction, two miles south of Winchester, 1955.

Top: Eastleigh locomotive works at about the time of its opening, 1911. Above: locomotives outside Eastleigh shed, 1957. On the left is preserved Great Western 4-4-0 City of Truro, withdrawn in 1931 but just returned to traffic to work special trains.

1881 the population was still only just over six hundred.

However, by then the London & South Western company was finding its works at Nine Elms in London intolerably cramped, and it considered moving them away into the country, as all other big railways except the Great Eastern had then done. It began to purchase land for this purpose at Eastleigh in 1886 and moved the carriage department down there in 1891.[12] The locomotive works followed in 1910, employing a much larger number of men, and that brought the population of the town up to 15,000.

Eastleigh was far from a model town in its early days. The railway company left building and services to be provided by speculators, and the result was wretched. After the town became an Urban District in 1894, however, things improved. The works lay east of the line, but the town grew mainly westwards, never fully engulfing Bishopstoke. The main entrance to the station is on this west side.

The locomotive works at Eastleigh had only just got fully going when the First World War broke out. They could have served the needs of the whole of the new Southern Railway after 1923, but that company continued to maintain the smaller works at Ashford and Brighton as well. After nationalisation everything was scaled down. The last new locomotives produced at Eastleigh appeared in 1950. Over a span of forty years 320 had been produced there in all. An annual production of eight looks diminutive, but for ten of those years the country was at war, and Eastleigh was then engaged largely on construction of another sort: parts for guns and shells in the first war and aeroplanes in the second, as well as landing-craft in advance of D-Day.[13] The works continue in use still, on a much smaller scale, for the repair of carriages and wagons.

SOUTHAMPTON AIRPORT, on the southern fringe of Eastleigh, has a station of its own, opened in 1966: it is small, but busy in the summer with passengers flying mainly to the Channel Islands and France. Two older stations follow in quick succession: first SWAYTHLING and then ST DENYS, where a line from Portsmouth comes in on the

SHAWFORD, the valley of the Itchen opens out on the down side, and the long descending gradient flattens out as the train runs along delightful watermeadows to Eastleigh.

EASTLEIGH is a railway town, the last important one to be developed in England – though Inverurie came afterwards in Scotland. A junction appeared here very early, named Bishopstoke after the neighbouring village to the east, with branches going off to Gosport (for Portsmouth) in 1841 and to Romsey and Salisbury six years later. For a while the arrival of the railway produced very little building. The first of the long rows of houses facing on to the line, Tait's Terrace, was not put up until 1864. Four years later an ecclesiastical district was established, named Eastleigh, but by

Dutch gable on Swaythling station (down side), 1982.

citizens discerned that clearly: it lay very far from all the country's main centres of industrial production. In 1845 they eagerly supported plans for a cross-country line to Birmingham and Manchester, avoiding London, but without success. When in 1848 the Dorchester company was bought up by the London & South Western, which had by then also swallowed up the Southampton company, there was one provider only of railway transport to the town. Southampton had passed under a 'railway monopoly'.

Henceforth whatever complaints there might be – about high goods rates or slow passenger trains or the services at the docks – were hurled at the South Western company. Its deficiencies, real or imaginary, became an element in local politics, well aired in the Parliamentary elections of 1857 and 1862.[15]

When the P & O company ceased to call at Southampton, transferring its services to London in 1875-81, the town cursed the inadequate docks and the railway alike. A plan was brought forward for ending the railway monopoly by means of the Didcot Newbury & Southampton line, connected with the Great Western; but it proved only a disappointment.

down side. The tall building on the up main platform at St Denys, erected in 1866, is strikingly handsome: of the same family as Tite's of the 1840s, but more assertive in strong red brick. As Edwin Course remarks, it 'retains its air of a solid, mid-Victorian residence in a favoured district'.[14]

The approaches to Southampton have been complicated, in one way and another, from the beginning. Everything looked easy: the London & Southampton line had an almost straight run in across the marshes of the Itchen until it curved round gently to its terminus close to the first dock, which began to be fully used in 1843. A second railway was opened in 1847, the Southampton & Dorchester, running westwards through a tunnel under the north end of the town and then along the shore, with a second station at Blechynden, which served a growing residential district. But the residents disliked the railway for its tunnelling operations and for its interference with their drainage system, which discharged into the Test.

Southampton had one great inherent weakness as a port in the Victorian age, and its more intelligent

St Denys station: building on up main-line platform, 1983.

The South Western company wisely now moved towards conciliation, gradually improving its main passenger services and then agreeing in 1892 to purchase the docks and to invest a great deal of money in extending and modernising them. The purchase went through, and before long the benefits arising from it became clear and abundant. Southampton began to wrest transatlantic traffic from Liverpool, growing after 1907 into one of the great passenger ports of Europe. It also rendered an immense service to the nation in both world wars (see p. 42). The mountains of containers, seen beyond the station as the train goes west towards Bournemouth, are impressive evidence today of the scale of the freight traffic still passing through the port.

The original terminus station down by the docks is now disused; Tite's good building survives, but it accommodates no trains. Although the railway still runs to the docks, all regular passenger services take a very sharp curve westwards at Northam Junction to join the old Southampton & Dorchester line to Blechynden. Another line comes in here on the down side. Out of use now and largely blocked up, it gave the Southampton & Dorchester access to the original station and the docks.

The Southampton tunnel, so unpopular with the town in the 1840s, comes next. A special difficulty in constructing it arose from the passage of another tunnel beneath, begun for the Salisbury & Southampton Canal in the 1790s and never finished.[16] The foundations of the railway were insecure, and two days before it was due to open in 1847 the whole work began to sink. More than two months' labour was required before repairs were complete. In 1964 it was found that the floor was moving again, this time upwards towards the roof, and for six months single-line working had to be adopted while the tunnel was repaired. Twenty years later the difficulties recurred, and single-line working was again introduced.

There has been one permanent change for the better. The tunnel was never equipped with ventilators, and the driving of steam trains through it was a tough and nasty task, particularly

for engine crews handling the up trains, which emitted heavy smoke as they gathered speed. The electrification of 1967 ended that curse for good.

SOUTHAMPTON station today stands slightly west of the old Blechynden. The London & South Western Railway rebuilt it in 1895 with a clock tower. It was enlarged to provide four through platforms in 1934-35; the down side of the station today is of that time, but the up side was wrecked by bombing in the Second World War, and it was not rebuilt until 1967.

Looking into the old 1895 Southampton station, with its sharply curved platforms, 1959. Behind, on the left, the Cunard liner Queen Mary *towers over everything.*

The new station cowers beneath a heavy office block. The entrance, booking office and other facilities are meagre, the ceilings very low and the floor-spaces quite inadequate. The information office is a ludicrous apartment: a dozen inquirers makes a crowd in it. Surely a station of this importance might be given a travel centre?

It is sad to find the railway so meanly provided here, when one thinks back over its history and over all that the railway has done, since 1892, for the town and port of Southampton.

Entrance to Tite's Southampton terminus. It is preserved today, though its surroundings are not exactly as they were when this photograph was taken in 1939.

ENGINEERING & ARCHITECTURE

The railway companies came to acquire widely varied interests, some of them apparently very remote from their proper business. They operated transport in all its branches, by water, by road, by air. They built churches, schools, hospitals, convalescent homes – one might almost say whole towns like Crewe and New Swindon. They made seaside resorts: the promenade at Cleethorpes was the work of the Manchester Sheffield & Lincolnshire Railway. They even went in for real estate development. 'Metroland' was not a mere catch-phrase to describe the suburban area served by the Metropolitan Railway. Within its bounds lay 14 estates, stretching from Neasden to Amersham, owned by a subsidiary of the railway, which put up 4,600 houses on them between 1919 and 1930.[1]

With such far-flung interests to pursue, a railway company's architects, builders and engineers had to be able to turn their hands to work of the most varied description. A railway might be found owning property of almost any kind. After nationalisation the British Transport Commission owned the greater part of the docks in Britain and the biggest chain of hotels in Europe. Tens of thousands of railway buildings remain today up and down the country, either fulfilling their original function or some other, or perhaps disused and in ruins. They include some of the most striking monuments bequeathed to us by the Railway Age.

But the greatest achievement of the railways, their main contribution to architecture in Britain, lies in the works that arose from their very nature, the bridges, viaducts and tunnels that carried the track. These structures represent the engineers' excited, sometimes inspired, answers to the challenges they faced. When the railway companies came to erect buildings of a more conventional kind, such as stations and hotels, they showed much less originality; and their architects and builders were often hampered by the companies' parsimony or – quite as bad – embarrassed by their insistence on opulent display. One of the sanest writers on 19th-century architecture observed that 'the civil engineering of early railways had aesthetic merit so considerable that the first railway stations seem somewhat tame and inappropriate in comparison with it'.[2] We may not always agree with this view, but it puts the history of railway architecture into its proper perspective.[3]

—— LARGE STATIONS ——

The earliest railways required no buildings of their own: all they did was carry coal from pit-head to navigable water. They still did not immediately need buildings even when they began to carry passengers. On the Stockton & Darlington and many other railways the passengers' needs were met by inns along the route. Occasionally these inns fetched up as railway property, like the Ashby Road Hotel on the Leicester & Swannington line, where the railway began by renting rooms and ended by purchasing the whole building to serve as Bardon Hill station.

The first railway to erect stations of its own, of the kind we think necessary now, was the Liverpool & Manchester. One of its original termini, at Liverpool (Crown Street), has disappeared; but part of the other, Manchester (Liverpool Road), survives, excellently used as a museum of science and industry. If words are to be chosen strictly, it shares with Mount Clare station, Baltimore, the title of the oldest railway station now extant in the world. But whereas the station at Mount Clare was 'hardly more than a box office for the excursion to Relay, which was the first business of the line',[4] that at Manchester bore the recognisable character of a modern

Previous page: the great curved iron roofs at York create one of Britain's most dramatic railway station vistas. the station was built in 1877 to replace an earlier one; the view here looks south along what is today platform 9. The semaphore signals have now gone; rail buses have replaced the wooden carriages on the right; the subway (the entrance to which may be seen between the two nearest columns) has given way to an ugly footbridge, and some of the decorative touches have disappeared. But in essentials the station remains as it was when it was opened. The signal box on the left is now used as offices and a bookstall. Modern lighting, new gable screens, carefully renewed roof cladding and an admirably renovated concourse made with specially matched bricks are the only real changes.

On 10 April 1840 Richard Doyle, aged 15, drew in his journal this sketch of the booking office at the original, temporary, Great Western terminus at Paddington. His buff-coloured ticket to Ealing cost 9d and would have been a paper one torn from a book. The premises look more like a shop, and the clerk behind the counter appears to be making an entry in his ledger.

railway station from the start, providing not only booking-offices but waiting-rooms and a platform that was sheltered with a roof.

Two other terminal stations survive, in part, from the 1830s. The Ionic portico of the entrance to Curzon Street station, Birmingham, built by Philip Hardwick in 1838, is still intact, though forlorn today in its modern surroundings. And at Newtyle in Scotland is a far more modest station building (now a warehouse), erected for the Dundee & Newtyle Railway in 1836.[5] All the early London stations have disappeared, either demolished or submerged practically without trace beneath later buildings: London Bridge, Nine Elms, the first terminus of the Blackwall Railway at the Minories have gone. So too has Euston, by far the most notable of these early terminal stations. Approached, when new, over open fields, its Doric portico, also to Philip Hardwick's design, was as grand a 'Gateway to the North' as could be imagined. But it was only a gateway. The buildings behind it, used by all those who had business with the railway or worked for it, were entirely dwarfed by it until the Great Hall was erected in 1849 by P. C. Hardwick, Philip's son. This, with attendant rooms leading off it on the ground floor, came to serve as a vast waiting-room for passengers. It was not, however, well adapted to that purpose, and was treated rather sombrely until the London Midland & Scottish Railway dropped a large and quite hideous booking-kiosk into its centre. In 1960-62, despite a loud public outcry – which went, in vain, as far as the prime minister – the great portico and all that lay behind and around it were swept away. An entirely new station then gradually emerged, to accommodate the electrically hauled trains serving the main line to Birmingham, Lancashire and Scotland. From the passenger's point of view this was, in almost every respect, a huge improvement.

Nine Elms was the first of these early termini in England to be designed to the U-shaped plan that is the essential feature of most such buildings now: the platforms flanking the tracks were joined at their head by a block containing entrance hall, waiting-rooms and offices. The next important departure in station plans came, independently and almost simultaneously, at Slough, Reading and Derby. For Slough and Reading, Brunel's plan provided for two separate station blocks, both on the south side of the line, one for up trains and one for down. As each town lay to the south of the railway, this arrangement had the advantage that no passenger needed to cross the lines, and it allowed non-stop trains to run past clear of the station. On the other hand, it involved much inconvenience in working, since the up trains had to foul the down lines twice, when they entered the station and again when they left it. Awkward though this was, more such stations were ultimately built on Brunel's pattern, for example at Taunton, Exeter and Gloucester.

For once, however, Brunel's conception was less grand than somebody else's. The 'Trijunct' station designed by Francis Thompson for three companies at Derby consisted of a single platform 1,050ft long, with a continuous brick frontage, correspondingly immense, on to the street. When Thompson came to repeat the idea, at Chester in 1848, he improved on it, at least from an architectural point of view. The facade of Derby station must have been squat in relation to its length, for it was no more than 40ft high. At Chester this defect was overcome by punctuating the front with towers, which gave the building a vertical 'lift'. The single-sided plan was also followed elsewhere – at Cambridge in 1845, at Huddersfield in 1848 and at Ipswich in 1860 - but then gradually abandoned, either by the rebuilding of the stations (as on the Great Western) or by the provision of additional platforms (as at Derby, Chester, Huddersfield and Ipswich). The original plan is still, however, to be seen in operation at Cambridge, modified only by the building of bay platforms at the north and south ends of the station.

In the meantime, what may be termed the standard U-pattern of the British terminal station had established itself firmly in London. A classic example is King's Cross, designed by Lewis Cubitt and opened in 1852. Although the station has been enlarged since, the original building can still be studied, and it takes a high place among the architectural monuments of 19th-century London.

The merit of King's Cross consists in its plainness: what today we call its 'functionalism'. It had two great sheds, one for departure and the other for arrival, roofed in glass that was originally set in a laminated timber frame. The yellow-brick facade was designed to display these two sheds quite openly, furnishing also a colonnaded entrance in the centre and – what could be more useful to the railway traveller? – a clock mounted in a small tower. Cubitt claimed with justice that the station would achieve its architectural effect through 'the largeness of some of its features, its fitness for its purpose, and its characteristic expression of that purpose'.

The magnificent classical station at Huddersfield, designed by J. P. Pritchett, senior, and shown here in about 1908, celebrates at its most monumental not only the early railways' sense of triumph and achievement, but, in this case, one of the first joint ownership agreements between rival companies. It was built for the Huddersfield & Manchester Railway & Canal Company, but shortly before its completion in 1848 it was taken over by the Lancashire & Yorkshire and the London & North Western companies. The central block behind the portico originally included a hotel. The glass-roofed porches on each side, later additions that did nothing to improve the architecture, have now been removed.

When King's Cross station was opened, it catered for 26 trains a day. Between the two original platforms, 14 tracks were laid down for the storage of rolling-stock. On the departure side there were waiting-rooms 'elegantly fitted up and furnished', and an ample booking-office. Across a small courtyard on this side the company soon erected the Great Northern Hotel, a gracefully curved building, particularly solid in its construction to guard against the dangers of fire. Goods traffic was handled at a large station in Maiden Lane, north west of the passenger terminus. Waterways were let into the floor of this building to provide easy communication, by means of the Regent's Canal, with the Thames. Stabling was also erected on the same site for three hundred horses, for the delivery of freight sent by rail.

It was not long before the two first platforms proved insufficient; but it was a simple matter to multiply them by encroaching on the siding accommodation in the centre of the building. In 1869-70 it became necessary to reconstruct the unusual roof on the eastern (arrival) side: the spring of the timber had produced a dangerous outward thrust in the wall, and there was no room to build flying buttresses. The wooden roof on the western side, where the wall was reinforced by the lower buildings containing the booking-offices, survived until 1886-87.[6] King's Cross station was much extended later, by the building of two platforms for trains running down to and up from the Metropolitan line, and of the new suburban station on the western side. The number of passenger trains that entered and left it had grown to two hundred before 1914.[7]

The great London termini that have been erected since have all been fundamentally of the same type, though they show many variations of treatment. Most of the railway companies, following the example set at Euston and King's Cross, built hotels at their stations; but unlike those, the later ones were incorporated into the fabric of the station itself, generally in the transverse arm of the U. The first of them was at Paddington, completed in 1854 to the designs of P. C. Hardwick and of great interest to architectural historians as 'one of the earliest buildings, if not the earliest building, in England with marked influence from the French Renaissance and Baroque'.[8]

Other railway hotels followed at Charing Cross, Cannon Street, St Pancras, Liverpool Street and Marylebone. The St Pancras hotel was designed and built separately from the station. W. H. Barlow was responsible for the station, which remains unaltered in any important respect since its opening in 1868. His glass and iron roof was of 240ft span – at that time the widest in the world – and has always been warmly admired as a triumph of technical skill and engineering beauty. Opinions have differed sharply on the hotel building that masks it from the Euston Road.[9] (How truly it is a 'mask' may be seen from the inside of the station, below the great clock, where the gap between the metal and glass screen of the station and the brick wall of the hotel is apparent.) The Midland company commissioned the best-known architect of the day, Sir Gilbert Scott, to design the hotel, and he sketched it out in the autumn of 1865. In his autobiography he wrote of it with a monumental complacency, saying that it had been excessively traduced and excessively praised. 'It is often spoken of to me as the finest building in London; my own belief is that it is possibly *too good* for its purpose.'[10] Some critics who are normally sympathetic to Victorian Gothic architecture have been tepid about this building. Yet St Pancras has two great aesthetic merits. Its irregular spiky outline is continually exciting, whether you are running into it by train, or playing hide-and-seek with it as you drive up behind the tall buildings to the south, or – best of all –

The soaring arched roof of the St Pancras trainshed dwarfs the mixed collection of carriages beneath it in this photograph taken in about 1890. Four- and six-wheelers are lined up at the platform, with pot-holes in their roofs for oil lamps; the long, curved clerestory roofs of Pullman cars are visible in the siding beyond. The Midland was the first British railway to introduce Pullmans, in 1874. The 240ft span of W. H. Barlow's iron-and-glass roof was the widest in existence when it was completed in 1868; it remained so for twenty years, until it was exceeded in the USA. The great clock (removed some time ago but now most happily restored) dominates the concourse; behind it is the hotel.

approaching it down the slope of Pentonville Road. And the rising curve of the front never loses the power to interest and quicken the spirit. Sir John Betjeman, too, pointed out the exceptionally fine quality of the brickwork of the goods station that adjoined it to the west.[11] A fragment of this noble piece of Victorian craftsmanship survives on the west side of Midland Road, not beyond repair; the new building for the British Library is being erected behind it.

At St Pancras both units, station and hotel, are gigantic. At Liverpool Street, its next successor in 1875, the trainshed was large, but divided into four parallel sections, and when the Great Eastern Hotel followed in 1884 it was much smaller than the Midland Grand.[12]

The last new station to be built in London, Marylebone, exhibits a comical disparity between its parts, the vast Great Central Hotel quite dwarfing the peaceful little station behind it. At Waterloo there was never a railway hotel. When that station came to be gradually rebuilt in 1902-22, it was on a plan like the segment of a cheese, with a curved concourse. It is now, in most respects, very convenient for the passenger: spacious, well-lit, easy of access to taxis and the Underground. Yet the architectural forms it displays are uniformly coarse, and its ornamentation is tawdry.

Though almost all great stations afford terminal facilities for some trains, few of those in the provinces are termini and nothing else. Glasgow (Central and Queen Street), Inverness, Swansea, Norwich, Hull, Liverpool (Lime Street), and Manchester (Piccadilly) are examples of stations that do

not provide facilities for through trains. But the characteristic large provincial station is different. Either it is a junction for through trains, like York, Carlisle or Crewe; or it is a station that serves primarily as a terminus but also affords through facilities, like Edinburgh (Waverley) or Aberdeen.

From an architectural point of view stations in large towns and at great junctions should be thought of side by side with the public buildings of their time, and a few of them can stand the comparison well enough. In two towns at least the railway station may claim to be the best building there. That is conspicuously true of Huddersfield; it is true of Stoke-on-Trent, where the station and the North Stafford Hotel (built by the railway) form a handsome group that rises proudly superior to its surroundings. To the student of railway history, however, the most interesting stations are those that have been built up from separate units on adjacent sites, owned by different companies. Bristol (Temple Meads) exemplifies railway architecture of four different dates, showing plainly how a modern layout may be determined by past history.

In the beginning Brunel had no hesitation in designing the station as a terminus, for it was then the end of the broad-gauge Great Western Railway, coming down from London. It was by no means complete when the Bristol–Bath section of the line was opened in 1840; in fact, the last rail was laid only half an hour before the first train left that morning, and the building was finished a few months later. The offices were in a stone building in the Perpendicular Gothic style. The trainshed contained two

The frontage block of St Pancras station, containing the Midland Grand Hotel, was designed by Sir George Gilbert Scott and completed five years after the trainshed. In Scott's own drawing of the eastern elevation, the gap between the two parts of the building is clearly visible. The platform, into which the ribs of the station roof are tied, is at first-floor level, providing a massive storage space beneath, used chiefly for Burton beer. Road vehicles gain access to it through some of the arches at street level; the other arches are fitted with shop fronts.

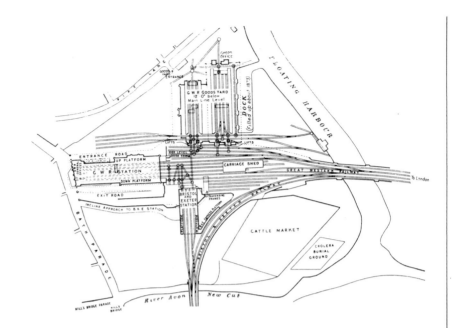

In this 'Plan of the Bristol stations', published in 1845, the difficulties of the site are revealed. The Great Western and Bristol & Exeter stations stand at right angles to each other, the two systems being linked by the curved stretch of track containing the Bristol & Exeter's 'express platform'. In 1854 the tracks in the Great Western station were converted to mixed gauge to accommodate through trains from a third company, the Midland Railway. 'Traversing frames' just to the right of the Bristol & Exeter station were used for moving carriages sideways from one line to another, while the Great Western goods yard, 18ft below the level of the main line, was provided with lifts to raise and lower freight wagons.

platforms with siding accommodation between them, covered with a wooden hammerbeam roof of the medieval kind: 72ft in span, wider than the one in Westminster Hall. This splendid shed is the noblest monument surviving from the early years of the Railway Age. Its preservation has been assured by an enterprising local trust aided by funds from British Rail.

By the time through trains began to run between Bristol and London on 30 June 1841, another railway had been opened, the first section of the Bristol & Exeter line as far as Bridgwater. This company, however, had no station of its own at Bristol. Its line ran in at right angles to the Great Western's, and a curve had therefore to be constructed to enable Bristol & Exeter trains to be manoeuvred into the Great Western station. The Bristol & Exeter company built its own station in 1845, though its Jacobean-style offices (still to be seen on the right of the modern station approach road) were not completed until 1854. For through trains from the west to London an 'express platform' was built on the curve, but it was not invariably used, for the down Flying Dutchman of 1862 ran to the end of the curve and then backed into the Bristol & Exeter station.

Meanwhile a third railway had arrived to share the Great Western station at Temple Meads: the Bristol & Gloucester, opened in 1844 and swallowed up by the Midland company in the following year. The Midland was determined to carry its narrow gauge into Bristol and, after much legal argument with the Great Western, succeeded in doing so in 1854.

Here, then, was a strange tangle: three railways operating in two stations, adjacent but at right angles, with separate booking-offices (there was even one on the express platform) and with track of two different gauges – all on a site a mile away from the centre of the city, reached only by a series of inconvenient lanes. A scheme for cutting a new 'Victoria Road' through them was authorised in 1847 and then deferred indefinitely because of ratepayers' opposition. Another plan for extending the railway system to a new central station in Queen Square was put forward in 1861 and backed by the Great Western company, but rejected by a narrow majority of the city council. The three companies then fell back on the idea of a new joint station at Temple Meads. The fulfilment of this plan took an extraordinarily long time. Four years passed before parliamentary sanction for the scheme was secured, ten before work was even begun, 16 before it was finished and opened in its entirety, on 1 January 1878. The new station was entered by a rising approach road and booking-office in the acute angle between the original station and the curve, on which the new platforms were placed. Stylistically the work stayed Gothic, the embellishment being entrusted to Sir Matthew Digby Wyatt, who had acted in a similar capacity with Brunel at Paddington in 1851-54. The station did duty without substantial change until it was much extended, on the side away from the original buildings, in the early 1930s.[13]

—— HOTELS AND REFRESHMENT ROOMS ——

In the provinces and in Scotland, a fair number of important stations had hotels attached to them just as in London, and the railways also owned a number of hotels intended to promote holiday traffic. In 1913 there were 92 of them in all, 67 in England and 25 in Scotland; the companies had spent just over £7,500,000 on them, on which they secured an average return of about 7½ per cent.[14] Fifty years later the British Transport Commission still had 36 hotels. In 1983, however, the government decided that the British Railways Board should divest itself of all it held, and they were then sold off.

With a few exceptions, these hotels had all been built by the railway companies themselves. An early one was the Zetland at Saltburn, put up by the Stockton & Darlington company at a cost of £30,000; it was an attractive white-brick building with central bow windows, standing high above the sea. The railway was extended fifty yards from the end of Saltburn station, to run into the hotel itself under an awning – an arrangement unique in England. Saltburn is, indeed, a very interesting example of a resort that owes its origin entirely to the railway and that has not been smothered

The Victorian splendour of the Royal Hotel, Sutton Coldfield, built in 1865 in the high Gothic style with Romanesque details, overshadows the station and the locomotives beneath it in this engraving of about 1870. The London & North Western's branch from Birmingham to this exclusive residential town, opened in 1862, was planned to carry businessmen to and from their work in Birmingham. It was regarded at first by some of the inhabitants as an unwelcome intrusion, but was well patronised by 1880, when the line was extended to Lichfield. The hotel became the town hall in 1903 but is now in private ownership.

under later development, like Cleethorpes. With its pretty wooded glen, its pier of 1867, and its modest streets laid out 'according to a plan by Mr George Dickenson of Darlington', Saltburn remains a perfect type of the small Victorian watering-place.[15]

As the railway companies began to develop their marine services, they frequently acquired or built hotels at the ports for the use of passengers and their friends coming down to see them off or to meet them. There was the Lord Warden at Dover, the London and Paris at Newhaven, the South Western at Southampton. At Holyhead the original Royal Hotel (owned by the Chester & Holyhead company) was superseded by the handsome Station Hotel, built in 1880 by the London & North Western Railway. A substantial part of the business done by the Midland Railway's Adelphi at Liverpool was with passengers on Atlantic liners; but that large caravanserai had many other functions to perform as well. The Great Eastern Railway began to operate steamers from Harwich Town Quay to the Low Countries in 1863; and as soon as they were regularly established it built a hotel there. This must have been welcome to a good many travellers, since the timing of the Rotterdam services was variable, depending on the tides, and the boat from Antwerp often arrived at two o'clock in the morning. At the hotel, we are told, 'the accommodation generally is such as to suit the requirements of the upper as well as the middle classes'.[16] The railway company soon found the Town Quay unsatisfactory, and in 1882 it completed a new packet station of its own, a mile higher up the river. This was named Parkeston Quay – after C. H. Parkes, chairman of the company – and the equipment included a new hotel. The old one was made into the Harwich town hall.

The railways had 11 hotels in London, one at every important terminus except Waterloo. They were generally well reputed, and they took their full share of helping London to become a great centre of international tourist traffic. But, like most other Victorian railway structures, they were built to last, and it did not prove easy to adapt them to the changing demands of their guests. The Midland Grand at St Pancras closed down in 1935, largely because it was judged too expensive to refurbish it and provide the private bathrooms and other facilities that guests were by then coming to expect.

The magnificent Great Eastern Hotel on the quayside at Harwich, built in 1865, is seen here in a delicate and atmospheric rendering by its architect Thomas Allom, who was also a painter. The Great Eastern had started a successful steamer service from Harwich to the Low Countries in 1863; the building on the left is the customs house. When the railway later moved its ships to a new quay higher up the river, this hotel became the town hall. It served that function up to 1983, but is now privately owned.

This coffee-pot in the form of a locomotive belonged to the Queen's Hotel, Swindon: its ownership is proclaimed on the boiler plate. The model, named Victoria, was based on the Great Western 'Firefly' class of 1840. The framing is simplified, some additional boiler mountings are incorporated, and there are regal flourishes on the firebox and at the chimney top.

Not all railway companies undertook the labour of working the hotels they owned. It was a common practice to lease them, along with the station refreshment rooms, to contractors. The most famous arrangement of this kind was made by the Great Western company at Swindon, requiring all trains to stop there for refreshments for ten minutes. When the company tried to maintain that this provision did not apply to expresses, the court upheld the lessees. Thereupon, for nearly half a century, the Great Western resigned itself to its bargain, which was a doubly bad one: it retarded the trains, without giving the company any effective control over the service rendered to its passengers. The lessees, meanwhile, made handsome profits, as can be seen from the prices paid for the lease when it changed hands: £20,000 in 1848, £45,000 in 1875, £70,000 in 1881. When at last, in 1895, the company could bear it no longer and finally bought the lessees out, it had to pay £100,000.[17]

The refreshment rooms at Swindon were considered very splendid when they were new. The food they purveyed, however, was usually something less than splendid. ('I did not believe you had such a thing as coffee in the place,' wrote Brunel once to the contractor, 'I am certain that I never tasted any.') Still, providing crowds of travellers with meals of the customary Victorian proportions must have been difficult in the ten minutes allowed. The same was no doubt true at Preston, Normanton and

This new tea room at York station was designed in the art nouveau style by William Bell, architect to the North Eastern Railway, and was opened on platform 4 (now platform 8) in 1906. Beneath filigree Moorish arches, passengers could partake of 'true North Country "teas" at moderate rates'. Elegant refreshment rooms such as these were already doomed by the increasing provision of food on trains.

York, where the passengers had twenty minutes. Large refreshment rooms were provided on those and other major stations, and they were liberally staffed. They are altered now, though not always beyond recognition. Cafeterias have been installed at Carlisle (how many passengers read the Latin tags carved incongruously on those Gothic fireplaces?), at Preston, Crewe and Rugby. 'Modernisation' has swept away most of the old character of all these rooms, but many of them have been greatly improved in the process. They are cleaner, brighter, more agreeable places to eat in, and certainly much easier to work. Yet we may still regret the passing of the old railway dining-room, with the tiled open fireplace, the lincrusta and mahogany and horsehair, the portraits of languid ladies in ostrich feathers eternally sipping Apollinaris, the Sheffield plate *épergne* on the sideboard, the snow-white tablecloths, the endless interest of the cutlery engraved with historic names and symbols – Highland, Caledonian, the London & North Western's Britannia. It was delightful to lunch at those places – at Bletchley, Leicester (Central) or Grantham – and now one can do so no longer.

—— SMALL STATIONS ——

For many years the minor stations of Britain were given second place by students of railway architecture, overshadowed by the much grander build-

ings of the big towns and junctions.[18] Christian Barman, however, insisted
gently that this emphasis was wrong. Whilst he paid tribute to the merits of
the great stations, he argued that 'these monumental fronts ... do not
reflect the characteristic architecture of the railways, the unique railway
style, with quite the same force as many other kinds of railway structures';
and he went on to claim that it was in country stations that 'the special
idiom of railway architecture is found in its strongest and purest form. No
country in the world has a collection of minor stations that can begin to
compare with ours.'[19]

That claim is perfectly justified. Such stations will repay all the study
that is given to them. The only difficulty they present is in the variety of
their forms – bewildering, intricate and endless. The station buildings on
each railway might conform to one general style – the plain classical of the
London & Birmingham and the London & Brighton, for example – but
within the series there would be constant changes of treatment.[20] Or
uniformity might be abandoned altogether. On the Great Western the
earliest stations fell into two main groups. Between London and Reading
they bore a classical character. West of Reading they were Tudor in inspira-
tion, with tall chimneys and high gables, but it was a Tudor style very freely
treated, with wide horizontal awnings to shelter the platforms that have a
strangely modern appearance. Three buildings of this series survive: the
'Wallingford Road' station-house on the up side of the line, three quarters
of a mile nearer London than the present Cholsey and Moulsford station;
the buildings at Steventon, much grander than the traffic to and from the
village warranted because it was originally intended to serve as the station
for Oxford; and the station at Culham (still almost complete), built a little
later, about 1845.

Even more interesting variations appeared on some other railways,
whose architects took pride in never designing two stations alike. Frederick
Barnes of Ipswich was one of these, as he showed at Needham, Stowmarket
and Bury St Edmunds; Francis Thompson was another. If Thompson's
Belper, Wingfield and Eckington stations on the North Midland were all
classical in character, each was still entirely individual. He served other
railway companies too: notably the Chester & Holyhead, for which he
designed all the original stations between Chester and Bangor, built in
1845-50. The most important of these to survive is Holywell Junction (on the
down side), a square brick building with stone-framed windows, which
takes its distinction from the free-standing turrets that flank it. Other
fragments of Thompson's work are also to be seen at Flint and Mostyn; and
it is pleasant to record that when Bangor station was reconstructed in 1924
his nine elegant 'C. H.' monograms from the old Chester & Holyhead
building, cut in stone and set in circular frames, were preserved and
re-mounted.

Thompson was an accomplished architect, but his very inventiveness
made him expensive to employ. It is no wonder that the North Midland
directors decided to abolish his post as architect to the company as soon as
the line was in working order, thus saving his large salary of £1,000 a year.[21]
By then the North Midland stood not for variety, which was extravagant,
but for its exact opposite – for economy through standardisation.

Railways facilitated standardisation in a way that had never been
possible before, by enabling cheap and durable building materials to be
carried all over the country, until nearly every town in England was being
roofed in slates from north-west Wales. The railways also introduced
standard designs for their own buildings. The reason for this was partly

Built for the Sutherland Railway and opened in 1868, Rogart station could be nowhere other than in the far north of Scotland, so reflective is it of the vernacular style of domestic housing. Together with the other stations between Inverness and Wick, it has been excellently restored without losing any of its distinctive Highland character.

Angerton station in Northumberland, seen here in the 1880s, was on the small Wansbeck Railway, opened in 1862 and in the next year incorporated into the North British Railway's system south of the border. Serving Angerton Hall, a few scattered farms and the village of Hartburn a mile away, it was a perfect example of the small, rural station, with a single line, two sidings, a combined station house and office, a tiny goods and coal yard, a level crossing and an ancient carriage body probably doing duty as a lamp room or store. The signals for each direction are frugally mounted on one post, operated by a lever at the bottom.

economic. It was also administrative – a consequence of amalgamation, which brought the original small companies together into larger and larger units. As a result no riotous proliferation of designs, like Thompson's, occurs after the 1840s.

Yet standardisation was neither immediate nor complete. As one travels up and down Great Britain, one is struck by the local quality of much railway architecture: a tile-hung front at Oakley station (now closed), west of Basingstoke; knapped flint at Micheldever (see p. 109); Midland brick on the Syston and Peterborough line, at Melton Mowbray and Oakham; iron pillars on the platform at Newtown, Powys, inscribed 'D. Edwards, Newtown Foundary'; pretty Broseley tiles to enliven the waiting-room at Shrub Hill station in Worcester; the diaper of blue bricks (a local speciality) on red in the North Staffordshire's Elizabethan stations; fierce and un-relieved Accrington brick at Bolton, and elsewhere up and down Lancashire; crow-stepped gables at Lockerbie and Stirling; Scottish baronial at Elgin. Most striking of all, perhaps, in the far north, were the stations of the late 1860s and 1870s, developed only a little way from the cottages of Sutherland. Built of huge blocks of stone, they stand low on the ground; and at Kildonan the attic rooms under the roof are reached by one of those external flights of stairs that were characteristic of Scotland for generations before railways were heard of.

In England, however, a change appeared about the middle of the century, when the companies began to adopt standard designs for their buildings. The reason for this was partly economic. It was also administrative – a consequence of amalgamation, which brought the original small companies together into larger and larger units.

An interesting transitional stage can be seen on the Midland line between Bedford and Leicester, opened in 1857. There the wayside stations (now closed) are all built to a common design, its hallmark the round-headed window with hexagonal and diamond panes of glass. But if the designs are the same, the materials vary. Glendon is built of limestone, Desborough of ironstone; Oakley is of red brick, Great Glen of white. This line also displays, at Wellingborough and Kettering, the platform roofs that were developed into a standard form by the Midland company: serrated, for drainage, and resting on a richly-decorated iron framework.[22] There is one piece of accidental variety here. The station at Market Harborough is quite different. It was the property of another company, the London & North Western, which had arrived at Market Harborough first, and accommodated the Midland as a tenant. When it was rebuilt in 1885 the work was naturally carried out in the manner prevailing on the London & North Western at that time. The station house, below the level of the track, is a well-proportioned building with a stylish air, in a fully-developed Queen Anne manner. The London & North Western company never went in for Gothic architecture. Its tradition, firmly founded by the sober, classically-minded London & Birmingham, had matured by this time into something very English and domestic. The building has now been admirably refurbished by British Rail.

Even when standardisation gained a firmer hold, it naturally varied from company to company. Each developed a recognisable style of its own. The Great Western and its associates had several, which succeeded one another: in the 1850s and 1860s it used timber or plastered buildings, with round-headed windows and awnings of a very solid appearance, beetling down low over the platforms. A number of these can still be seen at Charlbury, for example, at St Germans and Menheniot. Later, on its new 'cut-off' lines built in the twenty years before the First World War, the Great Western used hard red and blue brick for its stations (now almost all shut down). Aynho Park and Bishop's Cleeve, Badminton and Langport (East) were almost interchangeable, even down to the fir trees planted on their embankments. Here is the standardisation we know today. In the inter-war years the principle was carried further, particularly through the use of reinforced concrete. The buildings erected by the main-line companies in those years can occasionally be called inoffensive, like the station at Berwick and those rebuilt on the main line between Darlington and York. But what can be urged in favour of the monuments of the early Jazz Age, the stations at Leamington, Richmond, Surbiton, and those between Wimbledon and Sutton? They were cleaner, and easier to keep clean, than their predecessors. Architecturally, however, the only praise that can be given to them is to admit that they were less vulgar than the bloated Euston House erected by Lord Stamp and his fellow-directors of the London Midland & Scottish Railway within a stone's throw of the Great Hall they befouled and the Doric Arch they longed to pull down.

—— THE LONDON UNDERGROUND'S EXAMPLE ——

What makes this story so shocking is that all the time, in these years, quite excellent works of railway architecture were going up in London. The London Underground Railways and their successor of 1933, the London Passenger Transport Board, were building new stations and reconstructing old ones very fast as their tube lines reached further and further out into Middlesex and Surrey. The result was a series of railway stations more interesting and attractive for the variety of their forms than any seen in this country since the days of Thompson and Barnes. Arnos Grove and Southgate show fine drum-towers; Sudbury Town is a plain rectangle; at Osterley a slender square tower of brick is crowned by a totem-pole. One object lesson, in the treatment of a huge plain brick wall, is provided by the car sheds at Northfields and Neasden; another, in the use of concrete, by Uxbridge station.[23]

But these were not the only gifts made by the Underground to British architecture. A still more striking building was the huge block of offices, to house the whole group's headquarters, erected at 55 Broadway above St James's Park station. Ingeniously designed to economise ground-space, while letting in all possible light and sun, it is one of the most important buildings to be erected in that time anywhere in Britain.

The main credit for all this work rests with two men: Charles Holden, the architect chiefly responsible, and Frank Pick, managing director of the Underground group, an administrator of imagination and – what is even rarer – of almost unerring visual sense. Pick not only saw to it that the Underground had the best new buildings of any transport concern in the country, he watched over the design of everything it used in its stations and trains. In the closing years of his life (he died in 1941) he must surely have been puzzled and saddened to see how little influence his unceasing labours had had upon the practice of other organisations, and especially the great railway companies. The London & North Eastern, it is true, displayed an interest like his own in good lettering in its notices and literature; the Southern Railway architects perhaps learnt a little from Holden's example. If so, it was very little indeed.

But a more cheerful time was coming. After the war a fresh start had to be made, partly because of the destruction caused by the war itself, and partly owing to nationalisation, which brought in new arrangements and some new men, and opened up quite new possibilities. Nowhere has this been more obvious than in the station buildings we now see and use. Most stations were re-signed. One may be conscious that Frank Pick would have managed this more subtly, but the gain to the ordinary traveller was immense. It even became possible to read the names of many stations at night. The prevailing decoration was much improved. Some waiting-rooms were done up in such a way that it was no longer a penance to wait in them; new ones were built – combined sometimes, in a sensible manner, with a refreshment bar.

Much bigger things than this were accomplished. Among stations, the largest job was the completion of the Ocean Terminal at Southampton; but the plans for that were first made by the Southern Railway before the war, and anyway it was a station of a unique kind intended for ships more than for trains. A substantial number of ordinary railway stations were recon-

This cheaply constructed halt was opened at Ickenham on the Metropolitan line from Harrow to Uxbridge in 1905. It then stood out in open fields; a residential district was slow to develop. The wooden platforms, adequate for trains like this electric one with one first-class and two third-class carriages, were lengthened in 1922 when the line had begun to generate a profitable suburban traffic.

Charles Holden's station at Osterley on the London Underground's Piccadilly Line was opened in 1934. The slender tower was based on Dutch designs that Holden had seen on a European tour a few years earlier, and was intended to make the station visible some distance away from its site on the new Great West Road.

structed. Banbury affords a good example. Under the Great Western it had long been recognised as miserable, from the railwayman's point of view even more than the traveller's. Though a junction on a main line, used by expresses and carrying a substantial freight traffic, it had only two through tracks. The accommodation it afforded was mainly of ancient timber, with an inconvenient little over-bridge and an overall roof, infinitely dirty, of the old Great Western kind.[24] The company decided on its rebuilding in the 1930s. Gradually it worked its way to the head of the list, until in 1939 work began; and then war broke out. Another 15 years went by before the reconstruction was resumed. It was finished in 1958.

And a decent job was made of it, with four through lines and adequate bay accommodation, a pleasant refreshment bar and waiting-room on the bridge, and an ample forecourt for parking. The whole group of buildings presented an architectural elevation well worth looking at – the peer of anything else in the town. Other reconstructions of important stations followed shortly afterwards: at Stafford, for example, in 1962.

It was not only the large stations that benefited. A considerable number of smaller ones, too, were rebuilt, wholly or in part, such as Hawarden and Grays, Dovey Junction, Potters Bar, and Bury (Bolton Street), where the fine coat of arms of the East Lancashire Railway now occupies a place of honour in the reconstructed entrance. Signal boxes proliferated in new designs and materials – timber at Ashendon Junction in Buckinghamshire, light-blue brick at Barnes.

Bigger things were then undertaken: from the great reconstruction of Euston and Birmingham (New Street) stations, discussed on pp. 55, 117, to the new combined rail and ship terminal at Stranraer, completed in 1984. This is hardly less impressive in its way than the much larger and more lavish Ocean Terminal at Southampton, planned and built thirty years before – for a different kind of traffic, in a very different world.

The rebuilt station at Stevenage, opened in 1973 to serve the New Town, possesses three red-brick towers which create a striking landmark for British Rail on the East Coast main line. The station replaces the old wooden buildings of the Great Northern Railway which stood a mile away.

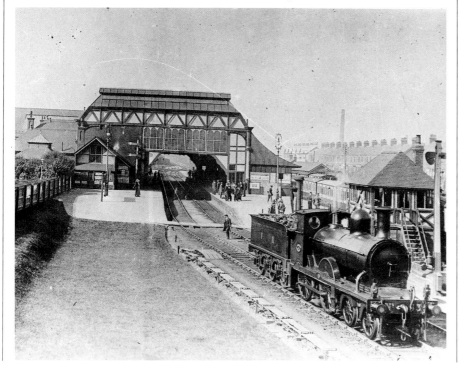

This scene at Barrow Central on the Furness Railway, with class K2 4-4-0 No. 33, built in 1896, letting off steam by the signal box, dates from about 1908 and recalls the vogue for wooden barn stations with overall roofs. The Great Western built the greatest number, but the Furness had elaborate examples here and at Coniston. Built in 1882 to replace an earlier station, Barrow Central exhibited elements of Swiss chalet styling which were thought appropriately romantic for a location close to the Lake District. The building was bombed during the Second World War and subsequently replaced.

MOTIVE POWER

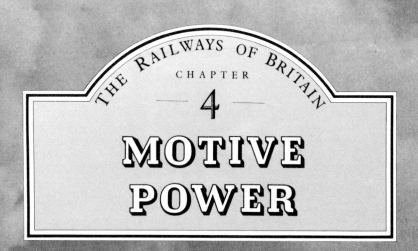

To many people the most interesting parts of a railway are not its 'static' features – the track, the works and the buildings – but its 'dynamics': the locomotives and vehicles that provide the means of conveyance. That is hardly surprising. The locomotive was one of the most splendid products of the Age of Steam; perhaps, with the steamship, it was also the most beautiful. It has now been superseded. In Britain the railways passed through a revolution in motive power during the early 1960s – later than in most other countries of western Europe and North America. The last steam locomotive in ordinary service in Britain ran in 1968. Since then electric and diesel locomotives have provided the source of power. They too have an interesting history of their own, which stretches back over more than a hundred years.

THE PASSENGER STEAM LOCOMOTIVE

The invention of the railway engine is not the achievement of any one man. But if a single 'inventor' must be named it should be Richard Trevithick. George Stephenson is the best known locomotive engineer, but his famous *Rocket* was by no means the first railway engine – it was something like the seventieth to be built in Britain.[1] Older locomotives are still to be seen: *Puffing Billy* at the Science Museum in London, its fellow *Wylam Dilly* in the Royal Scottish Museum in Edinburgh, *Locomotion* at Darlington. But *Rocket* marked the turning-point in the development of the locomotive from a machine designed entirely for the slow haulage of coal to one that was able to handle passenger and general goods trains, which required greater flexibility and speed. In earlier engines the boiler had had a single flue; the boiler of *Rocket* was multi-tubular.[2] This increased the capacity of the engine to produce steam so greatly that, 'at one bound, steam locomotives' speeds were raised from about those of a carthorse to more than those of the fastest racehorse'.[3] *Rocket* showed its capabilities at the Rainhill trials of 1829. These were important both as a scientific experiment and as a means of publicising the steam locomotive. Publicity was widespread throughout Britain, the Continent and America. *Rocket* is beyond question the most famous locomotive ever built – the only one whose name is familiar to everybody.

It was very quickly superseded, however. *Northumbrian*, built the following year, was the first railway engine to have a smokebox and the first in which the firebox was an integral part of the boiler. A month or two after *Northumbrian* came *Planet*, which, in the words of E. L. Ahrons, was 'the real point of departure from which the modern British locomotive has been derived, in so far as it combined horizontal cylinders encased within the smokebox, crank axle, multi-tubular boiler with firebox inside it, and a framing, which supported the boiler'.[4]

All these engines were built for the Liverpool & Manchester Railway. The man chiefly responsible for their design was Robert Stephenson, doubtless in consultation all the time with his father George. They had already established their works in Newcastle, which became one of the leading suppliers of engines to railways in this country and overseas. Such firms now began to multiply, and many engineers contributed to the notable developments of the 1830s and 1840s. The machines came to be more strongly constructed: that was the real merit of Bury's small engines on the London & Birmingham Railway. They were more reliable, and continued longer in service. Robert Stephenson's *North Star* – the first successful locomotive possessed by the Great Western Railway – began work in 1838, lasted in its original form until 1854, was then given a new

Previous page: storming up Prestleigh between Evercreech and Bath with a heavy northbound Somerset & Dorset express in August 1952, two locomotives emit clouds of steam and smoke as their crews stoke up for the long climb ahead: three more miles to go at a gradient of 1 in 50. The engines are Midland Railway 4-4-0 No. 40505 and Somerset & Dorset Railway 2-8-0 No. 53804, types doomed to extinction within a very few years.

boiler and cylinders, and ran until the end of 1870.[5]

With the rapid extension of the railway system in the 1840s, greater demands, in endurance and capacity for haulage, began to be made on locomotives. Apart from a few experimental machines – like those of T. R. Crampton, which were never as popular in Britain as they became on the Continent – the largest and most powerful express engines of the time were those of Gooch's 'Iron Duke' class on the Great Western Railway. The first of these, *Great Western*, appeared in 1846; the next was *Iron Duke*, a modified version of the prototype, followed by 28 others in 1847-55. Engines of the same general design worked almost the whole of the broad-gauge express service until 1892.

On the narrow gauge, perhaps the best known locomotives of the 1840s were the 'Jenny Lind' type, designed largely by David Joy and built by E. B. Wilson of Leeds from 1847 onwards. These were very much smaller than the broad-gauge engines. Their boilers had a heating surface of only 800 sq ft against the 1,945 sq ft of *Iron Duke*, but their steam pressure was higher – 120lb to the sq in compared with 100 (later 115) – and to this feature their success has been generally attributed. These engines were built in considerable numbers for several companies such as the York & North Midland and the London Brighton & South Coast.

In the same decade there emerged what became the standard Victorian type of goods engine: the whole locomotive carried on six coupled wheels, which gave the maximum adhesion without putting too much weight on a single axle. The earliest engines of this pattern had been produced by Timothy Hackworth for the Stockton & Darlington Railway in 1827-30. It was developed by Robert Stephenson's company to their 'long-boiler' design (in which all the axles were placed in front of the firebox) from 1843 onwards. Though the long-boiler passenger engines were not successful, chiefly because they proved unsteady at speed, the goods engines worked well and enjoyed a long life. One of them, North Eastern No. 1275, is

Comet, seen from two angles in this engraving, hauled one of the passenger trains on the opening of the Blaydon – Hexham section of the Newcastle & Carlisle Railway on 9 March 1835. Built by R. & W. Hawthorn of Newcastle-upon-Tyne, it was similar to the Liverpool & Manchester Railway's Planet. Both engines had their cylinders and frames placed inside the wheels, but Comet's four wheels were coupled, which made it the more powerful. Apparently too heavy for the track, Comet was rebuilt with an additional pair of leading wheels, but did not last long in regular service. In 1858 it was taken back by its makers and used as a stationary engine to drive machinery until 1877.

A reproduction of the 1847 Great Western express locomotive Iron Duke, made for the Science Museum, London, in 1985, stands on a stretch of broad-gauge track laid specially for it in Kensington Gardens. Designed by Daniel Gooch, the Iron Duke class were the first successful locomotives built purposely for express traffic anywhere in the world. They were evolved partly under political pressure: the company needed to show the full potential of its 7ft gauge, when that was under attack in 1845. A six-wheeled locomotive, Great Western, was produced in 1846, followed by Iron Duke and five others which ran on eight wheels, in order to spread the load on the track. With minor modifications, the type remained in the same express service until the broad gauge was abolished in 1892.

No. 175, Contractor, of the Stockton & Darlington Railway was an example of the long-boilered goods locomotive, with six coupled wheels sited ahead of the small firebox. The engine was built at the company's North Road Works in 1864. It was designed by William Bouch, brother of Thomas who built the Tay Bridge.

preserved in the National Railway Museum at York. The long-boiler design was by no means universally acceptable, however, even for goods engines, and in 1847-48 a number of new six-coupled goods engines were built with the longer wheelbase afforded by placing the rear axle behind the firebox. This then became the classic British type, appearing fully developed on the Leeds & Thirsk Railway in 1848. Engines of the same design – larger, but not fundamentally altered – were still being built when the railways were nationalised a century later.[6]

The years 1829-48 saw an extraordinary increase in the capabilities of the locomotive, from *Rocket* to *Iron Duke*. No comparable development occurred in the years that immediately followed. The rapid railway building of the 1830s and 1840s was succeeded by a reaction, with many of the companies financially embarrassed and all of them anxious to restrict their expenditure. The financial crash of 1866 again put a brake on fresh expansion. The speed of travel did not increase greatly during this period – some of the earliest expresses, such as those of the Great Western, were drastically slowed up – and consequently the demands made on the locomotives were not much more severe in 1870 than they had been in 1845. Moreover, the light and brittle track of the period imposed strict limits on the speed of trains.

Nevertheless a number of technical improvements were effected. Many experiments were carried out to find a satisfactory method of burning coal instead of coke (which was almost twice as expensive). McConnell on the London & North Western and Joseph Beattie on the London & South Western both struggled with the problem. It was successfully solved on the Midland and the Taff Vale Railways in 1856-60. At the same time steel began to be substituted for iron in several of the locomotive's parts. The steel tyre came to be adopted by British railways very generally about 1860; experiments with steel boilers began on the Maryport & Carlisle and London & North Western Railways in 1862-63. It was in these years, too, that the bogie, or truck of four small wheels, came into widespread use in Britain, though it was not generally adopted for locomotives hauling fast trains until after 1870. In that year Patrick Stirling produced the first of his famous 4-2-2 engines for the Great Northern Railway, which also happily survives at York. This notation gives the number of leading wheels (four), followed by the driving wheels (two) and the trailing wheels (two). The outstanding features of the design were its absolute simplicity and the enormous driving wheels, 8ft 1in in diameter. The engines were given leading bogies not in order to negotiate curves, of which there are few on the Great Northern main line, but to render them steadier in running on a longer wheelbase, and to distribute the weight more evenly. The weight on the single driving wheels had been increased to 15 tons, which would have been unthinkable in earlier days, but was perfectly safe on the steel rails, 80lb to the yard, that the Great Northern company was then laying down.

When bogies were adopted on other lines at this time, it was usually in conjunction with a pair of coupled wheels. The classic British express locomotive thus emerged in the early 1870s: the 4-4-0 with inside cylinders and frames, a pattern that for neatness and grace of outline has never been excelled. The type appeared first in Scotland, on the North British and Glasgow & South Western Railways, and then in England on the Great Eastern, the Midland, and the London Chatham & Dover. In succeeding years it spread to almost every major railway in Britain and was exported overseas – to the Netherlands, for instance, to India and Australia. Five fine examples of it are preserved from the North Eastern, the South Eastern &

Chatham, the Great Central, the North British and the Great North of Scotland Railways.

The work required of express engines became very much more exacting in the 1870s. Competition between railway companies grew, and one of the forms it took was competition in rapid passenger services. Another was in the comfort offered to the passenger, and that involved the provision of heavier rolling-stock – including, from 1874 onwards, the earliest Pullman and dining cars. Locomotives had to be more powerful, which meant that they cost more to build, consumed more fuel, and were more expensive to run. Railway engineers gave much attention at this time to the principle of 'compounding' as a device for reducing the consumption of coal by using the steam twice over. The compound locomotive received its most extended trials in Britain on the London & North Western Railway under F. W. Webb between 1879 and 1905. It was tried out there in all forms, for fast and slow work, heavy and light, passenger and goods. Some advantages it certainly displayed, but they were offset by great drawbacks that were never entirely overcome. Webb's compounds were less reliable in performance than simple engines, they were expensive to build, and they were complex to drive and maintain. It would, however, be wrong to deduce that the principle of compounding itself was mistaken. With systems different from Webb's it succeeded well, on the Continent (most notably in France) and on the Midland Railway and its successor the London Midland & Scottish, where a series of 4-4-0 compound engines (235 of them in all) handled much of the fastest work with success through the first thirty years of the 20th century.

The capacity of the locomotive for high-speed running was demonstrated in the 1880s and 1890s, most showily in the Races to Scotland of 1888 and 1895. Those, however, *were* races, a series of exciting stunts; and it is more useful to look at performances in normal service. The most spectacular were those of the Manchester flyers, run by the Great Northern and the Manchester Sheffield & Lincolnshire companies in conjunction, both railways using engines with single driving wheels. The credit for these trains must be shared equally by the two companies: the Great Northern for getting from King's Cross to Grantham at an average speed of nearly 54 mph; and its partner for taking the train to Sheffield and on over the Pennines – one of the hardest lines in England over which express running was attempted – at 45 mph. In consequence, these trains took four and a quarter hours to get from London to Manchester, not a minute more than the London & North Western's best expresses, whose route was 14 miles shorter and as easily graded as a railway could be.

But the London & North Western's service was by no means inferior in quality. At no time – except momentarily during the Races to Scotland, when 'this dignified corporation started up with the animation of a schoolboy'[7] – did that company attempt to compete for the first prize in speed. Its trains, however, were superior in three other ways. They were more comfortable to travel in, since they ran at a steady pace and their coaches were excellently built, unlike those of some other companies (Ahrons suspected that those in use on the Great Northern in the 1880s had octagonal wheels). They had a good reputation for punctuality, whereas those on the Midland line promised one thing and were apt to perform something quite different. Lastly, and perhaps most important of all, they were substantially longer than their rivals, and so brought a better profit to the company's shareholders through carrying more passengers.

Loads were growing greater, with a corresponding increase in the

Preserved Midland Railway compound locomotive 4-4-0 No. 1000 is given a careful cleaning outside the National Railway Museum at York, where it is kept. It was built in 1901, as No. 2631, and rebuilt in 1914. Compound locomotives used the same steam twice and were therefore economical on fuel. The Midland's design was the one really successful compound locomotive to run in Great Britain, designed to haul light, fast passenger trains. These engines were in servioe between 1901 and the early 1960s.

The immense driving wheel of Patrick Stirling's Great Northern Railway No. 1 locomotive is 8ft 1in in diameter. Built in 1870 and now preserved in working order by the National Railway Museum at York, this engine was the first of the class of 4-2-2s which handled a large part of the Great Northern's express passenger service over the next twenty years: the fastest in Britain, and perhaps in the world.

demands made on the locomotive. The Manchester flyers were compara-tively light, weighing no more than 80 to 100 tons. The corresponding North Western expresses of the 1880s were at least half as heavy again. The afternoon Scotch express from Euston came to weigh about 280 tons in the 1890s, and it should be remembered – to Webb's credit – that it was worked by one of his much-abused compound engines, *Jeanie Deans*, every week-day for eight and a half years on end (1891-99), during which time it rarely if ever arrived late at Crewe. The two principal expresses between Brighton and London Bridge (8.45am up and 5pm down, first class only) usually weighed 275 tons, and on a Monday morning the up train might be a good deal heavier still. Yet these were hauled for many years by what we should now regard as diminutive engines, of Stroudley's 0-4-2 'Gladstone' class.[8]

Nor was it passenger expresses only that were becoming heavier and faster. The same was true of ordinary goods trains; and fast freight was being carried at speeds higher than those attained by many main-line expresses – until Ahrons could declare, on a comparison of two schedules, that 'it is better to be a dead mackerel on the North Western than a first-class passenger on the London Brighton & South Coast'.[9] As trains of such size multiplied, however, it soon became clear that they could not be worked satisfactorily by small machines. The need for the big locomotive had indisputably arrived.

Much argument is possible about the date of its emergence. It could be put at 1894, with David Jones's 4-6-0 goods engines for the Highland Railway; at 1896, when McIntosh produced the first of his 'Dunalastair' 4-4-0 class for the Caledonian, incorporating a boiler materially bigger in diameter than any previously used on a British express engine; or at 1899, with Aspinall's Atlantic (4-4-2) No. 737 on the Lancashire & Yorkshire Railway, which not only had a bigger boiler still, but was the first loco-motive in Britain to be fitted with a superheater.[10] It is enough to notice that locomotives altogether larger than those previously used were being turned out in the closing years of the 19th century; and to add that two out of three of the important examples referred to come from Scottish railways, which made a particularly important contribution in the later Victorian age to the development of the British steam locomotive.

The first decade of the new century brought very rapid progress. In spite of the merits of the compounds built by the London & North Western and the Midland, British engineers clung resolutely to the simple engine, moving decisively away from the prevailing practice on the Continent. Directly Webb retired in 1903, his successor George Whale reversed his policy, and no further designs of compound engines were produced at Crewe. Careful comparative tests were made with French compounds on the Great Western; but their result was to confirm the view of its locomotive engineer G. J. Churchward that the simple engine was the best. Having made up his mind on this and on many other controversial issues (partly through a close study of what was going on in the USA), Churchward evolved a series of locomotives, for many types of traffic, at Swindon in 1903-09. These engines had a great influence on subsequent British practice. They incorporated all the new features of the period, including superheaters from 1906 onwards and a number of changes to the front end of the locomotive designed to improve its capacity to produce steam. The boilers were 'tapered', to give the maximum heating surface at the back near the firebox, and made in a small number of standard sizes so that – like almost all the other parts of the Swindon engines – they were widely interchangeable. Four of these early Edwardian locomotives have been

preserved: a Midland compound, a Great Northern Large Atlantic, Churchward's *Lode Star*, and one of his 2-8-0s.

The increase in the weight of the trains continued relentlessly. From 1907 onwards, for example, the 'Norfolk Coast Express' of the Great Eastern Railway made its non-stop runs from London to North Walsham with trains weighing at least 330 tons and on occasion 100 tons more. During the First World War trains grew heavier yet, until the Great Northern Atlantics were coping with loads of nearly 600 tons. When peace returned, such things came to an end, save at exceptional times like bank holidays. But on most lines rolling-stock continued to grow bigger, and the average express was heavier in 1922 than it had been in 1912. Once again there was nothing for it but larger locomotives, and two emerged at this time that were of great importance: the Pacific (4-6-2) designed by Gresley for the Great Northern and Collett's 'Castle' 4-6-0 on the Great Western. Gresley's engine did not attain complete success immediately; but with infinite patience he kept modifying it and its successors on the London & North Eastern Railway, until the type reached its zenith in the streamlined version built for the new high-speed trains of 1935-39. One of these engines hauled a train for 43 consecutive miles at an average of 100 mph; another, *Mallard*, holds the world speed record for a steam locomotive: 126 mph attained on 3 July 1938. The 'Castles' were hardly less remarkable. With their larger successors the 'Kings', they continued to handle the Great Western expresses – always among the fastest in the country – until the end of steam operation.

No new express engine was built for the London Midland & Scottish Railway until 1927, when the 4-6-0 *Royal Scot* appeared, followed at once (without the usual interval of experiment with a prototype) by 49 others of the same design. Though they did well from the first, they did not reach the peak of their achievement until they were rebuilt in the 1930s and 1940s with taper boilers deriving from the Great Western pattern. The man responsible for this was W. A. Stanier, who went from Swindon to become chief mechanical engineer of the London Midland & Scottish Railway in 1932. A Pacific locomotive was built to his designs in 1933. Like its London & North Eastern counterpart it was gradually improved, and some of the later engines of the class were streamlined for working the Coronation Scot

George Jackson Churchward's 2-6-2 tank engine No. 3118, built for the Great Western Railway in 1903, was one of a range of locomotives designed for all kinds of service from express passenger to heavy freight. Each type was tried out with a single prototype, and modified as necessary after extended trials in service. No other programme of locomotive building so comprehensive, so carefully planned and so intensely observed was undertaken by any other British railway company before 1914. Eventually some 450 of these engines were built – to the same general design though differing in detail. This type of tank engine, which continued to be built at intervals up to 1944, was intended for heavy local trains, and also came to be used frequently for assisting the long coal trains from South Wales up through the Severn Tunnel to England.

Heading north with the 13.05 Euston to Perth train on 9 June 1962, No. 46252 City of Leicester attacks Shap Bank in Cumbria. The locomotive, which is pulling 14 coaches and one van, is one of Sir William Stanier's 8P 'Coronation' class 4-6-2 express passenger engines.

The 'Schools' class locomotive Whitgift *(BR No. 30916) leaves Victoria station on 26 July 1958, heading the* Kentish Belle *for Ramsgate. The locomotives of this class, designed by R. E. L. Maunsell for the Southern Railway and introduced in 1930, were the most powerful 4-4-0s ever to run in Britain.*

express between London and Glasgow. These Pacifics too have remarkable records to their credit: such as a pair of non-stop runs on the London – Glasgow route, on each of which the four hundred miles were covered at an average speed of 70 mph, including the ascent of the great Shap and Beattock banks. These runs, moreover, were a quite exceptional test of endurance for the drivers and firemen, for no change of crew was possible on the way.

The first wholly new express engine designed for the Southern Railway (the very successful *King Arthur* 4-6-0 type was a slightly modified version of one built for the London & South Western) was the *Lord Nelson* of 1926, the precursor of a series of 16. These engines, though powerful, were never an unqualified success. Many experiments were made to improve them, with the result that no two engines of the class were exactly alike. Their designer Maunsell succeeded more completely with the 'Schools' class of 1930, the last and the largest engines of the 4-4-0 type to be produced in this country. Though designed particularly for the Tunbridge Wells and Hastings line, on which the weight and size of locomotives had to be strictly limited, they took their turn at express work on all parts of the Southern system, including the heavy trains to Bournemouth and the West of England.

Two further express passenger designs, both Pacifics, were produced for the Southern Railway by O. V. S. Bulleid: the last new express types evolved by any of the four companies before nationalisation. The 'Merchant Navy' class began to appear in 1941; the later, somewhat smaller, class in two series ('West Country' and 'Battle of Britain') from 1945 onwards. They were partially streamlined, and their motion had some features that were quite new – notably the chain-driven valve gear enclosed in an oil-bath. The wheels were of a new pattern designed to withstand the thrust of the flanges against the rails when rounding curves. All these special features except the last disappeared when, from 1956 onwards, the engines came to be rebuilt. Though highly successful in their original form simply as machines for hauling trains, their consumption of fuel was heavy and the streamlined casing in which the engine was enclosed made the internal parts difficult to reach. For ease of maintenance, therefore, it was removed. One further small change made at this time is of historical interest. The piston-rod and crosshead of these engines were originally manufactured in a single casting. When they were rebuilt, the two parts were made separate. The single-casting method had been peculiar to the Southern Railway, and its origin can be traced back clearly through the work of earlier engineers – Maunsell, Urie, Dugald Drummond – to Stroudley of the London Brighton & South Coast.[11]

Only one major new type of steam locomotive for heavy passenger work was built after nationalisation: the 'Britannia' Pacifics of 1951, designed by R. A. Riddles. These engines were in many respects simpler than their immediate predecessors. They had two cylinders only, and were designed so that all the working parts were as easy to reach as possible. As a standard British Railways type, they naturally saw service in all the Regions, but their performance proved somewhat variable. This was not a reflection on the engines themselves – their excellent qualities were demonstrated beyond argument on the Great Eastern line. It was, rather, an interesting reminder that engine-driving was a human business still, and drivers accustomed for a lifetime to one set of engines (such as those of Swindon, with all their strongly marked characteristics) did not always take easily to machines of a different pattern.[12]

The chief workhorse among British locomotives, the 0-6-0, is seen here near Rhayader in Mid-Wales with a 'pick-up goods' train, which stopped at each station to load and discharge. The locomotive, No. 2538, is one of the 'Dean Goods' engines (named after the Great Western's engineer, William Dean), which had large driving wheels 5ft 2in in diameter.

A more powerful three-cylinder version of the 'Britannia' type, No. 71000 *Duke of Gloucester*, was produced in 1954. By the time it appeared, however, the decision had been taken to turn over all heavy passenger working to diesel and electric traction. No. 71000 therefore remained unique: the last steam express locomotive to be designed for the British railways.

—— THE FREIGHT LOCOMOTIVE ——

Although the express passenger engine brought publicity and prestige to the British railway companies, the staple of their business was the carriage of freight. Moreover, passenger trains were by no means all express. Suburban trains were also important; and branch lines, even if they were

"Skibo Castle," Highland Railway

Painted on this 1905 postcard in familiar olive-green livery, the locomotive Skibo Castle was one of a large and successful class of 4-6-0s used for passenger traffic in the far north of Scotland. Belonging to the Highland Railway, they were developed from the famous goods engines designed by David Jones in 1894, which were the first 4-6-0 locomotives in Britain.

At Wolfhall Junction, built to connect the Great Western with the Midland & South Western Junction Railway just south of Savernake, a D800 'Warship' class locomotive heads a train for London in 1962. This type of diesel-hydraulic locomotive was peculiar to the Western Region; the majority of them were built at Swindon. They were used during the 1960s to haul main-line passenger trains.

The Great Eastern's Norfolk
Coast Express steams out of
Liverpool Street station for
Cromer, headed by No. 1888
of the 'Claud Hamilton'
class. In their royal blue
livery, set off with scarlet
and edged with copper and
brass, these engines,
designed by James Holden,
were among the most
handsome ever built. The
first of them was numbered
after its year of introduction,
1900, and subsequent ones
were numbered backwards.

A down London & South
Western Plymouth express
approaches Surbiton, in a
postcard by F. Moore. The
locomotive is one of the L12
class, built in 1904-5. 'F.
Moore', a name well known
for railway paintings based
on photographs, was a
pseudonym. The pictures
bearing that signature were
almost all the work of the
artist Thomas Rudd.

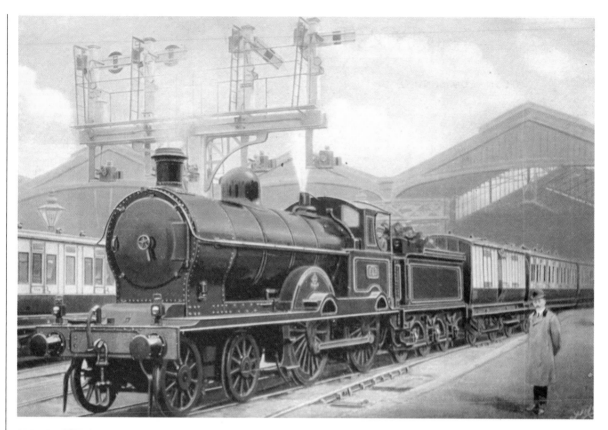

A London & North Western express leaves Euston station in 1905, in an F. Moore postcard. The engine is one of George Whale's 'Precursor' type, then very new; 130 were built of these strong, simple machines, which fast replaced F. W. Webb's compound locomotives on the principal trains. The North Western company had distinctive signals, introduced in 1883, with corrugated arms of pressed steel; the discs on the left hand pair indicate that they control the slow lines.

In another F. Moore postcard, a North British Railway express leaves the west end of Edinburgh (Waverley) station. The engine is one of the company's 'Atlantic' class, dating from 1906.

notoriously unprofitable, still needed locomotives for working them.

The standard British 0-6-0 goods engine, after its appearance in 1848, made its way steadily into favour, and by the 1870s was well established on almost all the English lines. The type was capable of great development; and the next attempt to secure still more power for the haulage of freight was based upon these engines. This was Sturrock's steam tender, tried on the Great Northern Railway in substantial numbers in 1863-66, which provided a second set of six-coupled wheels driven through a second pair of cylinders. The engines fitted with these tenders hauled heavy coal trains well, but on balance they were unsuccessful: their boilers could not supply enough steam, their consumption of fuel was high, and their crews' opinion of them was unprintable, since they entailed double labour and came near to roasting the men alive on the footplate.

The 0-6-0 engine was a peculiarly British machine. It worked well in its country largely because the railways are generally so straight. In the USA, where the track is lighter and curves sharper and more frequent, a leading four-wheeled bogie or a pair of small wheels called a pony truck became almost universal. Some American 'Mogul' (2-6-0) engines of this kind were built for the Great Eastern Railway in 1878 for working heavy coal trains between Peterborough, March and London. They were a disastrous failure; and, having burnt its fingers with this costly experiment, the Great Eastern then remained rigidly faithful to the end of its days to the 0-6-0 type for goods work. Three other companies – the Midland, Great Northern and Great Central – also tried the American 'Mogul' for goods traffic twenty years later. In 1899-1900, when their own works were fully employed and all British locomotive manufacturers stretched to their utmost capacity, these companies ordered between them eighty engines of this kind from the Baldwin and Schenectady Works. Those, too, proved expensive to operate and had a short life, the last of them being broken up after only 16 years. Moguls of British design came to be widely used, however, for mixed-traffic work on a number of railways like the Great Western, Great Northern and South Eastern & Chatham.

The Barry Railway in South Wales introduced the 0-8-0 tender engine into Britain in 1889 and the 0-8-2 tank engine eight years later. By 1900 the London & North Western, Lancashire & Yorkshire, and Great Northern companies had also adopted the 0-8-0 type. It was then developed on the Great Western by Churchward, who added a pair of leading wheels to improve the engine's capacity to take curves. This subsequent arrangement, the 2-8-0, came to be the most widely used for modern British goods locomotives. During the First World War the Great Central 2-8-0 was selected as the standard heavy goods engine for military use, and built in large numbers for the War Office. In the Second World War a 2-8-0 type was again used for this purpose – this time from the London Midland & Scottish Railway – and many of those made their way overseas to work in such unexpected places as Persia, where they carried supplies to the Russians for use on the Eastern Front.[13]

Between the wars a number of attempts were made to produce locomotives of exceptional power for dealing with the heaviest freight traffic. Gresley built a large 2-8-2 engine for the London & North Eastern Railway with a 'booster' for the second pair of small wheels – an auxiliary engine with additional cylinders, which could be used when greater tractive force was required. He also ordered a locomotive of the Garratt type, in which a very large boiler is mounted centrally on a girder frame, at the ends of which are two separate sets of cylinders and wheels. No more such engines were

Deltic No. 55017, The Durham Light Infantry, leaves King's Cross station for York. The Deltics were introduced in 1961, based on a mid-1950s prototype. They were diesel electric locomotives, containing two eight-cylinder Napier engines. The Deltics, designed especially for express passenger service, replaced steam engines and became the mainstay of the East Coast route to Edinburgh. The last of them was withdrawn in January 1982.

A British Railways 2-10-0 locomotive sweeps past Hatton station, between Birmingham and Leamington, with southbound freight. The last and most powerful of the standard steam locomotives built for BR, the class 9 2-10-0 was designed by R. A. Riddles and put into traffic from 1954 to 1960. There were 251 of these engines and they did their work very well; it is sad that they should all have had exceptionally short lives. This one, No. 92082, commissioned in 1954, was withdrawn in 1967. The cost of building it had amounted to £24,343, a sizeable investment to be discarded.

acquired by the London & North Eastern company, but the London Midland & Scottish used a series of 33 of them on the heavy coal trains between Toton and Cricklewood.

The standard large goods engine of British Railways was a 2-10-0 of the orthodox pattern, but considerably more powerful than any that had preceded it in Britain. A machine of very wide capabilities, it was normally used for the heaviest freight trains yet was able to take its turn at express passenger work too. It was the last of the British Railways standard designs, and the most successful.[14]

—— THE TANK LOCOMOTIVE ——

For suburban work, and light passenger traffic in general, a different kind of locomotive is needed, which may not be required to haul very heavy loads but must be nimble and easily manoeuvred. For this purpose the tank engine, carrying its own fuel – water in tanks and coal in a small bunker – soon proved preferable to the tender engine, for it could be readily driven in either direction without needing to be turned round.

The first tank engines to work in normal service in Britain appeared in 1847-48 on the branch line from Cheadle Hulme to Macclesfield and on the London & Blackwall Railway. A number of other small engines followed and then, in 1853, without the slightest warning, came the astonishing 4-2-4 express tank engines designed by James Pearson for the Bristol & Exeter Railway. Their driving wheels were 9ft in diameter and perfectly smooth, without flanges, the whole of the guidance of the engine being performed by the bogie wheels. Although reputed to have been unsuccessful, they formed nearly a third of the company's passenger locomotive stock, so they must have taken a large share of the work. They were all scrapped within twenty years, but six more engines of similar design were built between 1859 and 1873. One of these was derailed at Long Ashton in 1876, while hauling the up Flying Dutchman at a speed of 60 mph; but the subsequent inquiry showed that the accident was attributable to the bad state of the track and that the engine was in no way to blame.

In 1855 Robert Stephenson's company built five 4-4-0 tank engines for the North London Railway. Previous examples of the type had been undistinguished; these became the parents of a long succession, to different designs. All the passenger engines used by the North London to the end of its life in 1922 kept this wheel arrangement. It is much to be regretted that one of the later engines of this type, having been selected for preservation by the London Midland & Scottish Railway in 1929, should have disappeared three years afterwards.[15] One 4-4-0 tank engine, not very much later in date, does however survive. In its early days, London's Metropolitan Railway was operated with locomotives provided first by the Great Western and then by the Great Northern companies. In 1864 it acquired from Beyer Peacock some 4-4-0 tank engines of its own, which proved remarkably successful. With minor modifications, they remained in charge of the whole of the passenger traffic on the original Metropolitan line until its electrification in 1905.

The same type was adopted by the Metropolitan District company, which shared the responsibility for the Inner Circle. It spread to other railways, too: such engines were to be seen on the London & South Western (where they were known as the 'Plymouth Tanks') and on the Dutch Rhenish Railway in Holland. When the Metropolitan dispensed with some of them, after thirty or forty years of grinding hard work, they were still saleable, and they made their way to some improbable places. The Cambrian Railways, for instance, bought six of them. They were extraordinarily strong and well built engines. The first of them ran over 600,000 miles with its original boiler of Yorkshire iron; with a new one, it ran another 400,000 miles and then met death prematurely, as the result of an accident, after 33 years' service. When the last of these warriors came to be withdrawn in the 1920s and 1930s, they all retained intact the frames they were built with.[16] One of them has been preserved in the London Trans-

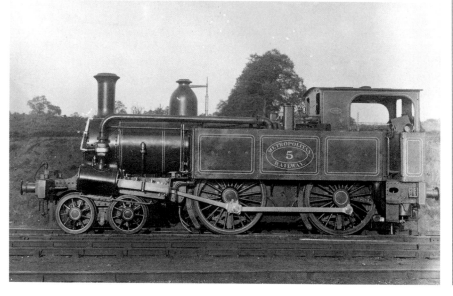

The 'A' class 4-4-0 tank locomotive, fitted with condensing apparatus so that it consumed its own smoke, hauled underground trains on the Metropolitan Railway from 1864 to 1905. Forty-four of these engines were built by Beyer Peacock & Co., together with another 22, very similar, of class 'B'. All at first had spectacle plates, and the engine crews stood in the open; the only important alteration made to this machine is the roofed-in cab added to provide some degree of protection.

port Museum in Covent Garden: both a demonstration of Victorian craftsmanship and a memorial to the first underground railway in the world.

Though these engines served their purpose well, on the Inner Circle
they were never required to run fast. The only express tank engines built
before the 1880s were those of the Bristol & Exeter Railway, but they were
always considered freaks and had an equivocal reputation. The first undoubtedly successful locomotives of the express kind were of the 4-4-2 type.
They appeared on the London Tilbury & Southend Railway in 1880, where
they worked all the traffic for many years (hence their name 'Tilbury
Universal Machines'), including some smartly timed short-distance express
trains. The design was modified in detail as the years went by, but
Thundersley of 1909, which has survived, represents a clear evolution from
the first engine of 1880.

From this time down to the First World War the great majority of the
tank engines that undertook fast passenger work were of the 2-4-2 or 4-4-2
type. One of the Lancashire & Yorkshire 2-4-2 locomotives, which were
among the most successful tank engines ever built, may be seen at the
National Railway Museum in York.

The Great Eastern Railway operated one of the densest of all suburban
services, in and out of Liverpool Street, for many years largely with 0-6-0
and 2-4-2 tanks. But though they were efficient machines, their capacity was
limited; as traffic grew heavier year by year the company had to consider
new ways of coping with it. The Great Eastern was far from rich, and it
shrank from the capital expenditure that electrification would involve. Its
locomotive superintendent James Holden believed in a cheaper alternative.
In 1902 he built a remarkable steam locomotive, which was capable of an
acceleration equal to that of an electric train. It was a ten-coupled engine
with three cylinders (known as the 'Decapod'), and it performed just what
he claimed for it. It imposed so heavy a weight on the track, however, that if
it and other similar locomotives had been used in regular service the lines
they worked would have had to be reconstructed, and that proved too
expensive to contemplate.[17]

Apart from the Decapod, which remained unique, the first really big
tanks appeared, for goods shunting, in 1907-09: the three-cylinder 0-8-4
engines of the Great Central Railway and the 4-8-0s of the North Eastern.
These were soon followed by similarly large passenger engines (4-6-2 and
4-6-4) for the London Brighton & South Coast, London & North Western
and other railways. Such designs were multiplied from 1917 onwards – by
the Caledonian and Glasgow & South Western companies, for example. In
terms of size, they culminated in the four-cylinder 4-6-4 tanks of the
London Midland & Scottish Railway, which appeared in 1924.

These very large tank engines were not, however, wholly successful in
passenger service. A distinct prejudice arose against their use on express
trains at high speed after the Sevenoaks disaster of 1927, when a 2-6-4 tank
jumped the rails. The Southern company thereupon converted nearly all its
large passenger tanks into tender engines. True, the London Midland &
Scottish and London & North Eastern companies, followed by British
Railways, built 2-6-4 tanks of substantial size; but though on occasion they
reached high speeds with perfect safety, they were employed very little on
true express work.

The tank engine was suitable for short hauls and intensive traffic. It was
developed more energetically in Britain than anywhere else in the world,
although very large tank engines were to be seen in Holland and France.

There was one other numerous and important family of British tank

Restored to its original condition by members of the Caerphilly Railway Society, this 0-6-2 tank locomotive was of a type greatly favoured by the railways of South Wales. It was designed for the Taff Vale Railway by T. Hurry Riches and built in 1897. When taken out of service on the Great Western Railway, it was sold to the Longmoor Military Railway in Hampshire; later it was put to work in a Durham colliery. Today it is part of the National Collection in the care of the Welsh Industrial & Maritime Museum.

locomotives. Though the older South Wales railways began life with tender engines, they adopted the tank engine with single-minded enthusiasm as soon as it had proved itself: the Rhymney Railway, for instance, never acquired a tender engine after 1868. The 0-6-2 type came to be particularly favoured on these lines. When they were absorbed in 1923 into the Great Western, three fifths of all their locomotives were of this arrangement.[18] The reasons for their partiality for the 0-6-2 are easy to understand. Running on eight wheels, the frame was large enough to bear substantial water tanks and a good-sized bunker for coal; since six of the wheels were coupled, great adhesion could be obtained for climbing stiff gradients, and the pony truck at the rear helped to secure flexibility in rounding curves. These engines were used for all traffic alike, passenger and freight. Toiling ceaselessly up and down the valleys, in and out of Newport and Cardiff, they were vital instruments in the world-wide export of Welsh coal and in the lives of those who produced it. One of them, immaculately restored, has a resting-place at Caerphilly. It is a memorial to the history of modern Wales.

—— ELECTRIFICATION ——

Other methods of traction for the railways were in use many years before the demise of the steam locomotive. Electricity came first, followed a generation later by the diesel engine. Passing over some interesting early experiments (a primitive electric engine was tried out by Robert Davidson on the Edinburgh & Glasgow Railway in 1842), the first successful electrically operated railways in the British Isles were opened between 1883 and 1886. Because they were so satisfactory, it was decided that the tube railway then under construction in London, the City & South London, should be operated by electric instead of by cable traction. It had been intended to incorporate the electric motors within the bodies of the coaches, but the Board of Trade required that separate locomotives should be provided. Fifty-two were built between 1889 and 1901. An example survives today in the Science Museum at South Kensington in London, and one of the original 'padded cell' coaches is at York.

A solitary traveller at James Street station watches a train of the Liverpool Overhead Railway pull in on its way to Dingle in 1947. Opened in 1893, this was the first electric urban railway in Britain outside London and the first electrically powered elevated railway in the world, of a kind that came to be much used in the United States. Originally it conveyed large numbers of dock workers at specially low fares imposed by Parliament, but its nimbler and more flexible competitors, the electric tram and the motor bus, killed it. Not nationalised, it was unable to pay its way and closed on 30 December 1956.

The next electric railway to be opened in Britain was the Liverpool Overhead Railway, which was brought into use in 1893-96; constructed on a framework raised above the road, it was the only example in Britain of a type more favoured in Germany and the USA. It is also unique as the only important stretch of electric railway in Britain that has had to be closed down. It conveyed millions of city workers into and out of Liverpool, and countless thousands rode on it for pleasure, for the unforgettable sight it afforded of the Liverpool docks and shipping. But its revenue fell far below its expenditure. Strenuous efforts were made to induce Liverpool Corporation and the British Transport Commission to take it over, but they failed and all traffic ceased on the line at the end of 1956. It is perhaps foolish to sentimentalise over the closing of a railway. Yet this dingy line, striding above the Liverpool streets, had a quite peculiar character. It unfolded before one's eyes so much of the history of England in the years of her greatest power. There were echoes and associations in the name of almost every station: Herculaneum, Nelson, Huskisson, Canada, Brocklebank, Gladstone.

The rest of the story of electric traction in Britain is one not of failure but of great success. The City & South London was the parent of a series of tube railways, all worked electrically, opened between 1898 and 1907. In those nine years the outline of the tube system of central London, as we know it today, suddenly took shape. Tube railways reached north to Golders Green, Highgate and Finsbury Park; south to Clapham Common; east to the Bank; west to Shepherds Bush and Hammersmith. By this time, moreover, the entire District system had been electrified, along with all the Metropolitan's lines except the long arm that stretched out into the country from Harrow to Verney Junction.

Meanwhile, electrification was going forward elsewhere. The leaders were three companies in the north of England: the Mersey, which began electric working in 1903, followed the next year by the North Eastern (Newcastle – Tynemouth) and the Lancashire & Yorkshire (Liverpool –

Southport). In London, electric traction began on the Brighton and South Western lines in 1909-16, and on the North London and London & North Western in 1916-22. Manchester got its first electric trains in 1915, on the Lancashire & Yorkshire line out to Bury. One other electrification, for freight service only, was the 18½ miles from Shildon to Middlesbrough (Newport), undertaken by the North Eastern company in 1915.

With trifling exceptions, all this work justified the heavy capital expenditure involved. But it had one disquieting aspect. At least eight different systems were used; and with the exception of one or two of the London tubes, no electric train of one company could have run successfully on the lines of another. The current was transmitted through overhead wires on the Midland, the Brighton, and the Shildon – Newport lines; through one electric rail on the London & South Western; through two on most of the rest. The Metropolitan and District companies quarrelled fiercely over the merits of alternating and direct current and in the end were obliged to take the matter to the Board of Trade for arbitration. Even those two ancient enemies recognised that it was hardly possible to work the Inner Circle except on a common system.

During the first thirty years, when electric traction was still relatively new, it was natural and proper for engineers to try out each successive improvement of it. But with amalgamation in 1923, the problem became more serious. On the new Southern Railway it was acute. For that company, immediate electrification seemed an absolute necessity if its swollen suburban traffic was to be handled at all, yet two of its partners had adopted diametrically opposite systems. In the event, it committed itself to the London & South Western's third-rail direct-current system, pushing it further out to Guildford and Dorking and introducing it on the South Eastern & Chatham lines to Orpington. At the same time, it carried out the plans already prepared by the Brighton company for extending its overhead system on the alternating current to Coulsdon and Sutton. The directors of the Southern company had complete faith in the principle of electrification. Although they had doomed the system, which would have to be converted before long (it lasted in fact only till 1929), they nevertheless went ahead and installed it on those two Brighton lines. What mattered most was that there should be electrification immediately in some form, to keep the packed suburban trains moving. All these important conversions were brought into use by 1925. The Brighton lines went over to third-rail traction in 1928-29.

Electrification was not always a comfortable business for the traveller. The trains were flimsy wooden affairs, reconstructed from the stock used for steam operation, and they creaked and pitched and banged with the electric motors built into them. But it represented a great and unquestionable improvement on the older means of traction, in cleanliness, speed and punctuality – and that was plainly reflected in the Southern Railway's receipts from passenger traffic. Encouraged by this success, the new company was soon undertaking the electrification not only of further suburban lines but of main lines too. By 1939 almost all the important routes within the triangle London – Portsmouth – Hastings had been electrified.

Other new companies were less enterprising. The Royal Commission on Transport said roundly in 1930 that 'it would be greatly to the interests of the railway companies, and at the same time tend to the great convenience of the public, if all suburban services were electrified, not merely in the London area but in every district where there is intensive suburban passenger traffic'.[19] In the provinces, however, the only new schemes of

A photograph from the Weekly Scotsman magazine shows passengers travelling on the Glasgow District Subway, shortly after electrification in the 1930s. When regular services began on 21 January 1897, cable-operated trains ran along a twin-tunnelled, four-foot gauge circle line that connected the central parts of Glasgow on both sides of the river Clyde. The Subway was closed in 1922 but reopened the following year after it had been bought and refurbished by the Glasgow Corporation. It was electrified in 1935.

electrification were on the Altrincham line out of Manchester, the lines at the north end of the Wirral Peninsula, and the ancient Swansea & Mumbles Railway, which was converted from steam traction in 1929. In Scotland the Glasgow Subway (still running on the rare 4ft gauge) turned over from cable to electric traction in 1935.

No further electrification was carried out before the Second World War, but in the late 1930s the London & North Eastern Railway began work on two big schemes, one in the London area, the other on the line from Manchester to Sheffield. The second of these projects was important as the first application in Britain of electric haulage to all forms of traffic, goods as well as passenger. When the work was finished in 1955 the steam engine practically disappeared from nearly seventy miles of railway. This revolutionised the handling of goods, which was the main traffic, passenger trains numbering only a tenth of all those passing through the Woodhead Tunnel. The time taken to haul a train up the very steep line from Wath to the goods yard at Mottram was reduced from 191 to 101 minutes.[20] The passenger benefitted too, if less spectacularly, with a quickened suburban service from Manchester out to Glossop and a greater number of trains, faster by about 15 per cent, between Manchester and Sheffield.

The system of electrification used on this line was direct current at 1,500 volts, supplied overhead. In 1932, acting on the recommendations of the Pringle Committee, the Minister of Transport required direct current to be used on all British main-line railways in the future, either on the 1,500-volt overhead system or on the third-rail pattern already established on the Southern Railway, with current at 750 volts. This was the first attempt by the government to rationalise the multiplicity of electric systems, a problem which was threatening to become almost as troublesome as the Battle of the Gauges had been a century before.

In 1951 a committee of the British Transport Commission recommended that all future electrification, except on the Southern Region, should be at 1,500 volts. Although this seemed unequivocal, proclaimed with all the authority bold type could give it in the committee's report, the force of the recommendation was somewhat weakened by the next sentence: 'It [the committee] does not wish to rule out, however, the possibility of using direct current at 3,000 volts or single-phase alternating current at low frequency, or at the standard frequency of 50 cycles, for secondary lines with light traffic.'[21]

This qualification reflected the interest British engineers were showing in the experiments that had been made before the war in Hungary and Germany, and were at this time being conducted in France, with new systems using alternating current. The French railways were as heavily committed as the British to direct-current electrification, then coming into use with brilliant success on the lines from Paris to Lyon and Bordeaux. Nevertheless, they equipped a mountainous stretch of line, from Aix-les-Bains through Annecy to Laroche-sur-Foron, on a 25kV alternating-current system; and this yielded such good results that alternating current was then chosen for the electrification of the Valenciennes – Thionville line, which carried some of the heaviest freight traffic in France. Brought into operation in 1954, this showed such notable economies in the cost both of fixed equipment and locomotives that the British Transport Commission felt obliged to reconsider its earlier decision. After bearing in mind all the difficulties that would arise from the introduction of yet another system, the Commission decided to use 25kV alternating current for its biggest new project, the lines from Euston to Birmingham, Manchester and Liverpool.

Considered historically, the electrification of railways in Britain seems to have been a curiously vacillating affair, displaying first the evils of separate development under private companies and then a want of firmness on the part of the government and the nationalised administration. But the changes of policy, the conversions and re-conversions that took place, should be more truly seen as reflections of a rapidly changing technology.

Most of the rolling-stock used on the electrified railways of Britain is operated by built-in motors, placed in compartments at the ends of each set of two, three or more coaches. The advantages of the built-in locomotive are clear enough: the train can be operated from either end, and no time need be lost in turning locomotives round at the end of the journey. The pattern was established very successfully on nearly all British metropolitan and suburban lines. It had, however, one drawback from the passenger's point of view. The vibration of the powerful motors, placed within the train, was uncomfortable; travelling was noisy, and subject to a plunging motion at high speed. It could hardly be expected that the wooden bodies of old South Eastern four- and six-wheeled vehicles, mounted on new steel frames, would be able to withstand the motors' vibration. The fine stock of the London & North Western Railway, used on the electrified North London and Watford services, proved more successful, though it had the advantage of running over some of the best laid permanent way in Britain. Rolling-stock could now be specially constructed wholly or mainly of steel. On the Southern Railway 55 new three-car sets were built for the extended electrification of 1925 and performed better than the old wooden carriages. But when electrification of the main lines from London to Brighton and Worthing began in 1933, troubles with the rolling-stock continued. No one could doubt the improvement in the service, in cleanliness, speed and frequency. Noise and rough riding were its faults and, though now a little reduced, those faults are still apparent, even in the new stock built in 1967 for the Bournemouth electrification.

The electric locomotive, as opposed to the built-in motor, did not cut much of a figure in Britain before 1967. The North Eastern company produced a fleet of locomotives for its Shildon – Middlesbrough line, together with one express engine, which never ran more than a few trials.[22] The Metropolitan Railway built a number in 1905-07, for handling the through trains that ran out to the edge of its newly electrified system and beyond. The trains consisted of ordinary rolling-stock, hauled by electric loco-motives as far as Paddington or Harrow (later Rickmansworth) and there taken over by steam engines. These electric locomotives were completely rebuilt from 1922 onwards and continued in operation until 1961: a familiar sight to Londoners, some of their names commemorating men and women connected with the city.

Between Manchester and Sheffield locomotives of two designs were in use, both developed from a prototype which was under construction for the London & North Eastern company when war broke out. Designed for mixed traffic, mainly freight, this locomotive was completed in 1941. Between 1947 and 1951 it was lent to the Netherlands Railways, then desperately short of motive power; they bestowed on it the name *Tommy*, which it kept after the war. Another 57 locomotives of the same type were built. Their maximum speed was 65 mph. At the same time seven new locomotives, similar but capable of higher speeds, made their appearance, chiefly for working passenger trains.

The main-line electrification carried through between 1967 and 1974 called for entirely new locomotives. They were of classes 81-87 and numbered just over two hundred in all. The earlier ones (classes 81-85) developed from 2,950 to 3,600 horse power (hp), which became 4,040 hp in class 86/2. It was 5,000 hp in class 87, which had a slightly higher permitted maximum speed than the rest, of 110 mph. The services between Euston and Birmingham, Manchester, Liverpool and Glasgow were maintained by these engines at average speeds of 70-75 mph.

Very much higher speeds than these were expected from the Advanced Passenger Train (APT). Designed from 1969 onwards at the Research Centre at Derby, the APT was intended to be a very high-speed train that could run on existing tracks, rather than requiring wholly new lines to be built as the Japanese had done in 1964 and the French were to do in 1981. The challenge was to find some means of negotiating curves at much greater speeds than before. A tilting mechanism was devised and successfully demonstrated in an experimental train driven by gas turbines. Production trains succeeded it, electrically powered, to run between London and Glasgow. In 1979 one reached a speed of 162 mph. After many delays, the APT entered regular passenger service on 7 December 1981. But it encountered so many troubles that it was withdrawn after only a fortnight – a miserable ending to a most imaginative and hopeful enterprise.[23]

—— DIESEL TRACTION ——

The use of oil as a fuel for locomotives was explored in the 1870s and 1880s, in Britain and in Russia. James Holden's apparatus, fitted in 1893 to a Great Eastern engine appropriately named *Petrolea*, was widely noticed. These experiments were intended to find a fuel that would be a satisfactory alternative to coal; the engines were conceived entirely in terms of the existing steam locomotive. At the same time, one or two engineers were beginning to envisage locomotives of quite a new kind, powered by petrol or heavy-oil engines. Gottlieb Daimler built a little petrol locomotive in 1891; W. D. Priestman produced the first oil-engined locomotive three years later, which was tried out as a shunter in the North Eastern Railway's Alexandra Dock at Hull. A number of oil-engined locomotives were built

The Metropolitan Railway's electric locomotive John Wycliffe arrives at Baker Street station in 1935 with a train from Aylesbury. This locomotive was written off in an accident on 31 December 1945, when it struck the rear of a train near Northwood in thick fog. Three people died in the ensuing fire.

On a northbound test run in October 1980, an Advanced Passenger Train (APT) leans into the curve at Winwick Junction in Lancashire. Heading in the opposite direction is a Glasgow to Euston express, hauled by a class 87 locomotive.

for the War Office, to work in Woolwich Arsenal, between 1898 and 1904.[24]

Meanwhile, Rudolf Diesel had begun his work in Germany, and from 1905 onwards he was proclaiming his belief in the far-reaching possibilities of applying the oil engine to railway traction. It is perfectly just that his name should have come to be attached to the heavy-oil engine, provided we remember that he did not invent it, and that among those who helped its development were British engineers like Akroyd Stuart, and British firms like Hornsby of Grantham and Hawthorn Leslie.

The development of the diesel locomotive was impeded in Germany by the First World War, but the neutral Swedes pressed on with it. The first diesel railcar ever built went into service in Sweden in 1913, and by 1920 seven more were working successfully. After the war the diesel locomotive was rapidly improved and adapted to a wider range of work, by American and German engineers and by the Soviets under Lomonossoff. It established itself most firmly in Germany, where nearly 2,000 were built for shunting duties in 1928-30, and where in 1933 the high-speed railcar known as the *Flying Hamburger* appeared, attaining speeds of 100 mph day after day in ordinary service.

In Britain a few isolated experiments were made, such as the Kitson-Still diesel steam locomotive of 1928. A four-coach train powered by a diesel engine (originally intended for an airship) worked on the London Midland & Scottish Railway between Preston and Blackpool for a few months in the same year. In 1933 the LMS acquired a diesel railcar called *Bluebird*, which ran quite successfully for two years and was then disposed of on the grounds – they sound curious now – that the traffic was too intensive for it, and that steam-operated trains of the traditional kind were more satisfactory. In the course of the 1930s the London Midland & Scottish did, however, acquire a number of diesel shunting locomotives. But the true pioneer in the use of diesel railcars for passenger services in this country was the Great Western company, which built them from 1934 onwards. They were used mainly for local traffic, for example from Oxford to Kingham and Princes Risborough, but the Great Western also maintained a fast service with three-coach diesel sets between Birmingham and Cardiff. These were the first diesel railcars in Britain that were not experimental but part of the normal service.

It may look odd that Britain, which had taken an important part in the early development of the oil-engined locomotive, should have made so little use of it in the years between the wars. But this new method of traction was especially valuable where the traditional fuels, water and coal, were lacking or of poor quality; it was the badness of the water on the Tashkent Railway that first turned Lomonossoff's mind to it. In Britain water and coal were cheap and good, whereas oil had to be imported and was expensive; and the initial cost of a diesel locomotive might be twice as great as that of a steam locomotive.[25] In the 1930s, therefore, there was no great incentive to adopt the new form of traction. After the war, the situation changed. Good locomotive coal became increasingly hard to get, and the economics of fuelling and maintenance began to work in favour of the diesel engine; it was naturally easier, too, to recruit good staff for diesel operation than for the dirty and arduous work on the footplate of a steam locomotive. In other countries, notably in the USA, the diesel was rapidly replacing the steam engine. In Britain the conversion took longer. The London Midland & Scottish Railway ordered two diesel locomotives for main-line work, completed in 1947-48. They were followed by three more, of a different type, delivered to the Southern Region of British Railways in 1952-54.

The experiments made with these locomotives, and the work being performed by diesel engines on railways in other countries, persuaded the British Transport Commission to invest heavily in diesel traction. In the Modernisation Plan it gave electrification first preference; but it recognised that diesel haulage could bring great immediate benefits at a lower capital cost. By the time the plan was published, the first of the new diesel railcars were in service in the Leeds – Bradford – Harrogate district, West Cumberland and elsewhere. Diesel shunting engines were being built in large numbers; and further plans were in hand for main-line locomotives. These began to appear on the Eastern Region main line out of Liverpool Street in 1957 (the Brush D5500 series), followed the next year by the more powerful English Electric D200 class and by the Swindon diesel-hydraulic locomotives of the 'Warship' class, which at once took their place on the Cornish Riviera Express and other Western Region main-line trains.

At first these machines proliferated in numerous different designs – too

numerous, in fact, indicating that each was experimental. Such experiment is always costly and the railways' losses were damagingly increased as a result. But presently a small range of satisfactory locomotives emerged. Two types came to bear the brunt of main-line long-distance work for both passengers and freight. The 'Peak' class 44 and its derivative class 45, with a slightly more powerful engine, were built from 1959 onwards and ran very steadily and dependably. The most numerous locomotives, those of the later class 47, were introduced in 1962 and made their way to every part of the system: twenty years later they were fitted up to provide the power for the fast push-and-pull trains between Edinburgh and Glasgow (see p. 221). New diesel locomotives were now required for freight traffic only. Class 58 went into production in 1982; its prototype was firmly named *Railfreight*.

The reduced demand for these machines in passenger service arose from the introduction of what were at first known as High Speed Trains (HSTs) and later, officially, Inter-City 125s. Run in standard formations with a diesel power-unit at each end and designed to travel at speeds of up to 125 mph, they were first introduced in 1976 and 1977 on to the Western Region main line between Paddington, Bristol and South Wales. They were next used on the East Coast main line out of King's Cross where they displaced the one class of British diesel locomotives that had been designed specifically for express passenger service: class 55, known as the 'Deltics' from the delta-arrangement of their 16 cylinders. These machines became very celebrated. There were 22 of them (excluding the prototype, built in 1955), and they ran on this route alone.

The HSTs proved generally successful, and they were put into service on all the chief main lines that were not electrified, as far north as Aberdeen, including the important cross-country line from Bristol to Birmingham and York. They form the basis on which the long-distance passenger train service principally rests, until they in their turn begin to be ousted by further electrification.

At Keswick station in 1963, the driver of a diesel multiple unit (DMU) leans out to collect the staff which will enable him to enter the single-track line to Penrith. The DMU on the left has just come off the Penrith line, the driver surrendering the staff to the railwayman on the tracks as he passed. DMUs were brought into general service in 1956 and immediately proved a successful alternative to steam locomotives. Their use on the Cockermouth Keswick & Penrith Railway, however, was not enough to prevent its closure in the late 1960s.

MANCHESTER · HALIFAX · BRADFORD

*('Down' = Manchester – Bradford; 'Up' = Bradford – Manchester.
The names of stations now open for passenger traffic are printed in
small capitals.)*

The line from Manchester to Bradford has two sections. They were planned by two companies and laid out separately by two engineers, each of whom was eminent in his time.[1]

The journey begins over the Manchester & Leeds Railway, built between 1839 and 1841. This was among the earliest trunk railways, and the first to pierce the Pennines. It was indeed the first railway to be completed anywhere in Europe through what may properly be called mountainous country. Together with the North Midland line from Derby to Leeds it was the last of George Stephenson's great works, and it bears some of the impress of his mind still.

Manchester (Victoria) station: 1909 façade by William Dawes, photographed in 1983.

At Milner Royd Junction, east of Sowerby Bridge, the route diverges, turning northwards – also through steep hills – to Halifax and Bradford. Most of this line was planned as part of the West Riding Union Railways and laid out between 1844 and 1852 under John Hawkshaw, who became one of the leading railway engineers of the second generation, following George Stephenson.

The need for a railway linking the Lancashire and Yorkshire industrial districts became apparent very early. It was thought of as a continuation of the Liverpool & Manchester. Though the Pennines had already been scaled by roads and canals the transit across them by coach or by boat was necessarily very slow. A steam-worked railway offered the prospect of a much quicker service.

All in all, George Stephenson made three different plans for building the part of the line for which he was responsible. The first, which was worked out in 1825, involved stiff climbing and long tunnelling. Stephenson turned in 1830, in association with James Walker, to an easier route, which required no tunnels at all but was very circuitous. In 1835 he produced on his own a new set of plans for a line somewhat more direct, without any very steep gradients but with eight tunnels. Though seven of these were short, the eighth, through the mountain chain, was to be more than one and a half miles long. This was the line actually built. Its layout was a victory for Stephenson's firmly held principle of resisting sharp gradients. Through all this very difficult country there are only two substantial stretches of line rising more steeply than at a gradient of 1 in 200.

It is right to speak of the Manchester & Leeds Railway as Stephenson's, for he was its engineer, he laid down its course, and he remained personally concerned in its construction. But like most other works of the kind, it owed much also to the engineer's colleagues: in this case particularly to T. L. Gooch (Sir Daniel's eldest brother), who was Stephenson's chief assistant. Many of the contract drawings are signed by Gooch, and his autobiographical sketch describes in some detail the work for which he was responsible. It does no injustice to Stephenson to say that the credit for the strong fabric of the line – many of its structures standing unaltered still – belongs also to Gooch.[2]

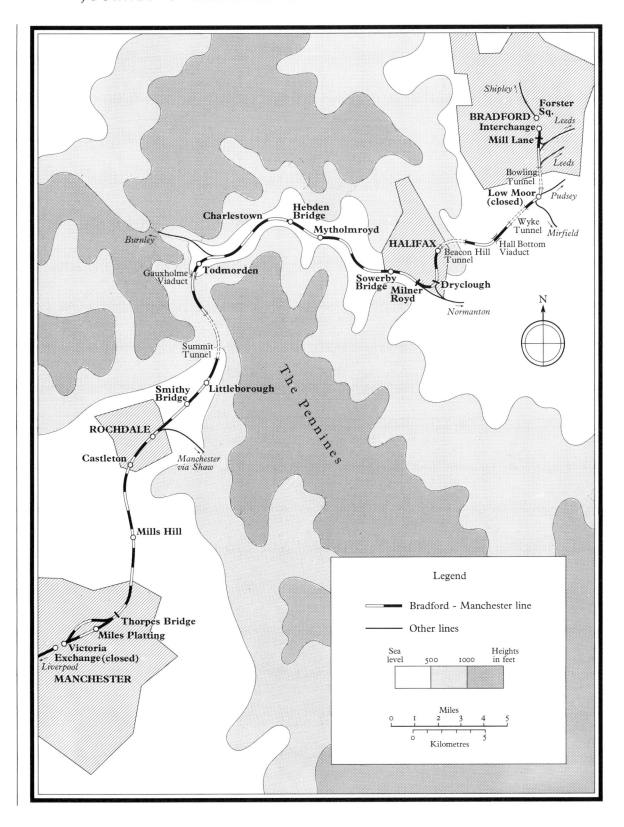

Shipley

Forster Sq.

BRADFORD
Interchange
Mill Lane

Leeds

Leeds

Bowling
Tunnel

Low Moor
(closed)

Pudsey

Wyke
Tunnel

Mirfield

Hall Bottom
Viaduct

HALIFAX

Beacon Hill
Tunnel

Charlestown

Hebden
Bridge

Mytholmroyd

Burnley

Sowerby
Bridge

Milner
Royd

Dryclough

Gauxholme
Viaduct

Todmorden

Normanton

The Pennines

N

Summit
Tunnel

Smithy
Bridge

Littleborough

ROCHDALE

Castleton

Manchester
via Shaw

Mills Hill

Legend

Bradford – Manchester line

Other lines

Sea
level   500   1000

Heights
in feet

Thorpes Bridge
Miles Platting

Victoria
Exchange (closed)

Liverpool

MANCHESTER

Miles

0   1   2   3   4   5

0   5

Kilometres

THE GRADIENT OF THE MANCHESTER–BRADFORD LINE

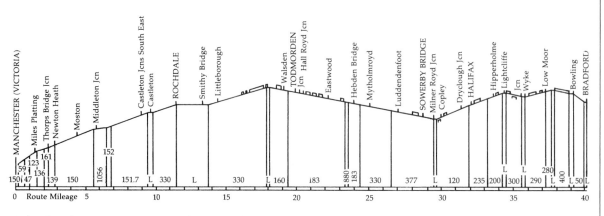

In this chart the figures above the base line should be prefixed with '1 in' to read off the gradient for each section. 'L' stands for level, and boxes along the upper line indicate tunnels.

Manchester (Victoria) station: iron-and-glass canopy showing destinations served by the Lancashire & Yorkshire company, 1980.

The original southern terminus of the railway was on Oldham Road in Manchester. When the line was to be joined to the older Liverpool & Manchester, a diversion was constructed to a new station at Hunt's Bank, opened on 1 January 1844 and named, after the young Queen, VICTORIA. This had a single platform 850ft long. In effect it was two separate stations linked together, the Liverpool & Manchester (part of the London & North Western Railway from 1846) running westwards from one end, the Manchester & Leeds (Lancashire & Yorkshire) eastwards from the other. There was no joint management. Here was a cause of endless trouble in operation, commented on by the government inspectors. One of them wrote bluntly in 1872: 'The station, as now divided and apportioned between the two companies, is bad and dangerous'.[3]

The London & North Western

company built a new station for itself, called Exchange, at the western end in 1884. Passengers had then a miserable walk of a quarter of a mile to the other one. The Lancashire & Yorkshire section was extended by stages, particularly in 1877-84 and in 1898-1904, including a series of shorter terminal platforms;[4] and an effort was made to render it imposing externally by a new facade designed by William Dawes and completed in 1909.

This building shows decent ashlar masonry, a feature not commonly seen on this scale in railway work. The light iron and glass canopy outside is adorned with the names of places to which services then ran from the station, at home and on the Continent (via Goole or Hull); inside, there is a huge wall map of the Lancashire & Yorkshire system, with the company's war memorial below it; the refreshment room retains a faint flavour of *art nouveau* through all the revamping it has undergone in accordance with succeeding fashions. For the rest it must be said that the exterior is heavy and coarse-grained, its dullness relieved only by vapid ornamentation. Much money has lately been spent on cleaning it all; the work was finished in 1980. But the building gazes glumly on to a large tract of waste ground and a row of dilapidated shops. Though British Rail began by doing its best here to cheer up a sordid quarter of Manchester, the job has been left unfinished.

The station lies low, not much above the level of the River Irwell, and a steep climb away from it is necessary in

the eastward direction. A stationary engine was provided at first to take the trains up to Miles Platting (as at Glasgow: see p. 214), but locomotives seem to have been in use on their own little more than a year after traffic began. The Bradford trains today avoid Miles Platting, taking a deviation, opened in 1877, to Thorpes Bridge Junction. There they rejoin Stephenson's original line, and they keep to it for about 28 miles, climbing almost uninterruptedly at a steady 1 in 150-57 to CASTLETON.

Here the railway begins to accompany the Rochdale Canal. This was the first canal to traverse the Pennines and was one of the principal works of William Jessop, opened throughout in 1804. The railway and canal competed energetically for traffic, but though the canal suffered severely its decline was gradual; the last working trip over its whole length was not made until 1937.[5] Parts of it are well maintained still.

A noble prospect of the Pennine foothills now opens up to the north. The station at ROCHDALE was placed well away from the large town it served and, though building has gone on all round it since, it remains rather off-centre. Most of the late-Victorian structure has been demolished, and meagrely replaced.

North of Rochdale the gradient becomes easier, with a two-mile level stretch followed by a steady climb up to and through the long Summit Tunnel at 1 in 330. A new station at SMITHY BRIDGE has been opened, replacing an earlier one on a different site, closed in 1960. The railway is carried on a handsome low masonry viaduct over the centre of LITTLEBOROUGH, where a plaque on the station wall commemorates the opening of the line from Manchester in 1839. It now turns north to enter a narrow defile, running side by side with the canal and the Todmorden road before entering the tunnel.

The Summit Tunnel took three and a quarter years to construct (1837-41). On completion it was longer than any other railway tunnel – 2,885yd against the 2,426yd of Robert Stephenson's Kilsby Tunnel on the London & Birmingham Railway; but Brunel's Box Tunnel on the Great Western, opened only four months later, outdid it with a

length of 3,212yd. Another railway tunnel through the Pennines was under construction at the same time, at Woodhead on the line between Manchester and Sheffield (begun under Vignoles and finished under Locke). That was much longer (5,302yd) and had taken seven years when it was opened at the end of 1845.

The Summit Tunnel, driven through millstone grit, was lined with brickwork throughout, most of it set in cement brought across from the neighbourhood of Hull. For the making of it 14 vertical shafts were sunk. The work continued round the clock, as many as 1,000 men being employed on it at once. The miners and bricklayers received the high maximum wage of 6s 6d for a ten-hour day. The original contractors, Evans & Copeland, proved inadequate

West portal of Summit Tunnel: lithograph by A. F. Tait, 1845.

and were superseded in March 1839 by John Stephenson (no relation of George), a man long experienced in railway building. The total cost of the tunnel is said to have amounted to £251,000, against the engineer's original estimate of £156,800.

In December 1840, when the work was nearly finished, part of the inverted arch below the track failed, giving rise to a wild rumour in Manchester that the whole tunnel had caved in and buried workmen beneath it. When a party of the directors went up with George Stephenson to inspect, they found that the damage was in fact not serious and had caused no deaths. Stephenson pointed out the treacherous nature of the shale through which the invert had been built and explained the reconstruction and strengthening that he proposed to make.

He took occasion at the same time to make a formal pronouncement about the tunnel as a whole: 'I will stake my character, my head, if that tunnel ever give way, so as to cause danger to any of the public passing through it.... I don't think there is such another piece of work in the world. It is the greatest work that has yet been done of this kind.... This is a dislocated part of a very high country, where the debris has come off at a time and in a place where we could have no chance of examining it, except by excavation. But this is the only weak part we have met with'. That was a defence and a cry of triumph. Both were justified.

The directors of the company and the engineer declared their pride in the great work by more than words. The south portal of the tunnel is an elaborate and splendidly powerful composition, the arch surmounted by a double horizontal gable, at once elegant and ponderous; the gable seems indeed to suggest that it is supporting the weight of the hill above. No ornament of any kind was applied here; instead the arms of Manchester and Leeds were carved above the southern portal of the short Summit West Tunnel, approaching the main one.

The great portal of the Summit Tunnel may be viewed from the road, which crosses the line a little way off, but it is black like everything round it, and cannot show itself boldly even in sunlight. Tait's fine lithograph, published in 1845, remains the best portrayal of it.[6]

George Stephenson's boast has stood. The tunnel has always been wet, and that has given some trouble. It had to be closed for substantial repair in 1984-85, but that was nearly 150 years after it was built, and was due primarily to a fire in a petrol train. During that closure, travellers who had to be conveyed from Littleborough to Todmorden by bus saw one thing hidden from them in their normal passage underground, moving here from Lancashire into Yorkshire: the wild and gloomy moorland pass beneath which the tunnel was built.

From the northern end of the tunnel the line begins to fall steadily. The difficulties confronting Stephenson and his assistants here in Yorkshire were different from those they had faced in Lancashire, but not less challenging. The railway had now to descend into the gorge of the Calder: narrow, curvaceous, already occupied by the Rochdale Canal and a main road, together with a series of villages and industrial buildings, among which it was obliged to pick its way. The approach to TODMORDEN, along the hills west of the river, called for two big bridges: one the impressive Gauxholme viaduct over the canal, built on

Two views of Gauxholme viaduct: above right, the iron span over the Rochdale canal with preserved Midland compound 4-4-0 No. 1000 heading a special train, 1985; right, masonry approaches with diesel multiple-unit train, 1985.

the skew, with machicolated turrets flanking a wide iron span; the other on the southern edge of Todmorden itself, a long masonry viaduct with a plainer iron section, again over the canal.[7]

Todmorden was well known for the Fieldens' cotton mills. The railway did not disturb them or the town, running high on a ledge in the hills and then curving over a good stone viaduct, beneath which a small market is held today. Just beyond, a branch goes off on the down side, climbing through the Cliviger Gorge to Burnley and Preston. It was opened in 1849. Having been closed for years to regular passenger traffic, it acquired a service again in 1985.

Three miles beyond Todmorden, at Charlestown, the engineers were confronted by a sandy hill, which proved too unstable to take the tunnel that was to be driven through it. The line was then made to skirt the hill in a cutting, on two reverse curves. A serious accident occurred here in 1912, when a Manchester to Leeds and Bradford express, hauled by one of the Lancashire & Yorkshire company's famous 2-4-2 tank engines, was derailed at speed and four passengers were killed.

The narrowness of the Calder Valley made the siting of stations difficult. Not a stick or stone appears to remain of any of the original structures. Whishaw remarked primly that the wayside stations of the Manchester & Leeds Railway resembled 'so many Elizabethan villas', with 'buildings . . . on a scale of nearly sufficient magnitude for terminal stations'.[8] True, he always pounced with relish on what he thought extravagance; and here he may have had an axe of his own to grind if – as seems likely – he had been removed for some reason as an assistant engineer on this line.[9] What were these stations like, one wonders?

They have all been replaced by later buildings. Each of the four still open from the Summit Tunnel down to Sowerby Bridge (there were originally six) is a curiosity in a different way,[10] largely because of the lack of space on the valley floor. At Todmorden the refreshment room customary at junctions was provided under contract with the railway company on the first floor of the Queen's Hotel, approached from the

platforms by a footbridge. HEBDEN BRIDGE was rebuilt in 1909 and provided with a ramp up to the platforms on one side and a staircase on the other. MYTHOLMROYD was erected partly on a viaduct with the subway connecting the platforms slung beneath one of its arches. The station building is a narrow, very tall structure, with five flights of stairs. These two have both been carefully cleaned and refurbished in recent years, which makes it a pleasure to use or visit them.[11] SOWERBY BRIDGE, now bereft of its Victorian buildings, has declined from a junction to little more than a wayside station.

From Milner Royd Junction, just beyond Sowerby Bridge, the original

Todmorden viaduct, built with nine arches and carrying a diesel multiple-unit train, 1985.

Hebden Bridge station, as restored by British Rail, 1985.

Manchester & Leeds main line (which ran on to Normanton) is disused for passenger traffic for eight miles eastwards. To reach Halifax and Bradford the train turns away on a spur built under Hawkshaw in 1852, crossing the Calder on a long, high viaduct. There is a fine panoramic view of the valley before the train burrows through the short Bankhouse Tunnel and climbs into the hills beyond. At Dryclough Junction it rejoins the original line into Halifax.

The Manchester & Leeds Railway had at first by-passed Halifax, an important textile town, but opened a branch to it in 1844. Laid out by Gooch, this branch faced eastwards down the line, towards Normanton, making it impossible for trains approaching from Sowerby Bridge to gain access to Halifax without reversing. It was to cut off this corner that Hawkshaw's spur was constructed.

Gooch's approach to HALIFAX was (like all approaches to that remarkable place, from any direction) difficult: his line rises on a gradient of 1 in 118, passing through a dramatically narrow rock cutting at Dryclough to a station on the south-western edge of the town. This was as far as the Manchester & Leeds was prepared to go. It refused to extend its line to Bradford, and built a terminus at Halifax, described at the time, perhaps fairly, as a 'filthy dog-hole'.[12]

After much argument between rival projectors, a West Riding Union Railways company was formed and

secured powers in 1846 to continue the line. It then ran into difficulties. Three months after its Act was passed it was amalgamated with the Manchester & Leeds, which was forced to take over the project. Laid out by Hawkshaw, the line was opened to Bradford in 1850. The old 'dog-hole' station was entirely removed and a new Halifax station built in 1855. Part of the main building, designed by William Butterworth, survives, now cleaned. The platforms and their superstructure, with the railway snaking awkwardly through them, were rebuilt in 1886.

The passage on to Bradford was in its own way almost as difficult as the rest of the route, from Littleborough northwards. This line had no gorges to negotiate, but it climbed over two saddles of hills and ended in a steep drop into Bradford. Originally it had seven tunnels, long and short; there are still six. The first of them, Beacon Hill (1,105yd), presents a frowning, castellated face to Halifax. The line then turns east, crossing the Clifton Beck on the Hall Bottom viaduct at a height of 114ft.

In this big work Hawkshaw made use of an uncommon technique, which he had already displayed in the superb Lockwood viaduct between Huddersfield and Penistone. The very tall piers were constructed of 'snecked' rubble, the regular courses of stone being broken to admit, here and there, 'jumper-stones' two or three courses tall. This was an economical practice, allowing the use of blocks of stone

Sir John Hawkshaw, in about 1852.

Halifax station, 1912.

irregular in size, but it was disciplined so as to provide interesting variation rather than crude irregularity.[13] After running on through Wyke Tunnel (1,365yd) the railway suddenly comes out into a strangely empty space, the disused site of what was once the most important junction on the whole of this section: Low Moor.

The name Low Moor was made famous by one of the biggest Yorkshire ironworks, founded in the 1790s and in high Victorian days employing 4,000 men. Low Moor iron was 'known wherever iron of great toughness and tenacity is required'[14] – and that might mean anywhere across the world. The Halifax – Bradford line was joined here by two others from the east, one from Mirfield (Lancashire & Yorkshire), the other from Pudsey (Great Northern). Trains coming up from Manchester were split into two portions at Low Moor, the front one going on to Leeds, the rear one to Bradford. For a long time all trains stopped here for this purpose, but presently the faster ones came to be divided and re-formed at Halifax instead.

The station at Low Moor was closed in 1965. It is now nothing but a grim ghost. Passengers often had long and gloomy waits there for those Leeds and Bradford trains to come up, for until the 1880s the Lancashire & Yorkshire's services were notoriously unpunctual; and they were solaced by no amenities like the billiard room provided by the company for passengers who were similarly delayed at Mirfield.

Turning now due north, the line soon enters Bowling Tunnel (at 1,648yd, the longest on this journey after the Summit Tunnel) and then it falls straight into Bradford for over a mile at 1 in 50, with the Great Northern line from Leeds coming in on the up side at Mill Lane Junction. At first there was another short tunnel here, notoriously foul, underneath the Wakefield Road, as well as a level crossing at Mill Lane.

The railways' arrangements at BRADFORD have been curious almost from the beginning.[15] The first of them to arrive was the Leeds & Bradford (later amalgamated into the Midland Company), which came in from the north via Shipley and was opened in 1846 with a station on Market Street.

Low Moor station, looking towards Halifax, 1962.

The second was the Manchester & Leeds, which established its station a quarter of a mile from the first one, on the opposite side of a valley then being developed as a new commercial district. In 1854 a third line arrived from Leeds, worked by the Great Northern, coming into yet another station inconveniently high up on the southern slope of the valley. Its route from Leeds was four miles shorter, but the Leeds & Bradford still took most of the traffic between the two towns because passengers did not have to climb the hill to the station.

The Great Northern then arranged to make a branch to Mill Lane Junction and to run some of its trains into the Lancashire & Yorkshire station. But that station was too small for its own traffic, let alone the traffic of a second company, and the arrangements for getting trains into and out of it became grotesque. They were described in the late 1870s by E. L. Ahrons, who savoured every twist of their absurdity. He put the usual time taken to get from the station to Low Moor – a distance of three miles – at 22 minutes.[16]

The Lancashire & Yorkshire secured powers to reconstruct and enlarge its station (by now called Exchange) for the use of both companies in 1873. The work took 15 years. It must have seemed an eternity to the railways' customers, but the task was complicated, involving the demolition of a great deal of property and the building of a new goods station as well as one for passengers. When it was at last completed in 1888 the dreadful Wakefield

Road Tunnel had gone, and the station had ten platforms against the old one's four, surmounted by an elegant iron-and-glass roof.

Here was certainly an improvement. But the central weakness in Bradford's railway system remained: the absence of any link between the northern and the southern lines, only a quarter of a mile apart on opposite sides of the valley. The idea of making one was talked about every twenty years from 1846 to 1884, and the Midland Railway actually took powers in 1911 to build a new line from Low Moor (reached from the south by running powers), crossing part of the centre of Bradford on a viaduct to a junction with its old line beyond.

This railway was never built. The proposed viaduct was a hideous structure, beetling low across Forster Square, which would have been greatly disfigured by it. Though a similar plan was examined in the inter-war years, it was rejected as uneconomic. It is never likely to be realised now, unless perhaps as part of some wholly new urban railway.

In the meantime trains to London have to go first to Leeds, where they reverse. Two Inter-City 125 trains run by this route very early in the morning, and a third uncomfortably late at night; there is no through down service what-ever from London until 3.50 in the afternoon. Otherwise, almost all the trains running in and out of Bradford nowadays are two-car diesel units.

Exchange station has been replaced by a very small building on a site close by, suited to the present very modest services. This new station is poky, but it has one great merit. It was planned integrally with a large bus station; the name 'Interchange' it bears is justified. It is the centre of public transport for this city and district, to a greater extent perhaps than any to be found elsewhere in Britain. Here is an admirable example, which surely deserves to be noted and followed in other places too.

If Exchange station has vanished, one piece of the Great Northern Railway's empire still stands here: the handsome Victoria Hotel, which used to face the station forecourt. It was built independently of the railway company in 1867, to the design of architects who did much striking work in Bradford – Lockwood & Mawson. The Great Northern purchased it in 1893, and the hotel remained in railway hands until 1952. It is pleasant to see it still in use, well kept inside and out. In the high days of railway travel it represented for a good many passengers a welcome promise of comfort, much desired at their journey's end.

Bradford Exchange station, 1957, with some of the newly introduced diesel multiple unit trains.

Bradford Interchange, with a diesel multiple unit train at the platform and the bus station in the background, 1981.

Victoria Hotel, Bradford, 1985.

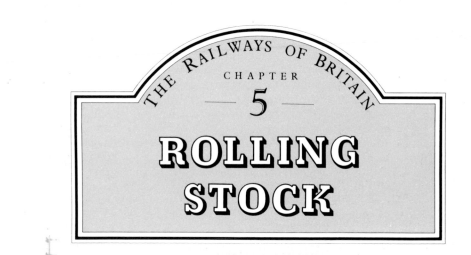

THE RAILWAYS OF BRITAIN

CHAPTER

5

ROLLING STOCK

—— THE EARLY VICTORIAN CARRIAGE ——

The first idea of accommodation for travellers on the railway was naturally based on what had been provided on the road. It was a coach, with wheels of a different pattern to run on rails, and until 1830 it was hauled not by machinery but by horses. The first railway to work passenger traffic in normal service by steam power was the Canterbury & Whitstable. It opened the service (from 4 May 1830), using stationary engines for four miles of the route and a locomotive for the other two. In the following September the Liverpool & Manchester company began operations on a very much bigger scale. Its first-class coaches were exactly like those on the road, though with stronger iron frames, and had names like stage-coaches: *Wellington, The Times, Victory*. The tradition died hard. Several words from the vocabulary of the coaching age survive in use today among passengers and railwaymen: 'coach' itself, for example, 'carriage' and 'guard'.

The earliest surviving passenger coaches in Britain are probably three from the Bodmin & Wadebridge Railway, dating from the 1830s. The first-class vehicle (afterwards altered to a composite first and second) has three compartments, and it is a piece of traditional coach-building with curved side-panels and windows. The second-class carriage is an almost square box, divided into just two compartments; the third-class carriage is no more than a simple open truck.

The railway coach developed in the 1840s and 1850s into something independent of its ancestor. The characteristic vehicle for first and second classes ran on four wheels, had such amenities as oil lighting and spring buffers, and carried its passengers' luggage on the roof. A good example of this kind of coach is one built for the Stockton & Darlington Railway in 1846 and now preserved at York. Some railways were already experimenting with substantially larger vehicles. The Great Western favoured the six-wheeled coach on its broad gauge from the start. Using the greater width available to seat six a side, it was possible to accommodate 72 second-class passengers in a vehicle weighing less than seven tons when empty. The accommodation was very bad – the seats were wooden benches 15in wide, the sides open to the weather. Yet it was better than what was offered on the outside of a stage-coach: at least the passenger had a roof over his head, and he made his journey in half the time, or less, at a lower cost. After 1844 the coaches were entirely enclosed, and glass windows were provided to give light and afford more heat.

Third-class travellers fared worse. At the beginning, on many lines, they occupied open wagons. Not all of these were provided with seats. In the vehicles known as 'Stanhopes',[1] which ran on many lines such as the Manchester & Leeds and the South Staffordshire, the passengers had to stand. Managements showed themselves fully alert to the economies to be gained from this kind of accommodation. In 1840 the directors of the Glasgow Paisley Kilmarnock & Ayr Railway decided that their new third-class carriages should in future be made without seats, and that where seats had been installed they should be removed.[2] In a timetable of 1841 the Great Western stated that 'the goods train passengers will be conveyed in un-covered trucks by the goods trains only'. One such train was involved in an accident at Sonning later that year, and the resulting publicity prompted the Board of Trade to undertake a general inquiry into the provision for third-class passengers on all railways. Its report led to measures in Gladstone's Act of 1844 which were effective in improving third-class travel (see p. 22).

Previous page: freight wagons stand in the busy shunting yard north of the station at Wellingborough in the early 1900s. This was a key point on the Midland Railway's system: it was half-way between London and the coalfields of Nottinghamshire and Derbyshire, and provided the junction for a line to Northampton. A large running shed was maintained to accommodate the coal trains, which usually changed engines there.

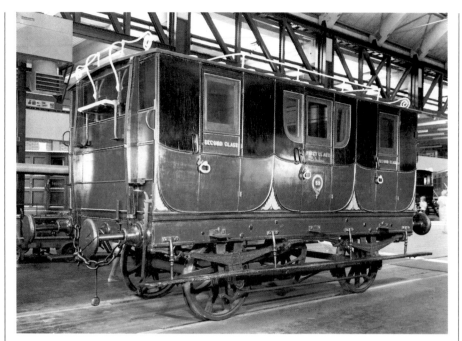

This early railway carriage from the Stockton & Darlington Railway dates from 1846 and is preserved in the National Railway Museum at York. Its curved side-panels clearly reflect the traditional design of the stage-coach, but the iron underframe and wheels are entirely of the railway. The roof, designed to take luggage strapped within its rails, provided no seats for passengers, as the stage-coaches did. The contrast between the first-class compartment in the centre and the second-class ones that flank it is marked: the first-class is much bigger and provides more light.

Although it cannot be said to have become a comfortable business until the last quarter of the 19th century (and on some lines it remained uncomfortable well into the 20th), at least the railways were now obliged to treat third-class passengers as human beings and not as merchandise. Some companies, including the Edinburgh & Glasgow and the Great Northern in Lincolnshire, now offered fourth-class travel at rates below the 1d a mile prescribed in the Act. For such passengers, and for excursionists, open wagons would do well enough. On the Sheffield Ashton & Manchester Railway the first cattle trucks, ordered in 1845, were 'to be fitted with spring buffers and drawbars, to answer occasionally for passengers'.[3]

Except for a small number of iron coaches built for the Great Western and Vale of Neath companies from 1845 onwards, all early coaches were constructed of wood and ran on open wagon wheels with spokes. In 1848 Richard Mansell, carriage superintendent of the South Eastern Railway, patented a wheel with a solid centre made up of wooden segments enclosed within an iron, or later steel, tyre. Wheels of this kind became accepted for use on most passenger vehicles within the next two decades. Otherwise the very light four- or six-wheeled vehicle remained the standard type on most railways.

Some interesting experiments were conducted, however, with more elaborate carriages running on eight wheels. In Britain the first eight-wheel vehicle was a freak built by the Liverpool & Manchester Railway for the Duke of Wellington on the occasion of the opening of the line in 1830; the second, the royal saloon built by the Great Western in 1840, was used by Queen Victoria on her first railway journey two years later. During the 1840s the coach resting on two four-wheel bogies became the accepted standard in the USA, because on the light, uneven and sharply curved American track only swivelling bogies could hope to keep the rails. In Britain, where the track was much better, the need for the bogie was not so great. Nevertheless, Joseph Wright and W. B. Adams both played with the idea, and in 1852 the Great Western built six eight-wheeled coaches for its express trains between London and Birmingham. The railwaymen dubbed them 'Long Charleys'. Though they did not rest, strictly speaking, on bogies, the wheels were given some lateral play. In 1863 they were sent to work on the Metropolitan Railway.

—— THE CARRIAGE, 1870-1914 ——

The trend towards greater sophistication in carriage design accelerated in the 1870s, producing a new generation of passenger vehicles which owed much to Continental and American practice and offered previously undreamed of comforts and facilities for all classes of railway traveller, especially the third. Several companies – the little narrow-gauge Festiniog in North Wales, the Great Northern, the Great Western, the Midland – began almost simultaneously to try bogie vehicles between 1873 and 1875. For the opening of the Settle & Carlisle line in 1876, the Midland built some striking coaches with bogies of six wheels instead of four. Other new coaches appeared at about the same time. The general manager of the Midland, James Allport, had just toured the railways of the USA. On his return, he persuaded the company to adopt the Pullman car. Introduced in 1874, this took two forms: the parlour car for day use and the sleeping car, with the berths placed in pairs one above the other and running the length of the vehicle. Both ran on four-wheeled bogies, as in the USA.

These Midland Pullmans were not, however, the first sleeping carriages of any kind to run in Britain. Apart from some special vehicles built for royalty, 'bed-carriages' had made their appearance on the London & Birmingham Railway as early as 1838, and continued to be built for its successor the London & North Western for over thirty years; and the North British and the London & North Western both built small six-wheeled sleeping cars in 1873. These were among the first vehicles in Britain to provide lavatories for the passengers. Carriages so equipped had already been built in Britain, but only for use abroad. One made in 1869, by the Midland Carriage & Wagon Company of Birmingham for Denmark, is to be seen in the Danish Railway Museum at Odense. In Britain they did not become common even on long-distance trains until the late 1880s.

Although the Midland Pullmans were not an unqualified success, they helped to popularise a number of most desirable improvements in British

At some time in the 1880s a Midland Pullman sleeping car waits in the trainshed at St Pancras station to be attached to a train; generally only one car was used per train. Imported as kits from the USA, and assembled at the Derby works under licence, Pullman sleeping and dining cars were first used in Britain by the Midland Railway in the 1870s. They were staffed separately by British employees of the Pullman Company, and passengers paid a supplement on top of the first-class fare to use them. The Midland also bought outright from Pullman 'day parlour cars', which it renamed with the more English title of 'drawing room cars' and equipped with individual, swivelling armchairs.

The Pullman car Glencoe was a typically luxurious example of the 'parlour cars' made in Britain under licence from the Pullman Company – this one was built in January 1914 by Cravens Ltd. of Sheffield for the South Eastern & Chatham Railway. During the First World War it was used, along with three others, to convey the king, the prime minister and high-ranking cabinet ministers. It was withdrawn from service in 1955.

carriage design. They were well ventilated; they were heated. The only heat ordinarily provided in British railway carriages hitherto had come from 'footwarmers', tins filled with hot water or, later, with acetate of soda. On the Great Western these were made available for first-class passengers in 1856; the second class got them in 1870; the third class not till 1873. A mid-Victorian journey from London to Wales or Scotland could still be formidably unpleasant in winter. The Lancashire & Yorkshire Railway did not provide even this kind of heating for third-class passengers until 1891.[4]

The Pullman cars also offered better lighting than had been provided in the past, from large paraffin lamps with Argand burners. Just at this time a German, Josef Pintsch, invented a system of oil-gas lighting, which was adopted on the Metropolitan and Great Eastern Railways between 1876 and 1878. Shortly afterwards the London Brighton & South Coast company led the world in a new development: in October 1881 the Pullman car *Beatrice*,

MIDLAND HOTEL
AND
REFRESHMENT ROOMS.
DERBY.
NOTICE.

On and after MARCH 1st, 1875,

LUNCHEON BASKETS

Will be provided at the DERBY STATION, at
the following charges:—

No. 1, containing Half-a-Chicken, with
Ham or Tongue, Salad, Bread, Cheese,
Butter, &c., and a Half-Bottle of Claret
or Burgundy. -   **3s.**

No. 2, containing Veal and Ham Pie, with
Salad, Bread, Cheese, Butter, &c., and
a Bottle of Stout. -   **2s.**

The Baskets will be fitted with the necessary appointments,
which it is earnestly requested may be replaced in their proper
position, and the Baskets handed to one of the Company's Servants
that they may be returned to DERBY.

WILLIAM TOWLE,
Midland Hotel, Derby

A Midland Railway notice at Derby proclaims the beginning of a new service for passengers in 1875: luncheon-baskets to be taken on to the train. Their contents may often have been dull and rather dry, but they probably provided a more satisfactory meal than one snatched during a brief dining-stop at Swindon, Normanton or York. The reputation of British railway refreshment rooms was poor: Trollope called the railway sandwich 'the real disgrace of England'. The Midland, however, was considered by many passengers to be the best company in terms of catering, its food and hotels being ably administered by William Towle.

running on that railway, was equipped with electric light drawn from a battery installed in the frame. Though the experiment was not wholly successful, the company's locomotive engineer, William Stroudley, thought it worthwhile to equip four more Pullmans on the same system before the year was out; and in 1883 he began to fit a similar installation into some of the ordinary Brighton trains. This example was imitated in Scotland. From 1886 onwards the North British fitted electric light, from current picked up on a rail in the track, to the trains on its Glasgow City & District line.

One further amenity for passengers appeared at this time: the dining car. The notion of supplying food to the traveller *en route* was not a new one. As early as 1845 an abortive proposal was put forward for a 'railway restaurant'.[5] Ten years later W. B. Adams, one of the most creative of railway inventors, remarked: 'For long journeys it is essential to avoid stoppages; yet it is essential to obtain refreshment. To devour refreshment hurriedly, as is now done at stopping stations, is not to be refreshed, but to be made ill. A free passage through the train would facilitate all this'.[6] His plea went unnoticed. In the mid-1860s Dickens commended the luncheon baskets available to railway travellers in France.[7] Spiers & Pond are said to have offered something of the kind in Britain in 1871; the railway companies themselves did not do so until 1875 and 1876, first at Derby and then at Chester.[8] By that time the energetic Midland company had served a meal on a train, to a party it took from St Pancras to Bedford and back to demonstrate the new Pullman cars in 1874. This was, however, a special stunt, and the food was not cooked on board. The distinction of running the first dining car in Britain in regular public service belongs to the Great Northern Railway, which introduced one between London and Leeds in 1879. The example was not followed quickly. Dining cars appeared on the Midland in 1882 and on the London & North Western in 1889, for first-class passengers only. The Great Eastern was the first company to serve third-class passengers, in the dining car it put on to its North Country boat train between York and Harwich in 1891.

That Great Eastern train is historically important in another way also.

At the Midland Railway's Derby station in 1908, a railwayman stands ready with a refreshment trolley. Food and drink were sold to passengers while the train was waiting in the station.

Its designer James Holden recognised, like Adams, that the dining car should be made accessible from the train. Otherwise the only passengers who could take meals would be those who entered the car at the start of the journey or at an intermediate station at which the train stopped. His dining car was therefore joined to two other vehicles, one on each side, by a corridor. The 'dining saloon' for first- and second-class passengers, together with a third-class dining compartment, gave 24 places; some fifty seats were available in the two flanking coaches. All these vehicles were six-wheelers; the Great Eastern did not adopt the bogie until 1897.

The provision of a corridor through these three coaches was taken to its logical conclusion by the Great Western very shortly afterwards. In 1892 it put into service between Paddington and Birkenhead the first train in Britain with corridors throughout. When the company introduced dining cars in 1896 it confined their use strictly to first-class passengers: a rule that was only gradually relaxed from 1900 onwards. The train of 1892 was also among the earliest in Britain to be heated throughout by steam, supplied from the locomotive.[9]

The combined influence of these examples induced the companies responsible for the Anglo-Scottish services to build some rolling-stock on the corridor principle, with dining cars, for service in 1893. One of these, the 2pm from Euston to Glasgow, became known as 'The Corridor', and that name stuck to it among railwaymen, who rightly ignored the fatuous title it came to bear officially in 1937, 'The Midday Scot'. What is a midday Scot, anyway?

These were important new amenities for the traveller, but they presented difficult problems for the management of the companies. They added greatly to the weight of the train that the locomotive had to haul. The

By the first decade of the 20th century, dining cars had become a well-known feature of most companies' rolling-stock, but the service they provided was not cheap. This luxuriously appointed Lancashire & Yorkshire dining car of 1909 ran on 12 wheels for extra comfort and smoothness, featured a built-in kitchen at one end, an electric fan and electric lighting; seating only twenty customers, it was costly both to build and to haul.

inclusion of a dining car, serving meals to passengers in other coaches, added nothing to the total carrying capacity of the train, while the provision of a corridor meant the sacrifice of two seats in every compartment. The West Coast Scotch express of 1893 weighed 252 tons empty and accommodated fewer than 200 passengers. For every passenger in a full train, one and a quarter tons of rolling-stock had thus to be hauled by the locomotive, whereas in the Great Western second-class carriages of the 1840s ten people were conveyed for every ton of dead weight. Many companies decided in 1893 to restrict second-class provision, or to abolish it altogether – that, at least, reduced the varieties of accommodation that had to be provided. It is no coincidence that notably bigger locomotives made their appearance at this time.

Not all the improvements came quickly into general use. No carriages were heated by steam on the South Eastern & Chatham Railway until 1903 – despite the fact that it was the principal conveyer of passengers to and from the Continent, where such heating was generally provided on main-line trains. While a number of the smaller companies – such as the London Tilbury & Southend, the North Staffordshire and the Great North of Scotland – moved straight from oil to electricity for lighting, others clung to gas, until a series of accidents occurred. It was shown beyond question that gas was responsible for starting fires after collisions on the London & South Western at Clapham Junction in 1896, on the Midland at Hawes in 1910 and at Aisgill three years later. Nevertheless, by 1900 the British express train as we know it had emerged. Its decoration may look ornate to us, with the liberal use of lincrusta and brass, the seats with opulent curves and buttoned backs. But the vehicles were not less comfortable than their modern successors, and the dining and sleeping cars running on 12 wheels rode better than those built today on eight. Some splendid examples of the railway coach-builder's art in the early 20th century have been preserved and well restored, among them the dining car built for the joint use of the Midland and Glasgow & South Western Railways in 1914.

—— SUBURBAN CARRIAGES ——

If we compare conditions of travel today with those in the late Victorian period, the really remarkable change in standards has occurred on short-distance and suburban trains. Many of the vehicles used on them years ago were indescribably uncomfortable: almost universally four- or six-wheelers, offering the minimum of space to the passenger. Among the last survivors of such trains were the sets of close-coupled carriages that ran on the North London Railway – which never owned a vehicle with more than four wheels. Carriages of this description were being built for the Broad St – Richmond line as late as 1910. In 1916 the line was taken over by the London & North Western and converted to electric traction: it would be hard to imagine a greater contrast than that between the hard, rigid, antiquated four-wheelers (with wooden seats in the third class) and the magnificent LNWR electric trains that succeeded them. On other North London lines, however, the four-wheelers continued in service, the last of them until the Second World War. Similar antiques were to be found elsewhere in the 1930s – on the Great Western branches in Herefordshire, for instance, where they bore equally antique advertisements to encourage the purchase of 'bottles of claret, price one shilling' from stationmasters. I can remember making the four-hour cross-country express journey from Reedham in Norfolk to Lincoln in a six-wheeler in 1932.

Another solution to the problem of moving large numbers of people over short distances as economically as possible was provided by the railcar, the locomotive built into a large carriage that was capable of hauling a trailer as well. Experiments of this kind began in the 1840s; but they were carried out on a large scale only from 1903 onwards. In that year the London & South Western company produced a steam-driven railcar for use on the Fratton and East Southsea line, where competition from the newly electrified Portsmouth trams was very keen. It was followed by a fair number of similar vehicles, notably on the Great Western, which used them extensively, for example on the Stroud Valley line in Gloucestershire. Their vogue was, however, short, and within twenty years most of them had disappeared. The type has been revived with great success in recent years in the form of the diesel railcar, a very much more powerful and flexible machine.

The gradual improvement of suburban rolling-stock, operated by steam locomotives, was well exemplified on the Great Eastern: a railway that vied with the London & South Western for the distinction of working the densest traffic into and out of a single London terminus. The first objective was that all trains should accommodate the utmost number of people, and in 1899 James Holden introduced a set of 15 six-wheeled vehicles, entirely third-class, seating six passengers a side, making 828 in all. Next year he followed this up with a similar train, for all three classes, consisting of eight coaches on bogies of four and six wheels. The second train was heavier than the first, and its design was not imitated subsequently. Instead, the Great Eastern stuck to the old small carriages and continued to build them in large numbers until 1911, when a new and more economical set of bogie coaches appeared. This then became the standard pattern; and from 1915 onwards the bodies of the old four-wheeled carriages were made up in pairs to form new vehicles resting on bogies.

In 1920 the whole service was reorganised to cope with continually increasing traffic: between 5 and 6 o'clock in the evening, 11 passengers were presenting themselves at Liverpool Street every second. It was asserted by the company that this represented 'The Last Word in Steam-

A crowd of city workers, homeward-bound after the week's work, board a train at Liverpool Street station one Saturday afternoon in 1910. A few women are discernible in the sea of men. The Great Eastern's four-wheeled close-coupled carriages were exceedingly uncomfortable, but the journeys out to the eastern suburbs of London were short. The trains were smartly managed and, as a rule, admirably punctual.

Operated Suburban Train Services'. That was true. Yet the slogan was double-edged: for, as suburban travel continued to grow relentlessly, it became clearer and clearer that the only possible answer was to abandon steam altogether and turn to electric traction. Moreover, the continual need to economise on space meant that the second- and third-class compartments were uncomfortably narrow. In the 1920s and 1930s the Liverpool Street commuter looked with increasing envy at his fellows who were beginning to taste the advantages of electrification on the Southern lines.

In steam days the rolling-stock provided by the South Eastern & Chatham and the London Brighton & South Coast on their suburban services was dreary and often dilapidated. Ahrons wrote an inimitable description of the South Eastern trains in the late 19th century: 'The best view of one of these travelling panoramas was to be obtained from the end of one of the Brighton platforms at London Bridge. . . . The trains . . . were formed of coaches of so many varying heights, they seemed to give the impression of moving castellated walls. . . . [The interior of the third-class carriages] took the form of a cheerless bare rectangular box with hard wooden seats and "half-way" partitions separating the compartments. The partitions were so low that when the passenger sat down with his back to one of them, his head nearly collided with the back hair and best hat of the female in the next compartment. The carriage floor was constructed on the atmospheric principle, and when the train was moving a violent gale frequently raged in those latitudes which lay below the seats. There were usually two oil lamps of about half candle-power to each carriage, and as there were four compartments, the allowance of light was 0·5 lamp per compartment.'[10]

The Brighton company began to reform when its electrification began in 1909; but the main task had to be tackled by the Southern Railway after 1923. It was out of the question, for financial reasons, to build entirely new stock. Some fifty new three-coach sets were built in 1925; for the rest, old coaches were amalgamated in pairs to run on bogies and were fitted with motors. It was not until 1932, with the first stage of electrification to Brighton, that rolling-stock of a genuinely new design (incorporating lavatories) was built, and conversion of old 'steam' stock continued up to 1936. Much of this converted stock ran until quite recently; and it is curious to think of the long history of these vehicles' bodies. Once, under Queen Victoria, they were hauled painfully along by staggering tank engines. Now they were clattering down the bank from Forest Hill at 50 mph, carrying their passengers in conditions of comfort unimaginable to the Victorian commuter: seats sprung and upholstered, compartments warmed in winter and lighted adequately by electricity. And all this for the equivalent of Victorian third-class fares!

The rolling-stock available to the passenger on the main-line slow trains and the branch lines also improved. That was largely because, as new coaches were built for express traffic, the old ones displaced by them made their way on to the secondary services; the Southern Railway in its quarter century of life never built a single new 'steam' coach except for express trains. But much good rolling-stock was designed by other companies for secondary services such as these: especially the type of coach with a side corridor giving access to lavatories but no gangway from one coach to the next. Fine vehicles of this kind were built by the North British Railway for the opening of the West Highland line to Fort William in 1894. Communication throughout the length of the train was not needed, since no dining car was put into service on that line for another 35 years; the passengers

This composite carriage, built for the Great North of Scotland Railway and seen here at Boat of Garten in its London & North Eastern Railway days, has a lavatory at each end, one each for the first and third class, with frosted glass windows. The lavatories were accessible to all passengers via an internal corridor, but there was no connection between the carriages; Scottish companies rarely built trains with full corridor linking.

were well catered for by breakfast baskets at Arrochar and by full meals served during the waiting of trains at Crianlarich. Scottish railways in general had little to do with corridor carriages, except on a few long-distance services, such as those from Aberdeen to Glasgow. The Caledonian and Glasgow & South Western companies both built sets of non-corridor 12-wheelers for their rival services to the Clyde Coast. The Glasgow & South Western coaches were 70ft in length, among the longest passenger vehicles built in Britain at that time.

—— THE CARRIAGE SINCE 1923 ——

Apart from the electric stock of the Southern Railway, no striking new passenger carriages were produced by any of the four great companies created by the Railways Act of 1921. All four companies developed the use of the open coach, with the corridor down the centre, for third-class passengers. The London Midland & Scottish and London & North Eastern companies regarded these vehicles as excursion stock, for they accommodated four passengers in a row, two on each side of the gangway, whilst as a general rule the northern companies provided space for third-class passengers to travel three-a-side, with arm-rests, so blunting the distinction between third and first class. The Great Western and the Southern, on the other hand, continued to offer four-a-side accommodation in the third class and three-a-side in the first. This distinction was also accepted by British Railways, which built two versions of the same stock, one for service on the northern lines, the other on the southern. Ultimately, however, the southern companies' practice prevailed.

The London & North Eastern Railway, under Sir Nigel Gresley's direction, made a number of innovations. It developed articulated sets of vehicles, close-coupled and mounted on bogies that supported the ends of two neighbouring coaches – a practice that substantially reduced the dead weight of a train, but was inconvenient when one vehicle developed a defect and put the whole set out of service. But reduction of weight was an urgent necessity in the 1930s as coaches continued to grow heavier and the number of passengers they carried grew smaller. The standard Great Western coach of that period seated 64 third-class passengers and weighed just under 33 tons; the typical London Midland & Scottish or London & North Eastern coach, weighing a trifle more, seated only 42. The principal expresses out of King's Cross were frequently made up to 18 coaches weighing some 600 tons, and the bill for coal and for more powerful locomotives was correspondingly increased.

The nationalised railways soon began to reverse this tendency. Their standard coach for the northern lines, introduced in 1951, had eight compartments instead of seven, so seating 48 passengers – a gain of six. In common with most Continental railways, British Railways turned 'third class' into 'second class' in 1956. Four-a-side open coaches of the southern type were introduced in large numbers even on the northern lines, and the average express train came to have no more than 12 coaches.

The 1951 carriage was no different, except in details, from pre-war designs. Some cautious experiments were made with new patterns and arrangements from 1957 onwards, but it was not until 1964 that something really different began to emerge. The old compartment and corridor design was discontinued. The open coach took its place. From the passenger's point of view the change was most marked in two ways: the suspension was improved and the spacious new interiors were air-conditioned. There was good evidence that dislike of the older vehicles had been causing passengers to desert the railways, a trend that became especially serious as the conditions of long-distance car driving improved in the 1960s. Now the railways had something substantial to offer in the way of new comfort. In the exceptionally hot summers of 1975 and 1976 an air-conditioned train was one of the few cool public places to be found easily in city centres.

The coaches on the High Speed Trains and the unfortunate Advanced Passenger Trains were based on these designs. Early in the 1980s a re-arrangement of second-class accommodation began, to provide more seats by reducing the space available to the passenger, and a new type of sleeping car, based largely on these day coaches, went into service in 1982. Special attention was paid to the reduction of noise and to fire precautions, which had been reviewed carefully after an accident to a night express at Taunton in 1978. These new cars were widely advertised. They were an effective instrument in the hands of the railways in their continual struggle for long-distance traffic against the airlines.

—— FREIGHT VEHICLES ——

The evolution of railway vehicles for goods traffic in Britain has been little studied.[11] Until quite recently the majority of British goods vehicles showed hardly any sign of evolution. Britain was unique in clinging to the open wagon, which represented no more than a minor modification of the colliery wagons that ran on railways before ever the first locomotive appeared.

The first wagons used on the modern railway were of two types: the chaldron (for coal) and the flat truck. The chaldron wagon was so called because it was designed to carry one imperial chaldron, or 2 tons 13 cwt, of coal. The upper part of the sides usually tapered outwards. Such wagons continued in use, even on great railways, until late in the 19th century: in 1872 nearly two thirds of the mineral wagons in use on the North Eastern Railway were of this type, without springs or buffers.[12] The flat trucks were intended for any kind of merchandise that could be lashed securely to them under tarpaulins.

Very early, however, a third variant appeared, which was the direct ancestor of the standard open wagon; it had straight sides high enough to hold its contents in securely. A number of such vehicles are illustrated by Whishaw about 1840, of which the one running on the Birmingham &

In a print of 1773, a chaldron wagon waits to be unloaded at a riverside near Newcastle. The horse has hauled it down from the colliery, and is now tethered behind it. This type of wagon was in common use on the early railways of Tyneside before mechanical traction was introduced. Modern wagons of the chaldron pattern still have the same open-topped, sloping-sided design.

Gloucester Railway may be taken as typical. It was 10ft 3in long and 7ft 9in wide; the sides were 3ft 5in high. The Great Western, on its broad gauge, was unusual in favouring six-wheeled open wagons. Many of them were built of iron instead of timber. They had a capacity of nine tons, against the six tons of the broad-gauge wagons on four wheels, and they cost about a third as much again to build. Gooch described them in 1845 as 'probably the most economical we have for carrying loads'.[13]

In the 1830s and 1840s the companies differed widely in their practice concerning the ownership of wagons. Some, like the Ardrossan & Johnstone and the Durham & Sunderland, owned no wagons whatever – all those used on their lines were the property of private owners. The Leicester & Swannington built sixty wagons for itself in 1832 and then sold them, at a considerable loss, to the colliery owners two years later. The Garnkirk & Glasgow hired out wagons to its customers at 3s a week; the Newcastle & Carlisle itself hired chaldron wagons and then sub-let them.[14]

Most railway companies accepted wagons owned by industrial and commercial concerns, charging merely for their haulage, and this practice continued until the problem of private owners' wagons – many of them badly constructed and maintained – became extremely troublesome. In 1875 the Midland company embarked on a policy of purchasing them from their owners,[15] and the Caledonian subsequently did the same; but neither was able to carry it through to completion.

As early as the 1850s D. K. Clark was urging that a railway's wagons should be made as near as possible to a standard pattern: 'Whatever may be the upper works, the underframes of the whole wagon stock, like those of the carriages, should be entirely uniform.'[16] It was a counsel of perfection. Though the general design of all wagons might be similar, in detail it differed from one railway company, and one owner, to the next. As most wagons ran from one railway to another up and down the country, the supervision and maintenance of such a heterogeneous collection of vehicles was no easy matter.

Other sorts of wagon had by now come to be designed – the covered wagon, for instance, for merchandise that could not safely be exposed to the elements, and the flat timber wagon with iron stanchions, which – except that it became longer and ran on bogies – altered little in a hundred years.

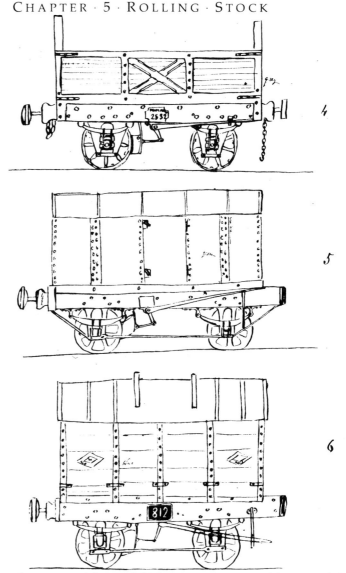

These sketches of wagons were made in about 1848 by E. T. Lane, a sharp-eyed pupil engineer still in his teens. The top one is an open 'tilt' wagon, with high ends to which a bar could be attached to support the tilt, or awning. The other two are covered by curving roofs. Each has its own hand-brake.

The standard cattle wagon of the mid-20th century was very like that of the mid-19th. There was some variety of design here, however: the Glasgow & South Western Railway denied roofs to the cattle in the 1870s, whereas the Highland went in for a 'valuable cattle wagon' with a roof and for double-decker vehicles for sheep.[17] Many kinds of more specialised wagons were built, for ballast and bicycles and bullion, for gunpowder and corpses.

Some early efforts were made to develop the use of wagons of large capacity, in order to reduce the tonnage of dead weight. The Caledonian company experimented with a thirty-ton wagon in 1858. The Great Western turned out four twenty-ton wagons, running on six wheels, in 1871; and in 1888 J. L. Wilkinson, who had become the company's chief goods manager after serving on the Buenos Aires & Pacific Railway, persuaded his directors to allow him to build a 25-ton open wagon on bogies. But it proved difficult to get satisfactory loads to make the use of so large a vehicle economic. The ordinary ten-ton wagon, which by then had become the standard on the Great Western and many other British railways, was still perfectly adequate for general merchandise traffic. But it was possible to handle coal, especially

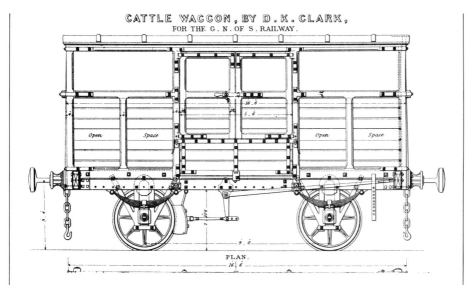

CATTLE WAGGON, BY D. K. CLARK,
FOR THE G. N. OF S. RAILWAY.

This cattle wagon was designed for the Great North of Scotland Railway in the early 1850s. A type of vehicle that reached its standard form very early, it remained essentially unchanged for the next hundred years.

Private-owner wagons full of coal cram the sidings at Goole Docks in about 1910, ready to be unloaded into ships bound for London, the Baltic and elsewhere. Goole Docks, owned by the Aire & Calder Navigation Company, were used by the Lancashire & Yorkshire Railway to handle the coal it carried from the mines of South and West Yorkshire. The wagons remained the property of the collieries whose names were painted on the side. Coal still produces revenue for the railways, but in different ways. Private-owner wagons are now a thing of the past and Goole Docks are in sad decline.

for the use of the companies' own locomotives, in larger loads – and several railways, such as the Caledonian, the North Eastern and the Great Western, built large steel wagons with capacities of up to forty tons at about the turn of the century.[18]

At the same time a start was made in tackling a much larger problem. Continuous brakes were now coming to be accepted for all passenger trains, but only after a long struggle and much argument (see p. 195). There was no question of extending them to goods trains, on which braking was still of the simplest design. Each wagon had its own brake, which could be applied by hand in shunting operations or if the train stood still before descending an incline. The engine in the front had brakes and could slow the train up gradually by its own weight; a brake van was marshalled in the rear, controlled by a guard. On steep inclines, catch-points were installed to derail any wagon that ran backwards if its coupling broke. But that was all. Under such conditions it was impossible to contemplate any really fast freight running. Indeed it is a wonder that there were regular express goods

Two remote control 'merry-go-round' trains on parallel tracks carry coal into Eggborough Power Station, near Pontefract, West Yorkshire. When the wagons pass under the bunker (background), automatic doors in the wagon floors open and discharge the coal directly on to a conveyor belt which runs beneath the train, comes up from underground and passes overhead, taking the coal into the power station inside the sloping covered way. The empty wagons return to the colliery where they are filled automatically with another consignment, the train being kept at a constant speed of 4mph by a slow-running mechanism.

trains at all – and that they ran in safety. To take a train of 26 wagons from Camden to Stockport or from Paddington to Exeter at a speed of over 30 mph, with brakes so inadequate, was a stout achievement.[19]

As the speed of passenger trains increased towards the end of the 19th century, the slow goods trains became more and more troublesome. The Midland company resigned itself to the nuisance, and on those sections of its line where there were four tracks it segregated goods rigidly from passenger traffic: a logical arrangement, but one that was attended with numerous inconveniences in working. The only satisfactory solution in the long run was to make the goods trains move faster, and this could not be achieved unless they were fitted with continuous brakes. It was a dauntingly expensive operation for the companies to undertake on their own wagons, and quite out of the question for the private owners. All that could be done was to fit the brakes to just a selection of the wagons regularly in use in express service. The Great Western embarked on this policy in 1903; other great companies also cautiously adopted it, as did their successors formed under the Railways Act of 1921. But progress was desperately slow. At nationalisation the British Transport Commission took over the private owners' wagons, and about two fifths of them were quickly scrapped. The Commission could then realistically contemplate the great task that had proved beyond the powers and resources of its predecessors.

The fitting of continuous brakes to all goods vehicles became an important object of policy, expounded in the Modernisation Plan of 1955: 'Great Britain is the only major industrial nation in which a large proportion of the freight traffic on the railways is still carried in loose-coupled wagons not fitted with continuous brakes. The absence of continuous brakes on freight trains necessitates slow timings and, consequently, undue occupation of the track. The additional headway required by the faster-moving trains introduces a further serious source of delay to the slower-moving loose-coupled trains. As a result, not only are the running times of the latter unduly protracted, but the trains have to be set aside in refuge sidings or running loops awaiting a margin to precede a faster-timed train.

'The chief advantages of fitting continuous brakes are increased line capacity for all services, passenger and freight, because of more uniform speeds; better transit times for freight traffic; improved punctuality; and greater safety in train movement.' The cost of this great measure was reckoned at £75 million. By the end of 1959 nearly a third of British Railways' stock of 945,250 wagons had been fitted with continuous brakes.

The standard open wagons of British Rail today, for the conveyance of coal or road-stone, are built of steel. They are a good deal larger than most of those owned by the old private companies, with capacity ranging from 16 tons upwards. The old pick-up goods train, stopping to shunt single wagons at wayside stations, is dead, like many of the stations themselves, with their sidings and little yards. The basis of those trains was a very miscellaneous traffic, often in small consignments, and the railways carried much of it in specially designed vehicles. Now they have given up conveying cattle and fish and fruit, whether in goods or in passenger trains. Their milk traffic, once so important (see p. 234), was finally discontinued in 1980. The specialised vehicles required today are of very different kinds: flat wagons for carrying containers, tanks for oil and chemicals. As far as possible they run in trains made up in fixed formations. They travel briskly over long distances without stopping, controlled by continuous brakes. They are trains of an entirely different species from the goods trains of the Victorian age.

The lion rampant and wheel, photographed on a tender at Battersea in 1957, was first used with the new green livery of British Railways on nationalisation. A more elaborate totem including a crown had appeared for use on carriages in 1956. Variations on this regal theme lasted until 1966, when the double arrow logo was introduced.

A train of oil tankers near Milford Haven oil terminal in 1968 exemplifies the new type of freight business developed by the railways since the Second World War. The wagons were built to Gulf specifications by British Rail but, unlike the old private-owner wagons, they are railway owned as well as railway operated. As many as 25 or 30 wagons might be included in one train, providing a carrying capacity in keeping with the modern requirements of a port like Milford Haven, whose deep-water channel can take tanker ships of up to 250,000 tons.

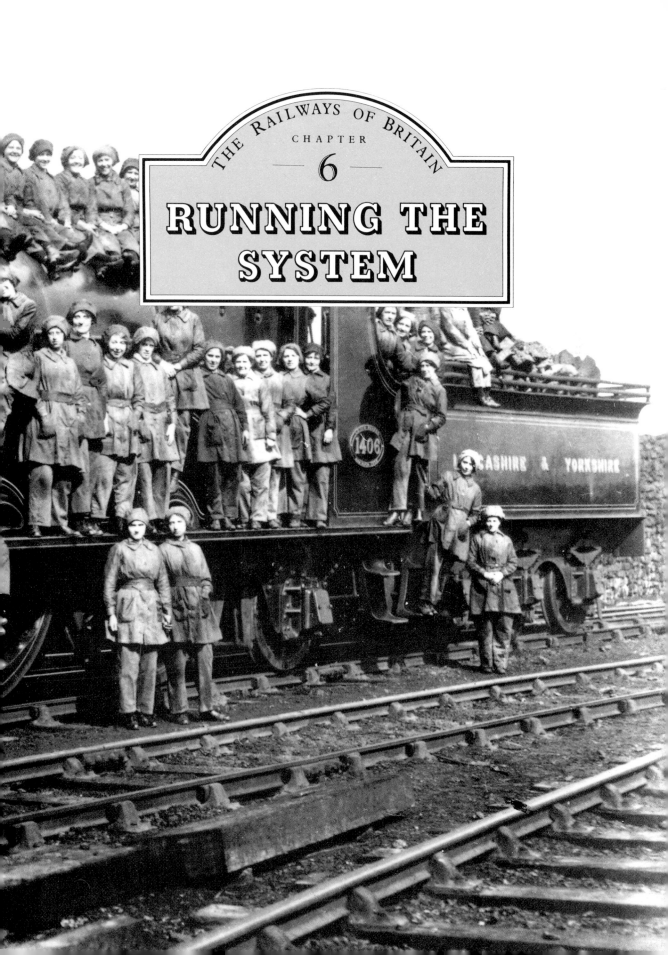

RUNNING THE SYSTEM

Previous page: ranks of women engine cleaners, hired to replace men fighting in the First World War, pose with an example of their handiwork at Low Moor engine shed, near Bradford. The engine, No. 1406 of the Lancashire & Yorkshire Railway, is an Aspinall 4-4-2, known as a 'Highflier' on account of its large driving wheels and high speed.

These three types of early signal were all in use by 1842, when Francis Whishaw published the second edition of his Railways of Great Britain and Ireland, *from which the drawings are taken. The one on the left has a projection marked 'red flag' (probably a painted board) to indicate danger; it was turned through ninety degrees to indicate 'all clear'. The other two are night signals: the central one consists of a lamp only, the one on the right comprises a lamp on a tripod at a junction (the arrow indicates the direction in which the train was permitted to travel). The left and right signals were on the Liverpool & Manchester Railway, and the central one on the Leigh & Kenyon line, which joined it.*

railway, with its own track, vehicles, locomotives, buildings and other fixed equipment, is an immensely complex mechanism. It relies for its daily operation on a large body of employees, all of whom must be supplied with suitable machinery and properly trained to use it if the passengers and goods entrusted to their care are to be carried safely and efficiently. Over the past 150 years the railway service in Britain has built up a reservoir of human and mechanical experience that can be observed both in the old *esprit de corps* that is still to be discerned among railwaymen and in the many relics of past operating practice ranging from early semaphore signals on branch lines to more incidental, but no less interesting, items of equipment, such as station signs and redundant water towers.

The most important requirement governing the operation of a railway is to ensure its safety, and that requires an adequate system of signalling and traffic control. The earliest signalling was by motions of the hand and by flag, without fixed equipment of any kind.[1] The first fixed signals seem to have been installed on the Liverpool & Manchester Railway in 1834; they consisted of boards on pivots which were turned at right angles to the track to stop an approaching train. The traffic was operated on a basis of fixed time intervals, and the signal remained at 'danger' for five minutes after a train had passed. Provided the rules framed by the companies for the safe working of trains were exactly obeyed, and provided the traffic was light and its operation uncomplicated by junctions, such a simple plan worked well enough. It was not long, however, before more elaborate arrangements became necessary. When the London & Croydon Railway was opened in 1839, it formed one of the first railway junctions that could truly be called busy where it branched off from the London & Greenwich at Corbett's Lane, one and three quarter miles south east of London Bridge. Disc signals were adopted here, worked by a pointsman from a sort of lighthouse that may claim to be the earliest of all signal boxes. The disc was painted red and indicated 'stop' when it was at right angles to the line. When it disappeared from the driver's view through being turned parallel with the line, the train was free to proceed. At night it showed a red light for 'stop', and a white one for 'go'.

After one or two experiments of another kind, the Great Western Railway adopted an improved version of this type of signal early in 1841. A disc, denoting 'go', was placed at right angles to a crossbar, which indicated 'stop'. This represented an improvement on the previous signals in that it gave a positive indication for 'go' as well as for 'stop'. The signals were mounted on very tall masts, forty to sixty feet high, in order to be visible

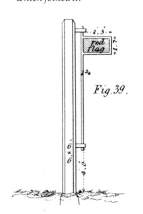

Fig. 39.

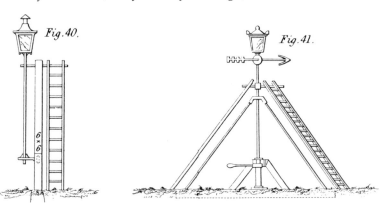

Fig. 40. *Fig. 41.*

One of the last disc-and-crossbar signals to remain in use in Britain was this one at Blackwood Crossing on the North Eastern Railway; the level-crossing gates are shut to allow the passage of a train. When they were open, the red discs were swivelled through ninety degrees, to warn any approaching train to stop. By the time this photograph was taken in 1907, such signals had given way almost everywhere to semaphores.

from as great a distance as possible. Once adopted, these signals remained standard on the Great Western for a generation, until they were gradually ousted by semaphores from 1869 onwards. They were also used on other railways, such as the Furness, and versions of the disc-and-crossbar principle were widely adopted on the Continent, especially in France. Disc signals, without the bar, were in use on the Sheffield Ashton & Manchester Railway in 1846.

Meanwhile, the semaphore had made its appearance, first in 1841 on the London & Croydon Railway, under the direction of its engineer Charles Hutton Gregory, then on the South Eastern and London & Brighton. This was an adaptation of a form of signalling that had been employed for half a century past for naval and military purposes, deriving from the 'telegraph' invented by the Frenchman Chappe in 1792. As applied to railways, it was perfectly simple. The semaphore moved through a quarter-circle. When it was horizontal, at right angles to the post, it indicated 'stop'; when lowered 45 degrees, 'proceed with caution'; when lowered completely, so as to fall within a slot in the post, 'all clear'. The equivalent lights at night were red, green, and white. The three positions gave a more precise indication than the disc and crossbar (though the Great Western soon developed a 'fantail' signal to indicate 'caution'). On the other hand, the semaphore was open to the objection that when it was in the 'all clear' position it gave a merely negative indication. In this form, however, it lasted on most British railways until the development of the separate distant signal, with a fishtail notched into its arm, to indicate 'caution', in the 1870s.

Two years after he had installed semaphores, Gregory began to experiment at Bricklayers Arms Junction with a device to prevent signals from being moved in conflict with one another – what came to be called 'interlocking'. A number of other engineers elaborated and improved on his notion. In 1856 John Saxby took out a patent for a mechanism by which 'the semaphore signals, the coloured glasses of the signal lamps, and the

At Old Kent Road Junction on the London Brighton & South Coast Railway in 1892, posts carrying semaphore signals rise directly from the roof of the signal box; they were controlled manually by levers inside the box. The posts were slotted and so allowed each semaphore arm to retract completely; when required to show 'stop', the arm was raised to a fully horizontal position. The disadvantage of this system was that there was no positive signal to indicate that it was safe to proceed. A more modern replacement signal box has been built in the fork of the lines.

"points" are all actuated by a single motion of the lever, thus rendering the duties of the signalman of the most simple character and making it impossible for an accident to arise from the signals and the points differing'.[2] Four years later this was improved by Austin Chambers of the North London Railway, whose mechanism absolutely prevented a second movement of points or signals from beginning until the first was completed. Chambers's device was installed at Kentish Town Junction, and in the same year, 1860, interlocking machinery also appeared at Yeovil Junction and in the box at Victoria station known as the 'Hole in the Wall'.

By this time the crude early method of working trains simply on a basis of time intervals was being slowly superseded by a new system. The electric telegraph was now available. Railways played a very important part in the establishment of this new device. The Cooke and Wheatstone telegraph was first tried on the London & Birmingham line out of Euston in 1837, and in the following year it was laid down from Paddington to West Drayton on the Great Western. Neither of these installations was entirely successful, but the potential value of the invention for controlling trains by transmitting information about their movements down the line was clear. The first railway to be worked throughout by telegraph was the London & Blackwall in 1840 (see p. 65).[3] In 1844 the Yarmouth & Norwich opened with a new system of controlling its trains, based not on time intervals but on intervals of space. The line was divided into sections, a second train not being admitted into a section until the preceding one had moved out of it. This was what came to be called the 'block' system, and its adoption was made possible only by the use of the telegraph, which enabled the signalman at one end of a block to know when a train had passed out at the other.

Although the block system found general favour, it did not become universally accepted. For a long time it was a common practice to mix the time-interval and the block systems. This was a main cause of the dreadful Clayton Tunnel accident on the Brighton line in 1861, in which 23 people were killed. When the Board of Trade's inspecting officer criticised the company for failing to adopt block-working throughout the line, the directors replied that 'they still fear that the telegraphic system of working recommended by the Board of Trade will, by transferring much responsibility from the engine drivers, augment rather than diminish the risk of accident'.[4]

This argument, frequently advanced, merits some attention, since it impeded the adoption of many mechanical improvements. There were perhaps two considerations that lay behind it: one hidden, the other open. The hidden argument was that such installations were often expensive to install. Economy therefore suggested that the old system should be retained and made to work satisfactorily through a rigid and ruthless insistence on exact attention to existing safety rules. But the open argument was a genuine one, however mistaken it may appear when we look back on it now. James Allport of the Midland believed quite sincerely that the whole interlocking system was wrong, on the ground that it fettered the signalman's discretion to act in an emergency, for example by diverting one of two approaching trains on to another line in order to avoid a collision. After the Board of Trade had refused permission to the Midland to open a new line at Birmingham in 1866 until the junctions had been interlocked, the company agreed to accept these requirements but only under protest, and with the distinct proviso that it 'must decline to be held responsible for their adoption'.[5] For some time to come, many prominent leaders of railway opinion such as Edward Watkin of the Manchester Sheffield & Lincolnshire and the general manager of the London & South Western, Archibald Scott, opposed such innovations as tending to reduce the alertness and sense of responsibility of signalmen and drivers.

The Board of Trade won its battle with the Midland company, and it may be said that the general acceptance of interlocking in Britain is to be attributed, in large measure, to its consistent advocacy of the principle. Its absolute powers of command were limited, but it acted as a steady and watchful critic of railway management, particularly in the matter of safety devices.

The Board of Trade's influence was not invariably fortunate. After much agitation, arising from such horrors as the murder of Thomas Briggs by Franz Müller on the North London Railway in 1864, it insisted that means of communication should be provided on all trains between passengers, guard and driver. This was written into the Regulation of Railways Act, 1868. The system approved by the Board employed a rope which ran outside the carriages and was connected to a bell on the engine, whose ringing warned the driver that the cord had been pulled. It proved hopelessly unreliable, and in 1873 the Board revoked the approval it had given. More than twenty years elapsed before an efficient device emerged, and that was made possible only by the adoption of continuous brakes.

As soon as trains began to run at high speeds, the necessity of some additional brake-power beyond that on the engine or its tender became plain. Many systems were devised by rival inventors, who tried with varying degrees of success to sell them to the British railway companies. But none of them proved completely satisfactory. Meanwhile, in accident after accident, the need was demonstrated for a brake that should be continuous

SHOWING WHAT A WONDERFUL IMPROVEMENT THE HOLES IN THE RAILWAY CARRIAGES ARE, PARTICULARLY DURING THE HOLIDAYS.

A cartoon in Punch *in 1868 makes fun of one of the newly installed 'port-holes' between compartments. On 9 July 1864 Franz Müller had robbed and murdered Thomas Briggs in a first-class compartment on the 9.50pm North London train from Fenchurch Street, and had thrown the body out on to the line near Bow. The brutal attack went unnoticed by the other passengers on the train, since they could neither see nor hear what was going on in adjacent compartments. To reassure the frightened public, some companies, notably the London & South Western, immediately made unglazed holes in the partition walls. Known popularly as 'Müller's lights', they were viewed by passengers as a very mixed blessing.*

throughout the train and 'automatic', i.e. instantly applied of itself to any vehicle that became detached from the rest. Disasters caused by the absence of such brakes included those at Round Oak in 1858, at Manuel and Shipton in 1874, at Abbots Ripton and Arlesey in 1876, at Lockerbie in 1883, at Armagh, on the Great Northern Railway of Ireland, in 1889. The last of these disasters was the most terrible: eighty people, many of them children, were killed when ten carriages of an excursion train ran away backwards down a steep gradient. As L. T. C. Rolt said, this was probably the most important single accident ever to occur on the railways of the United Kingdom: for it led immediately to the passing of the Regulation of Railways Act, 1889. This made both continuous automatic brakes and absolute block-working compulsory on all lines throughout the country. 'In those shattered coaches of the ill-fated excursion train', he wrote, 'the old happy-go-lucky days of railway working came to their ultimate end and the modern phase of railway working as we know it began.'[6]

—— TOWARDS AUTOMATION ——

By the time the Act of 1889 was passed, most British railways were in fact already complying with its safety provisions on their main lines. In the preceding ten years automatic brakes had become general; but in Britain, unfortunately, not to a uniform pattern. Two different brakes, working on opposite principles, came to be used. The vacuum brake was favoured by all the English companies except the London Chatham & Dover, the London Brighton & South Coast, the London Tilbury & Southend, the Great Eastern and the North Eastern, which all went in for the Westinghouse air brake. Each brake was in some ways superior to its rival; both were defensible choices. What was indefensible was the failure to agree, especially in a small country where so much through working of vehicles took place between one company's lines and another's. Only when the railways were nationalised did it become possible to make braking systems uniform. The British Transport Commission decided to adopt the vacuum brake, even though most of the other great railway systems of the world used air brakes and though they were almost invariably employed with electric and diesel traction.

In conjunction with continuous brakes a really effective emergency alarm system was at last devised. In the years after the rope-and-bell system was discredited, several companies had adopted alarms that made use of electric bells. The Brighton and South Eastern companies employed a much better mechanism than the companies north of the Thames. But no bell-type alarm could compare with the system the Great Western installed in its first corridor train of 1892. A chain was led along the inside of each carriage above the windows. When pulled it caused an immediate partial application of the brakes. It was so obviously superior to all that had gone before that it quickly passed into general use.

Meanwhile, a number of important advances were taking place in signalling. As with communications between passengers, guard and driver, the southern companies (with their heavy and intricate suburban traffic) did much more than their share of the pioneer work. W. R. Sykes of the London Chatham & Dover Railway now moved another stage towards automatic signalling with his 'lock-and-block' system. Though he met with strong opposition from the chairman of his company, J. S. Forbes, the Board of Trade supported him. Largely through its insistence, Sykes's scheme was tried. By the summer of 1882 the whole line from Victoria to Dover had been equipped with it. The mechanism was designed to reduce the risk of human failure even further by extending the interlocking system to govern not only signals and points but the block instrument itself. Sykes was a pioneer in the application of electricity to signalling, and he also deserves much of the credit for the invention of track circuiting, which enables a train to indicate its position automatically to the signalman.

The pattern of the semaphore, meanwhile, developed two fresh variants. After the Abbots Ripton accident of 1876, which was due in part to the failure of the signal wires and arms to move when clogged with snow, the Great Northern company went in for the 'somersault' type of semaphore. This was centrally balanced on a bracket attached to the post and swung to 'danger' at once if any of its mechanism failed. Such signals had also the merit of giving a strikingly clear indication to the driver in the 'go' position, for the arm fell quite clear of the post. The pattern was taken up by one firm of signal engineers, McKenzie & Holland of Worcester, and through them made its way on to many of the South Wales railways and even out to Australasia.

Somersault signals were clear, but they were complicated and expensive to maintain. Early in the 20th century another expedient was adopted. Hitherto, all the semaphores used in Great Britain had moved downwards from the horizontal position, which always indicated 'danger'. Experiments were now made with signals in which the arm moved upwards. These 'upper-quadrant' signals were installed on the Metropolitan Railway between Finchley Road and Neasden in 1910. A number of other companies – the Great Central, South Eastern & Chatham and Great Northern for instance – made trials of similar signals in succeeding years. Upper-quadrant semaphores became the standard pattern on the London Midland & Scottish, London & North Eastern and Southern Railways after grouping in 1923.

A train from King's Lynn to Peterborough North passes from a stretch of single line to double at Sutton Bridge, between King's Lynn and Spalding, in 1959. At the head of the train is British Railways class 4MT 2-6-0, No. 43107. The transition from single to double line was regulated by somersault semaphore signals from the box in the foreground, while the swing bridge in the background was controlled from the box immediately above it.

Each of the great companies had a distinctive signalling practice of its own. The London & North Western on its main lines favoured very lofty posts, with 'repeating' arms below to give an indication nearer ground level in conditions of bad visibility, and at places like Rugby, Nuneaton and Lancaster it put up great gantries straddling half a dozen tracks or more. The Great Western also used very tall posts originally, but when it changed over from the disc-and-crossbar to the semaphore, it abandoned them in favour of short ones; and though it put multiple signals on brackets it never went in much for gantries. Its signals were simple and never ambiguous. A Midland or a Great Eastern arm would often droop from the horizontal; there could never be any doubt whether a Great Western signal was 'on' or 'off'. In the years between the wars, when all the other companies turned over to the upper-quadrant signal, the Great Western remained faithful to the older pattern, and the same practice still survives on the minor lines of the Western Region of British Rail.

There were distinctive patterns of signal box also. The London & North Western made high brick fortresses of its important boxes, such as the surviving one at Shrewsbury. Most other lines contented themselves with timber, the Midland decking out its boxes with finials on the roof. One of these timber boxes, from Haddiscoe on the Great Eastern Railway, is now installed at the Science Museum in London. At the opposite end of the scale, in time and in mechanical development, stand those built in recent years at Sittingbourne, Potters Bar and West Hampstead.

Automatic signalling made its appearance before the end of the 19th century – it was first brought into use on the Liverpool Overhead Railway, opened in 1893. Electro-pneumatic power signalling was installed at Spital-fields on the Great Eastern in 1899, and then on the London & South Western between Andover Junction and Grateley in 1902. Two years later it was introduced on the North Eastern, between Alne and Thirsk. One of the original electro-pneumatic semaphore signals from this stretch of line is in the Museum of Science and Engineering at Newcastle – together, incidentally, with three lever-frames of the 1860s. What strikes one about this signal is its surprising combination of the old and the new. The principle is

Steaming in from Bury St Edmunds to Ipswich in 1954, a rebuilt Great Eastern Railway Class B12/3 4-6-0, No. 61569, passes under the Ipswich Goods Junction Box gantry. The gantry bears a fine array of Great Eastern lower-quadrant signals in one direction and three later, upper-quadrant, signals in the other.

modern, but the instrument itself curiously antique: though mounted on a tubular metal post, the semaphore is made of wood. It was operated by carbon-dioxide gas.

The underground railways became interested in automatic signalling very early. The pioneer City & South London tube, it is true, was no great pacemaker in signalling methods: when it was opened in 1890 its signals were lit by oil. They were readily extinguished by the draught set up by passing trains, and soon oil was replaced by gas. Only when this, too, proved unsatisfactory was electricity, which had provided the whole motive power from the beginning, applied to the signals. Automatic electric signalling was tried on the District line (modelled after the system in use on the Boston Elevated Railway) in 1903 and extended to the whole of the company's system in 1906. In tunnels the signals were lamps, whose colour was changed by means of movable shutters. In the open, semaphores were used, until they were gradually replaced by colour-light signals in more

The spiked finials adorning the top of the signal post and the box at Ketton & Collyweston station on the Leicester – Peterborough line are typical features of the Midland Railway. Each company had its distinctive designs for buildings and equipment. The modest station waiting room is in the foreground.

recent years; the last of the semaphores did not disappear until 1953.

The use of coloured lights alone for signalling, without semaphores, began on the Waterloo & City line of 1898. Although some experiments were made in Britain not long afterwards with the use of signals of this kind in the open air, they were not installed permanently out of tunnels until after the First World War, on the Liverpool Overhead Railway in 1921 and on the London & North Eastern Railway between Marylebone and Neasden in 1924. The Southern Railway first adopted them on the line between Holborn Viaduct and Elephant and Castle two years later. They have now come to be widely used in all parts of the country, and they have replaced semaphores on main lines.

One of the most valuable developments at the turn of the century was the system of automatic train control introduced by the Great Western. This was designed to give an audible warning to the engine driver in his cab if he passed a distant signal at danger, the device being electrically operated from a ramp laid between the rails. It was tried in its earliest form on the Henley branch in 1906. The plan was later improved so that not only was this warning given but at the same time the steam brakes were automatically applied. The Great Western steadily spread the installation over the larger part of its network, but remained unique for many years among British railways in adopting it, in spite of the comments of the railway inspectors that accident after accident on other lines might have been prevented by its use. A system with the same purpose was introduced on to the Tilbury line by the London Midland & Scottish company in 1938; and the Modernisation Plan of 1955 allocated £20 million to the installation of an automatic warning system, on a somewhat different pattern, throughout the country.

—— THE WORKING OF SINGLE LINES ——

The working and control of trains on single lines presents special problems of its own. In 1858 the Board of Trade decided that it would not allow new single lines to be opened for passenger traffic unless they were worked on the strict condition that only one engine might be in steam on the line at a time. This was perfectly acceptable on a country branch with little traffic; but no main lines could possibly be managed in such a restrictive fashion. If they had been, the maximum number of trains, passenger and goods, that could have been run, say, across the Grampians between Perth and Forres in 24 hours would have been only two or three in each direction. In fact, when this main line was opened in 1863 block signalling by telegraph was adopted. Fixed crossing places for the trains were laid down in the timetables; but they might be varied, owing to late running or to other causes, on the instructions of the traffic superintendent at Inverness, who had control of all movements made on the entire system of the Highland company. Eight hundred telegrams or more might be dispatched from the superintendent for this purpose in a single day, and no accident was ever caused by a failure of the system.

That was a special arrangement, however, adopted to meet the unique requirements of the Highland company, whose mountainous main line and Strome Ferry branch comprised by 1874 no less than 370 miles of single track, with crossing places only at the stations. What was needed on the ordinary short stretch of single line or branch was a simple and effective device for preventing two trains from occupying the same section at once. When the firm position it had taken up in 1858 had proved untenable, the Board of Trade agreed to accept the 'staff' or 'tablet' system in a number of forms, under which the driver could take his train into a section of single line only if he held a staff or a tablet permitting him to do so. After spectacular accidents on single lines at Norwich in 1874 and at Radstock in 1876, these systems were widely extended and improved, especially through the inventions of Edward Tyer, tried first on the Cockermouth Keswick & Penrith Railway in 1879, and of F. W. Webb and A. M. Thompson, developed particularly on the London & North Western from 1888 onwards. By 1895 more than half the single lines in the country were worked on some staff or tablet system. Even this was not proof against human fallibility, however, as a shocking accident at Abermule in Montgomeryshire showed in 1921.

All devices of this kind had one serious drawback from the operator's point of view. They forced every train to enter and leave each section of the line at low speed, to enable the 'token' to be exchanged with a signalman or porter. This mattered little if the section ended at a station at which the train was stopping; but it meant that all trains must travel very slowly over crossing loops between stations, and it rendered express working over a single line impossible. Even at slow speeds, the operation required some dexterity, and a mistake in catching the instrument sometimes resulted in a broken arm or a dislocated shoulder.

A solution to these difficulties was found by James Manson of the Great North of Scotland Railway. Having tried unsuccessfully a plan that had long been in use for the picking up and dropping of mailbags by the side of the line, he developed a machine derived from one used in cotton mills. It was a post ending in a fork, with one arm for receiving the dropped tablet, and the other for holding the fresh tablet to be picked up. A corresponding fork was fitted to the side of the engine, and as the two forks made contact the exchange was effected. This equipment was first tried out in 1889 and proved successful, enabling the exchange of tablets to take place at speeds up to 60 mph. Manson, a generous and honourable character, declined to

Inside the signal box at Fambridge in the depths of rural Essex, on the Wickford – Southminster branch line, the levers are still worked in the old-fashioned way. In order to enter the stretch of single track, the driver must collect a 'staff', which is given up again when he re-enters double track. This safety device is intended to prevent two trains travelling in opposite directions from entering the same stretch of line; dating from the 1860s, it has remained virtually unchanged (see page 161). The 'staffs' are issued automatically from the two machines on either side of the signalman, one for each direction.

take out a patent for this valuable device, hoping to encourage its adoption and so prevent the injuries caused to railwaymen by the old manual methods of exchange.[7] His apparatus came to be widely employed in Scotland on the Highland and the Caledonian Railways in addition to the Great North of Scotland where it originated, and it is still in use. One of the things that most impresses an English traveller on Scottish railways today is the efficiency of single-line working. The trains can move at substantial speeds, and they do not lurch or jerk disagreeably when they run through loops and past stations at which they are not stopping. All the loops on the Highland main line were excellently designed to permit fast running.

Elsewhere in Britain, single track was not found on main lines except in a very few places. The Royal Albert Bridge at Saltash has never been widened to take two tracks, and two curious survivals of single-line working are still to be seen, between Ely and Soham in East Anglia and on nearly two miles of the steep climb out of Montrose up to Usan box, on the line from Aberdeen to Edinburgh. Since nationalisation, some formerly important main lines carrying a reduced traffic have been made single: those from Salisbury to Exeter, for example, and from Oxford to Worcester. Otherwise single track is found only on secondary trunk routes, like that from Shrewsbury to Pwllheli or the Central Wales line from Craven Arms to Llandovery. The last of these was by far the most substantial single-line section on the whole system of the London & North Western Railway, which doubled the track even on quite obscure branches, as did its neighbour the Lancashire & Yorkshire. Perhaps the most efficiently worked single-line routes were those of two joint railways,[8] the Somerset & Dorset and the Midland & Great Northern. The Somerset & Dorset had not always been efficient. The disaster at Radstock in 1876 exposed a complete irresponsibility and incompetence of management. When it occurred, the Midland and London & South Western companies had just assumed the joint ownership of the line, and they immediately set themselves to modernise its equipment and impose some discipline on its staff. With success: for no accident fatal to a passenger occurred again on this railway between 1876 and its closure to passenger traffic in 1966. That was a more

Carved birds swooping down to refresh themselves decorate a drinking fountain at Gleneagles station in the Scottish Highlands. Installed by the Caledonian Railway and still in place in 1983, it continues to exhort passengers to 'Keep the Pavement Dry', but the drinking vessel that once hung from the hook has disappeared.

An ornate cast-iron urinal at Garston station, south of Liverpool, provides a reminder of the days when carriages had no lavatories. Such conveniences were needed by passengers, especially on long-distance trains, until well into the 20th century.

than satisfactory achievement, for though the Somerset & Dorset never came to resemble a goldmine, it carried heavy summer traffic between Bournemouth and the North over a line that was almost wholly single, and was in addition very steep as it climbed over the Mendips.

On the Midland & Great Northern less than a third of the system was double-tracked, but the running of the trains over it was smart. In the 1880s there was an express timed between Peterborough and Cromer at 30 mph, including six calls at stations and 12 more delays for exchanging the staff on single lines – 'as fast as we are sometimes allowed to go on the great thoroughfares of Europe when we pay "first class only"'. Before the end of the century a train was running from Peterborough to Melton Constable at 43 mph.[9] The Midland & Great Northern was shut down in 1959. It was a modest affair as trunk railways go, and certainly uneconomic towards the end of its life. Yet those who travelled over the line will always remember the journey: the climb over the Wolds by Castle Bytham, the drop down to Bourne (a rural Clapham Junction, now obliterated from the timetables), the run across the level fenland by the tulip fields of Spalding, the stiff pull beyond South Lynn up to the heaths of Norfolk, and then the long undulating descent through Melton Constable and North Walsham to the sea.

—— MISCELLANEOUS EQUIPMENT ——

A railway contains many small items of furniture which are, by comparison with its signalling and operating equipment, of trivial importance. Just because they are insignificant, signs, nameboards, water towers, benches, iron-tyred trolleys and other pieces of platform equipment sometimes survive to a great age unnoticed, and they represent an endlessly interesting branch of industrial archaeology.

The provision of adequate signs to show the names of stations has been attempted in many different forms, with generally poor results. The nameboard appears quite early in the history of railways, but it always seems to have been customary in Britain to place it parallel with the track and not, as on the Continent, at right angles to it, on the gable-ends of the station building. The name was seldom obvious. One architect advised that it should be cut in the stonework: 'instead of having the name of the station

At Wolferton in Norfolk, the station for the royal family's home at Sandringham, a sign lamp is emblazoned with royal coats of arms. Such ornate ironwork and lavish ornamentation was unknown elsewhere on the Great Eastern Railway. On the London & North Western line from Stockport to Buxton, clear easy-to-read black letters proclaim the name of Disley station. The names were designed to be illuminated by oil or gas light from behind, but the device must still have been barely adequate as a means of keeping night travellers informed.

painted sometimes on one part of the structure and sometimes on another, we would have had it sculptured on a conspicuous part of the front . . . ; and we would have had the name itself in sunk or in raised letters; coloured, if it should have been thought necessary'.[10]

The Great North of Scotland Railway painted the names of its stations in gilt letters on glass panels over the entrance doors, so that they could be illuminated from behind. Many varieties of small plates and boards were produced, usually attached to lamp-posts, in the hope that they would be visible after dark. Where oil lamps were used that hope was slender from the start. With gas and electric light the job could be done if the design and planning of the signs were intelligent. It was managed best, as a rule, on those lines where it was essential to move the passengers on and off the trains as quickly as possible: on the Great Eastern, for example, which used in the London area a semi-circular metal plate fixed round the lower half of the lamp-bowl. But no really satisfactory system of the kind was devised until modern times. A sustained and serious effort was made up and down British Railways to place clear name-plates of standard design immediately underneath an adequate lamp; and some stations enjoy a really effective set of indicators, with the name painted on a glass box or tube, through which electric light shines.

These are not the only means, however, by which the railway traveller can learn his whereabouts. He can be informed audibly as well as visually. On the Edinburgh & Glasgow Railway, we are told in 1861, starlings and parrots were trained to scream out the names of the stations.[11] This device did not meet with general favour. The usual method of announcement was the human voice; and its effectiveness has varied with the voice employed. The name often became unintelligible to strangers through mere repetition, like the patter of a tourist guide who has told the same story many times a day for many years. There was once a porter at Balham on the London Brighton & South Coast line who walked up and down the narrow wooden platforms saying nothing but 'Balammbalamm'; and another at Bow in North Devon who surprised strangers by repeatedly calling out in a flat tone of voice 'Bo Bo'.

The introduction of the station-announcer, speaking over a public address system, was in general a great improvement. But even then strange things happened. A young woman at Guildford during the Second World War always used to refer to a station called 'Arkwright' (meaning Arkwright Street, Nottingham); and another at Paddington who was a martyr to gentility spoke of Teignmouth as 'Teen-ah-mowth', to the astonishment of the people who lived there and had never known it as anything but 'Tinmuth'. It would be captious to multiply such examples. If there are announcers who can make it a penance to use their stations (I think particularly of Sheffield), the public address system has done much to ease the problems of travellers. It is capable, too, of extensions beyond its proper use, like the 'paging' of passengers and staff, and even the broadcasting of news. I happened to make a long cross-country journey on the day follow-ing each of the general elections of 1950 and 1951, and I remember getting the latest results through the loudspeakers at each of the large stations we stopped at: at Taunton and Exeter I heard that the two parties were running neck and neck in 1950, and at Doncaster I learned that the Conservatives had just established a clear lead in 1951.

Many pieces of ironwork that survive on the railways have the ad-vantage that, in addition to pleasing the eye, they can be read. Sets of initials cast into decorative spandrels supporting the roofs of station canopies and worked into the ornamental legs of platform benches are a source of information about the lines over which we travel, long after the death of the companies that built them. Often the water towers and storage tanks that were universally required for the service of the steam locomotive bore dates and makers' names, and one could trace the evolution of par-ticular types until in the end they came to be standard throughout the system of a whole great company – like the simple water-column with a square capital bearing the initials 'M.R.' of the Midland Railway. Some companies went to outside manufacturers for these things. The Great Eastern bought a number from Dodman's of King's Lynn; the Cornwall Railway went for theirs to Bridgwater; one survived into the 1960s at Liskeard. At Haltwhistle a large iron tank on a stone base was inscribed not merely with the name of the makers R. Wylie & Co. of Newcastle, but with that of the Newcastle & Carlisle Railway's engineer, Peter Tate, and the year of building, 1861. The Cambrian company, on the other hand, constructed its own, mounting on the roof of the station building at Portmadoc a tank that bore the legend 'Cambrian Works Oswestry 1872'.

—— EMPLOYMENT ——

The history of railways, like that of most other instruments of our social and economic life in the past 150 years, has been in great measure a history of automation, of gradual reduction in the number of men needed to operate them. This is particularly well exemplified in the development of signalling. In hand signalling, with which it all began, one man gave each signal. In the old 'A' box at Waterloo in the 1880s, ten men were making five million signalling movements a year; in 1908 the whole of the workings into and out of Glasgow Central station were brought under the control of a single box with 374 levers; four signalmen and one traffic regulator controlled 33 miles of track from the box at York that was brought into use in 1951.[12]

But British Rail still employs nearly 150,000 men and women, and it would be both ungrateful and historically wrong to close an account of the operation of the railways without saying a little about the human beings who have managed them and kept them going. The history of the railway

Employees of the North Eastern Railway at Fence Houses between Durham and Sunderland pose for a group portrait in the 1890s. The senior staff sit in front while the rest stand behind; the man on the extreme right is probably a 'ganger' in charge of the permanent way for this section of the line. The headgear of these dozen men is a fascinating index of social and economic class, from the silk top hat of the young station-master, through billycocks and bowlers, to the company's uniform caps of several different designs.

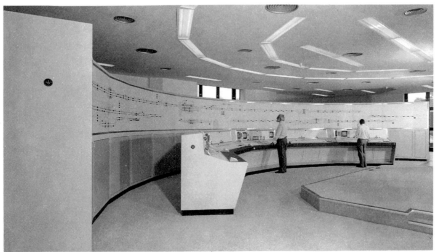

Two signalmen operate the modern panel signal box at Exeter on the Western Region. The new electronic system has gradually replaced most of the larger, manually operated, boxes, bringing large districts under central control. The signalman no longer needs any view up and down the line through windows at eye level; instead his attention is fixed on diagrams and display panels.

service is a little-explored subject, but one of great interest. We know something of the men who built the railways: a good deal about a few of the engineers,[13] a little about one or two of the contractors, and about the navvies who performed the manual labour of raising embankments and excavating cuttings and tunnels.[14] But when we turn to the railwaymen themselves, they are strangely anonymous. How were the staffs of the early railways recruited? Did experienced railwaymen move much from one line to another? How early did that *esprit de corps* develop which was so striking a feature of the old railway companies and is not by any means dead now?

Among early railwaymen the technical staff were paid highly and worked hard. A 12-hour day was usual, and sometimes a double shift had to be worked. As late as 1871 the chief inspector of railways remarked in an official report to the Board of Trade: 'Eight hours of continuous duty at very busy signal-cabins and 12 hours in any signal-cabin, are sufficient; but periods of 18, 25 and even 37 hours, for which men have been known to be regularly or periodically employed, principally during exchange of duty, once in two, seven or 13 weeks, are inexcusable.'[15] These hours seem incredible to us now. Though the Board was never in a position to dictate to the companies, it exercised a great influence over them, especially through its inspecting officers' reports on accidents, which were written with an Olympian candour, sparing neither the shortcomings of the men nor, on occasion, the harshness of their employers. The Royal Commission on Trade Unions in 1867 showed concern about the hours of labour of railwaymen; in 1891 a Select Committee of the House of Commons was set up to investigate the whole problem, and its report led to the passing of the Railway Servants' Hours of Labour Act of 1893. Railwaymen were slow to organise themselves into effective trade unions, but one of the grievances that led them to combine was the burden of intolerably long hours of work. The general public, too, had something to say on the matter: not so much from an altruistic sympathy with the men (though that was not wanting) as from the natural and well-justified fear that over-long hours of work on the part of railwaymen reduced their vigilance and increased the danger of accident.

Yet on the whole the railways were reckoned to be good employers. If their servants were subject to arbitrary dismissal, that was true of almost all workers in Victorian England. As the organisation of the companies grew bigger and their business expanded, they showed a general desire to retain their employees, even when they were found faulty, if they were men of good character. Men who failed as drivers, for example, were repeatedly offered other employment as an alternative to dismissal; the pay might be lower, but at least they still had jobs. The companies came, moreover, to assume responsibilities for their men that were not at that time usual among private employers. By 1870 eight of them maintained savings banks, and fifty or more had established friendly societies, which they subsidised. At least a dozen schools had been set up by the companies for their employees' children in railway towns like Wolverton, Ashford and Doncaster. The Great Western gave £3,000 in 1853 to found the New Swindon Improvement Society. This provided a building for the Mechanics' Institute, established ten years earlier, and other amenities like public baths.[16]

There was prudence in all this as well as philanthropy. The directors were for the most part hard-headed businessmen, and even if they were minded to be generous to the companies' servants, there were always shareholders to criticise them for extravagance. Good facilities were part of a policy designed to secure good service. The companies exacted rigid obedience from their servants to rules that ranged far beyond the technical business of running railways. The Taff Vale company, for example, promulgated a code of eight hundred rules in 1856,[17] which required that its employees should keep their hair cut and warned them that 'not any instance of intoxication, singing, whistling, or levity, while on duty, will be overlooked'. How dreadful is the implication that the company's officers are ubiquitous, to report every misdemeanour at once! In Rule 26 'it is urgently requested of every person . . . on Sundays and Holy Days, when he is not required on duty, that he will attend a place of worship; as it will be the means of promotion when vacancies occur'.

The companies had no scruple about interfering with the private lives and thoughts of their employees. The Taff Vale thought it best in 1856 to forbid its servants all political activity. But the Reform Act of 1867 gave many railwaymen the vote, and one company at least tried to induce them to use it in accordance with its directors' wishes. The London & North Western put the most direct pressure on its servants to vote at the general election of 1868 for the Conservative candidate at Carlisle.[18] At the same time, however, the North Eastern and North Staffordshire companies did

At Euston station in 1906, a guard of the London & North Western Railway checks his watch, flag at the ready to send the train off. Porters behind him load luggage into the guard's van. All station staff were expected to present immaculate appearances and be on their best behaviour while on duty.

exactly the opposite, leaving their men to vote exactly as they chose.[19]

In spite of the drawbacks of railway employment, the great majority of men and women, once they had entered it, stayed: for, above all, it offered them a degree of security that few other private employers could match. Many railwaymen brought in their sons and grandsons, until 'the railway service' came to mean something just as settled and established, in a social and economic sense, as army service in a military family or Admiralty employment in Portsmouth or Devonport. There was always, indeed, something military about it; the servants of the Taff Vale company, for example, were required to salute their directors and officers. For this there were two reasons. In the first place, in both employments the element of danger required a most strict discipline in the common interest. Secondly, the railways were moulded in very large measure not by the engineers – the Stephensons, Brunels and Lockes – but by their early managers, and a fair number of them were military or naval men: Captain Huish of the London & North Western, Captain Laws of the Manchester & Leeds, Captain

O'Brien of the North Eastern, Captain Coddington of the Caledonian. One man who turned from soldiering to join the North London Railway described the servants of the company as 'a regular little army'.[20] The phrase can stand for the British railway companies as a whole. They inspired a loyalty that went beyond the necessities of the job. This loyalty was seldom expressed, yet on occasion it could be demonstrated. In 1887 the employees of the Manchester Sheffield & Lincolnshire Railway volunteered to forgo a day's pay to help the company meet the expenses arising from an accident at Hexthorpe in Yorkshire. This generous offer was very properly declined by the directors, but it exemplifies the corporate feeling that pervaded the railway service: compounded of discipline, interest, family tradition, and the sense of being engaged in a common task, the special skills and mysteries of which marked railwaymen off from their fellows.

Particular railway servants appear from time to time in the histories of the railways. Acworth gave a sketch of one, named William Chadband.[21] His simple biography covers the first half-century of the London & South Western company's life: for he was born in 1817, worked on the building of the railway, went to its Nine Elms depot in 1839, rose to be yard foreman at Waterloo and, when Acworth wrote, was still employed on a light task in the 'Crow's Nest' signal box there although he was over seventy years old – receiving from his decent employers the same rate of pay as he had earned as a foreman.

Coming down to more recent times, there is the story of George Morse, who retired in 1954 from the post of shop inspector in the Carriage and Wagon Works at Swindon after 51 years' service.[22] In his time there was nothing exceptional about his career. He was paid 5s a week when he went into the Works at the age of 14; by the time he was 21 he was getting 18s. The working hours were from 6am to 5.30pm; and on top of that there was often night-school (or, for the men who lived out in the villages, a five- or six-mile walk home). The pay was never high, and the hours were long, but 'the great thing was, we were never out of work. If new construction fell short, we were put on to repairs.' As a railway coachbuilder, he learnt his job with timber and never cared for the steel that replaced it. 'When I came to do inspecting work,' he said, 'I found I always knew if I was working at a job done by a man of my own age. In the old days, you see, when we were brought up on wood, it had to be finished ready for painting. That meant there was a higher standard demanded, for you can have a few bumps in a steel panel and nobody'll notice.' Outside his work his interests lay in Methodism and music; for a quarter of a century he conducted the Swindon (GWR) Male Voice Choir. Here is a life lived entirely within a railway community: the life of a craftsman who gave back to his community all that he had to give.

Though the railways are pieces of machinery, the men who run them are not mechanised. Many of them have been 'characters', showing their character in the very handling of their machines. I think, for example, of two commemorated by E. L. Ahrons. The first is a North Eastern driver of the 1880s, known in York and Harrogate by the name of 'Sammy Sit-up'. He drove his little engine over the not very arduous road between those two towns in a way quite peculiar to himself, losing with great regularity two or three minutes on his schedule by the time he reached Dragon Junction, three quarters of a mile from Harrogate at the bottom of a stiffish bank. At this point he would observe to his mate that he was now going to 'make the old girl sit up', which meant that he would open the regulator and cause the engine to emit a fearsome roar as it climbed the hill. He was thus able to

Captain Mark Huish (1808-67), one of the ablest of the early railway managers, served as secretary of the Grand Junction Railway before he became the first general manager of the big London & North Western combine in 1846. He championed its interests with energetic persistence; always pugnacious, he was also shrewd, intelligent and, in some directions, far-sighted. But the company dropped him, on most ungenerous terms, in 1858. 'We have made Huish the scapegoat for the difficulties we are under,' wrote one of the directors, 'And why? – because he has too pertinaciously stood up for our interests, against our adversaries.'

recover perhaps ten seconds of the time lost; and the guards, who all knew him well, would forget to record the late arrival in their journals.[23]

The other character comes from South Wales: Cornelius Lundie, general manager of the Rhymney Railway. 'He might have been described', says Ahrons, 'as the Rhymney "Pooh-Bah", but he considerably outdid that celebrated character by being not only "Lord High Everything Else", but Lord High Executioner, Mikado, Chorus and Band all rolled into one. Presumably he was the "General Manager", but he was also the Traffic Manager and Superintendent of the Line. Further, if you consulted Bradshaw, or a railway directory, you also discovered that Mr Cornelius Lundie was the Chief Engineer, and that the Chief Locomotive Superintendent was also named Cornelius Lundie.... Mr Lundie was a marvellous old man, and he lived absolutely for the Rhymney Railway, the welfare of which was everything in life to him. In 1904, at the age of 89, after more than forty years' service as General Manager, he nominally retired from that position, and a grateful Board very naturally elected him a director. But if report is to be believed, the change was somewhat more nominal than real, and the old gentleman continued to do a good deal of "general managing" as before, and was in regular attendance at the head offices. Two days before he passed away, at the age of 93, he was to be seen at his old headquarters.'[24]

—— MEMORIALS ——

One does not naturally think of looking in churches for railway history. Yet that branch of history, like almost every other, is reflected in church monuments. You will come upon railwaymen there: in the churchyard of St Breock, Hayes Kidd, for fifty years superintendent of the Bodmin & Wadebridge Railway; in the glorious chancel of Salle, Douglas Earle Marsh, locomotive engineer of the London Brighton & South Coast Railway, whose father was rector of that Norfolk parish for many years. The east window of the parish church of Holyhead is a memorial to William Watson, chairman and managing director of the City of Dublin Steam Packet Company. The inscription states that he 'proposed and carried into effect the new and improved mail and passenger service between England and Ireland via Kingstown and Holyhead, which commenced October 1, A.D. MDCCCLX'.

Many railway accidents, too, are commemorated. In the churchyard of Abergele 33 people killed in the disaster that occurred there to the Irish Mail in 1868 are buried in a common grave; in the north aisle of Salisbury cathedral the citizens erected a momument to the 28 victims of the accident to the American boat train in the early morning of 1 July 1906; a stained-glass window was given to the church of Appledore in Kent as a thank-offering by a survivor of the Sevenoaks accident in 1927. Less famous accidents are also remembered on these walls. At Chapel-le-Dale under Ingleborough is a tablet to the memory of the men who lost their lives in the construction of the line between Settle and Dent Head in 1869-76. At the other end of England, at Bere Ferrers, one reads of ten privates of the New Zealand Expeditionary Force who were killed in the station getting out of a troop train in 1917; they had just landed at Plymouth and were on their way to join their comrades on Salisbury Plain.

Behind the brief inscriptions on these monuments there lie sometimes extraordinary tales of fortitude and devotion. I single out one from Soham in Cambridgeshire, a small town of 5,000 people, with four windmills (one of them working still), some pleasant old yellow-brick houses in the main street, and a fine church whose richly decorated tower dominates the flat landscape for miles around. Inside the church, on the north wall of the nave,

This memorial to driver David Fenwick of the Caledonian Railway was erected by Queen Victoria, indicating her appreciation of the services rendered to her by individual railwaymen, from chief officers to enginemen. It serves as a reminder of the dangers to which crews were continually exposed. On 21 June 1898, on a southbound journey just past Aberdeen, the royal train's communication cord became twisted. Fenwick, who had climbed on top of the coal in the tender in order to disentangle it, struck his head on a bridge and was killed instantly.

Fire consumes part of the remains of the Irish Mail at Abergele on 20 August 1868, an hour and a half after one of the most horrifying accidents that has ever occurred on any British railway. Two wagons loaded with paraffin had run backwards down an incline and collided head on with the express. The paraffin ignited, and all 33 passengers in the first three carriages were burnt to death. Nothing remained of them except, in the inspector's words, 'charred pieces of skin and bone'; an Irish peer, Lord Farnham, and his wife, were alone identified – from the crests on their watches, which survived. Responsibility for the disaster rested wholly with the London & North Western company, its unsatisfactory regulations and the misbehaviour of its servants. The accident was the first in a terrible series, occurring year after year up to the Tay Bridge disaster of 1879, which shook public confidence in railway management and helped to force an improvement in safety precautions.

is a simple mural monument commemorating the heroic action of Driver B. Gimbert and Fireman J. W. Nightall, which 'saved the town of Soham from grave destruction' in the small hours of 2 June 1944. They were taking an ammunition train of 51 wagons from March to White Colne in Essex. The story can best be told in Driver Gimbert's own words: 'After passing the Soham distant signal, which was off, I thought I noticed some steam coming from the injector and looked out and saw that the wagon next to the engine was on fire. The flames appeared to be getting all over the bottom of the wagon and seemed to be spreading very rapidly which seemed to suggest that something very inflammable was alight. I sounded the engine whistle to notify the guard and immediately took steps to stop the train carefully, knowing what the wagons contained, and stopped the train by the station end of the goods shed, where my mate, under my instructions, uncoupled the wagon from the remainder of the train. I told him to take the coal hammer with him in case the coupling was too hot to handle. On his having done this and rejoined the engine, I proceeded with the wagon which was on fire intending to get it well clear of the station and surrounding buildings, and leave it there and proceed to Fordham. The signalman came from his box on to the platform and I said, "Sailor, have you anything between here and Fordham? Where is the mail?" I did not get a reply from him as the explosion occurred at that moment. The engine and wagon were moving slowly at the time and the regulator was shut. I did not notice if he had a bucket, which I understand was found outside the box. I should estimate that from the time I first saw the fire in the wagon to time of explosion would be about six or seven minutes. The fireman uncoupled and was back on the engine very quickly.'[25]

The blazing wagon contained forty 500lb bombs, the next two another 74; behind them was a wagon carrying detonators, followed by further consignments of bombs. The explosion demolished the station completely, making a crater 66ft across. The words of the memorial tablet are well within the truth. If that wagon had not been detached, most of the town would certainly have been destroyed. Fireman Nightall was killed, but Driver Gimbert miraculously survived, much injured. Both were awarded the George Cross. In the records of such devotion to duty there can be no degrees of comparison. All that can be said is that no decoration could ever have been more fairly earned.

GLASGOW (QUEEN STREET) · EDINBURGH (WAVERLEY)

('Up' = Glasgow – Edinburgh; 'Down' = Edinburgh – Glasgow.
The names of stations now open for passenger traffic are printed in
small capitals.)

This journey is different from the others described in this book in two important respects. For one thing, the line was built in a single operation: of its 47¼ miles, 46 were opened at once, on 21 February 1842; the remainder only four years afterwards. And secondly, with the exception of the original Great Western Railway east of Wootton Bassett, the Glasgow–Edinburgh line is the most nearly level of any first-class main line in Great Britain.

Between Cowlairs and Edinburgh (Haymarket), a distance of over 43 miles, there is only one very short stretch graded as steeply as 1 in 600. All the rest is at 1 in 809–960, and 15 miles of the line are completely level. This is not to be explained solely by the fortunate configuration of the country. It is due also to the skill of the engineers, Grainger & Miller (John Miller being principally responsible),[1] backed by the substantial funds that the first proprietors of the railway had at their disposal.

To anyone with a sense of history, this railway has a special interest, for it moves along one of the oldest and most important natural lines of communication in the country, across the 'waist' of Scotland at its narrowest point. For twenty miles it runs close to, and it twice intersects, the Antonine Wall, built by the Romans in the second century AD; and for much of its course it is within sight of the Forth & Clyde Canal, one of the great engineering works of the 18th century.

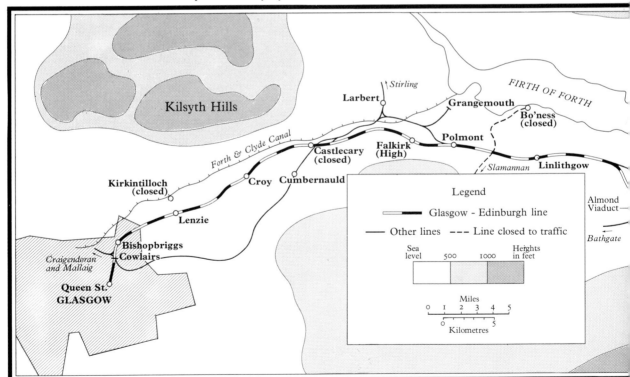

Serving two large cities, moreover, each with a peculiar physical character of its own, it exemplifies some of the general problems faced by engineers in driving their railways into towns. One of the most important difficulties has been solved here with triumphant success: each terminus is conveniently situated near the centre of the city it serves.

The Edinburgh & Glasgow was the only railway of any importance to be incorporated in the year 1838, in the dead time immediately following the first Railway Mania. Like many large Scottish transport undertakings, it drew its capital mainly from England.

It was not the first railway in the waist of Scotland. The Monkland & Kirkintilloch, the Ballochney and the Slamannan Railways were already in operation or at least projected. But they were local lines only, built to handle the transport of coal from the Lanarkshire pits to the Forth & Clyde and the Union Canals. The Edinburgh & Glasgow was a much bigger concern, and it was intended for the conveyance of passengers as well as freight.

Among its English predecessors, it

Glasgow (Queen Street) station: entrance, 1985.

resembled most closely the Liverpool & Manchester, being a short-distance line between two great towns that could immediately offer traffic fully adequate to support it. And just as the Liverpool & Manchester came together with other lines to form the London & North Western company in 1845-46, so the Edinburgh & Glasgow became by amalgamation part of the North British Railway in 1865. In one feature of its layout, too, it was very like the Liverpool & Manchester: it was generally a level line, but it had a very steep drop through a tunnel to its western terminus. QUEEN STREET station, Glasgow, and Liverpool (Lime Street) are very similar in plan, fanning out from the narrow mouths of their approach tunnels. No matter what effort was made to cheer them up with paint, they remained gloomy and sulphurous as long as the steam engine lasted. After its disappearance, however, Queen Street station was splendidly cleaned, and the roof was revealed for what it is: one of the most beautiful iron-and-glass structures in Britain. It is a shallow ellipse, somewhat like Fowler's roof at Victoria station in London, which was built in 1862. The engineer was James Carswell, and his reconstruction of the station was completed in 1877.

There are really two Queen Street stations, one above the other. Beneath the one from which the Edinburgh trains leave is the 'Low Level' station, running roughly at right angles to it. It serves the suburban trains from Motherwell and Airdrie on the east, running along the north bank of the Clyde to Helensburgh, and to Balloch at the southern tip of Loch Lomond. Before the electrification of 1960, the Low Level station was notable for the foulness of the air in its tunnels, remi-

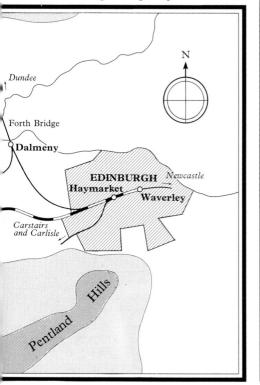

THE GRADIENT OF THE EDINBURGH–GLASGOW LINE

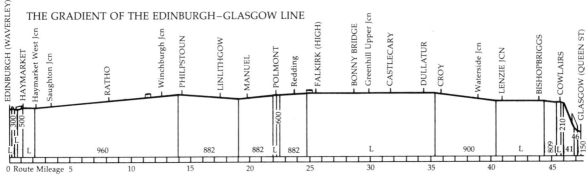

Station labels along the top: EDINBURGH (WAVERLEY), HAYMARKET, Haymarket West Jcn, Saughton Jcn, RATHO, Winchburgh Jcn, PHILPSTOUN, LINLITHGOW, MANUEL, POLMONT, Redding, FALKIRK (HIGH), BONNY BRIDGE, Greenhill Upper Jcn, CASTLECARY, DULLATUR, CROY, Waterside Jcn, LENZIE JCN, BISHOPBRIGGS, COWLAIRS, GLASGOW (QUEEN ST)

Gradient figures: 300, 500, L, 960, 882, 882, 600, L, 882, L, 900, L, 809, L, 41, 210, 46, 150

Route Mileage: 0 ... 5 ... 10 ... 15 ... 20 ... 25 ... 30 ... 35 ... 40 ... 45

In this chart the figures above the base line should be prefixed with '1 in' to read off the gradient for each section. 'L' stands for level, and boxes along the upper line indicate tunnels.

Men splicing the cable at Cowlairs, about 1900.

Two North British 4-4-0s ascending Cowlairs incline, assisted by cable, about 1900.

niscent of conditions on the old Metropolitan and District lines in London in the days of steam.

On leaving the main station, the Edinburgh trains face a gradient of 1 in 41-46. The ascent is just over a mile long, and more than half of it is in tunnel. It was not originally intended that locomotives should be used on this incline – like the similar one at Liverpool, it was first worked by cable. The rope, however, gave trouble, and in 1844 it was discarded in favour of powerful banking locomotives of a special design. Mechanically they were equal to the work, but they proved unsatisfactory in other ways, and cable haulage was reinstated in 1847. With one more brief interlude, it lasted until 1908. For all those years it was the practice to haul the locomotive – itself, of course, exerting all the power it could – up the incline along with its train. After 1908, the shunting engine bringing the empty coaches into the terminus acted as a banker in the rear of each train, assisting it to the top of the incline, where it quietly fell behind.

At the top is Cowlairs. Its rural name is to be interpreted literally:

before the railway arrived, it was a place where cattle were penned. On the down side of the line is the Eastfield motive-power depot; on the up side formerly stood Cowlairs works, which were among the earliest to be established by any railway for the building of its own locomotives. The Edinburgh & Glasgow company decided to undertake this task for itself in 1841, and the first engine emerged from the works in 1844. Though no locomotives were built at Cowlairs after 1923, when the North British became part of the London & North Eastern Railway, the works continued to be extensively used for servicing and repairs. That business was removed to the works of the old Caledonian Railway at St Rollox in 1968 and the Cowlairs works were then closed.

Although the works have gone, there is still an important junction here, at which the line to Craigendoran, Fort William and Mallaig diverges on the up side. The junction is made conspicuous by a large modern brick and concrete signal box. Close to it stands one of the original mile posts of the Edinburgh & Glasgow Railway; one of a number that survive on the up side at the Glasgow end of the line. Made of iron, with polygonal heads on a narrow stem, these posts are of exceptional interest, for they demonstrate how the railways took over and adapted for their own use

CROY, the railway comes into sight of the Forth & Clyde Canal, which is here making use of the valley of the River Kelvin, running under the steep Kilsyth Hills. It also follows the line of the Antonine Wall. When the canal was being cut in 1771, four Roman altars were found near this point and presented, with handsome rhetoric, to the University of Glasgow.[2] Not many railway companies, making discoveries of this kind when building, were as scrupulous as the directors of the Forth & Clyde Canal.

The line now enters a cutting over a mile long through Croy Hill. It is driven through solid rock. When it was being made, the blasting was likened to a military operation. 'The frequent discharge of the shots, which were generally fired in numbers varying from six to 18 or 20, resembled the operations of a battery train of artillery. This military similitude was greatly heightened by the trumpet sounds preceding the

Iron mile-post, Edinburgh & Glasgow Railway.

Cowlairs station, with locomotive works to the left, about 1900.

techniques that had been long established on the roads. This particular post is inscribed on one face, looking eastwards, 'Glasᵂ 2'; on the other, looking in the opposite direction, 'Edinʳ 44'. The total mileage of 46 refers to the railway as it was when first opened, with its terminus at Edinburgh (Haymarket). An extra one and a quarter miles were added to bring the line into what is now called Waverley station. That extension was opened in 1846, so these mile posts must date from the very earliest years of the Edinburgh & Glasgow Railway. They are the oldest anywhere in Britain still in use.

After Cowlairs the line curves away to the north east, through BISHOPBRIGGS station. Two miles beyond are the Cadder sidings, occupying what must previously have been a wild tract of boggy moorland. The place has a macabre memory: two navvies were publicly executed here after being convicted of murdering their 'ganger' (foreman) during the building of the railway in 1841.

The next station is LENZIE. Half a mile beyond it a bridge carries the line over the old Monkland & Kirkintilloch Railway, now closed: it was the earliest in Scotland authorised to work its traffic by locomotives. Incorporated in 1824, it passed into the control of the North British in 1865.

Between this and the next station,

The mile-long Croy cutting, September 1985, with a diesel multiple unit on local service between Glasgow (Queen Street) and Falkirk (Grahamstown).

Linlithgow station, August 1985: the old station building on the up (right-hand) platform has been restored and a new one built opposite.

1966, diverting the services that had run from there to Perth and Aberdeen into Queen Street.

A great urban spread opens out on low ground away to the north. The heart of this is Falkirk, whose tentacles have stretched out to touch Larbert on the north west and to embrace the historic Carron Works to the north. North east of Falkirk and almost continuous with it is the modern port of Grangemouth on the Firth of Forth, the most successful of the ports that have tried to capture the eastward sea-going trade of mid-Scotland.

Running into Falkirk the railway picks up another canal, this time on the down side: the Union Canal, which runs into the sea at Leith. Close to its starting-point here at Greenbank, the Battle of Falkirk was fought in 1746. Falkirk has two stations, one (Grahamston) on the northern line from Stirling and Larbert, the other (on this line) known today as FALKIRK (HIGH).

Passing through Falkirk Tunnel, the railway runs on to POLMONT, where it is joined by the line from Larbert. From this point to Haymarket West Junction, the Caledonian had running powers over the North British lines, enabling it to bring its trains from Stirling and the north into its station in Edinburgh (Princes Street). Two miles further on, the Edinburgh & Glasgow line crossed the older Slamannan Railway, part of a route from Airdrie down to the Forth at Bo'ness. The station at this crossing, Manuel (now closed), was a curiosity: a double station in a single structure, serving both lines one above the other.

The line now runs into LINLITHGOW on a gentle curve crossing a long via-

explosion, to warn the workmen of their danger.'[3] With its jagged vertical sides, Croy cutting is an impressive piece of work, most of all during severe winter weather, when the walls are so thick with icicles that the trains seem to be running through a trough of glass.

Two miles further on, Castlecary station (now closed) was an important point, standing on the boundary between the counties of Dunbarton and Stirling. The station was built close to the Wall and, six hundred yards to the east, the railway cut across a Roman fort.[4] The main road from Glasgow to Stirling (A80) runs below, and just beyond it is the corresponding railway, the Caledonian line from Glasgow (Buchanan Street).

A spur runs off on the up side two and a half miles further on at Greenhill Upper Junction to join the Caledonian line. This was always an important link, for it allowed North British trains (exercising running powers over the Caledonian line through Larbert) to travel from Glasgow into Fife. By means of this link, too, British Railways was enabled to close the Caledonian's old Buchanan Street station in Glasgow in

duct over the River Avon. The best view of the church and the great ruined palace in which Mary Queen of Scots was born is to be had by the traveller sitting on the up side of the train, facing west. Rather more than three miles further on, the line enters a cutting nearly four miles long. It is on this section that one can see most clearly how great an effort was made to keep the railway level, to ease the running of the trains. It would have cost far less if the line had been taken higher. As the cutting curves round to the south, a branch strikes away to the north to Dalmeny and Queensferry.

Out of the cutting, the line runs on to a high embankment and so on to a viaduct over the River Almond. This is one of the finest stone, or stone-clad, viaducts to be found anywhere on the railways of Britain – as fine as the Ouse viaduct in East Sussex and the Royal Border Bridge at Berwick (p. 88). The design of Miller's masonry was first class, in the best Scottish tradition; the bridge exemplifies it magnificently. Few engineering structures are more beautiful than a curved stone viaduct. This one is over a third of a mile long, and is carried on 36 arches.

As the line runs across the plain lying directly to the west of Edinburgh, in the narrowing gap between the Pentland Hills and the Firth of Forth, another line runs into it from the south. This is the Edinburgh & Bathgate Railway, which was opened in 1849 and ultimately formed part of an alternative route between Edinburgh and Glasgow, by way of Airdrie and Coatbridge. It is now closed to passenger traffic.

The suburbs of Edinburgh now begin to appear. The line from the Forth Bridge (opened in 1890) comes in on the up side, running parallel for a mile until it joins the main line at Haymarket West Junction. At this point, too, the Caledonian company's line diverged to Princes Street. The two routes were once hot competitors, but when Princes

Avon viaduct, west of Linlithgow, 1982.

Almond viaduct, looking east, 1985.

Edinburgh (Haymarket) station: main building at street level.

Overall trainshed from Haymarket re-erected by the Scottish Railway Preservation Society at Bo'ness, 1984.

Street was closed in 1965, the old Caledonian services from Glasgow via Shotts ran on to this line at Haymarket East Junction.

HAYMARKET station was the original terminus of the line. The trainshed of 1842 survives in the care of the Scottish Railway Preservation Society; it has been re-erected at Bo'ness. Above, at street level, stands the entrance building, a handsome stone structure exactly of a piece with the westward extension of the New Town of Edinburgh, in progress at the time it was built. Together with the station at Cupar in Fife, this is 'probably the most important early station building' in Scotland.[5]

When it first applied to Parliament, the Edinburgh & Glasgow company tried to secure powers to extend its line to the North Bridge. But this was vehemently opposed by the proprietors of Princes Street: they declared that the gardens on the south side of the street, which they owned, had been laid out at a cost of £7,000. Not unnaturally, they felt that this amenity would be destroyed if a railway ran through them. The company tried to propitiate the proprietors by offering to screen the line from sight with a wall and an embankment planted with trees and shrubs. As for any possible nuisance from the smoke of the engines, they dismissed that, stating that 'owing to the improved construction of the furnace the smoke is now scarcely seen'. The proprietors, however, remained unconvinced. They were joined in their opposition by various public bodies, such as the Society of Antiquaries of Scotland, and their views prevailed. When the railway company renewed the attempt in 1842, however, it was successful. It made similar promises: the embankment was to be high enough to hide the trains from the drawing-room windows of the houses in Princes Street, and its rawness was to be tempered by 'a profuse use of ivy, evergreens and trees'.[6]

So the railway was extended, through two tunnels and the long cutting through Princes Street Gardens to the North Bridge, with a terminus on the site of the present WAVERLEY station.

This short extension was brought into use on 1 August 1846.

The first 'General' station was a small one, lying between Waverley Market and the North Bridge, shared with the North British Railway, which ran on to Berwick. Presently a third company appeared, the Edinburgh Perth & Dundee Railway, with a terminus adjacent but at right angles to the General station. When all these companies had been united to form the enlarged North British company, an attempt was made to draw the three lines together into a single 'Waverley' station, but with very imperfect success. Among the principal stations of Great Britain, none surpassed it for inconvenience. Foxwell's joyous account of the proceedings there will stand quotation once again:

'On the platform of the Waverley station at Edinburgh may be witnessed every evening in summer a scene of confusion so chaotic that a sober description of it is incredible to those who have not themselves survived it. Trains of caravan length come in portentously late from Perth, so that each is mistaken

A 'Black Five' 4-6-0 heading a train past the Princes Street Gardens in 1955.

for its successor; these have to be broken up and re-made on insufficient sidings, while bewildered crowds of tourists sway up and down amongst equally bewildered porters on the narrow village platform reserved for these most important expresses; the higher officials stand lost in subtle thought, returning now and then to repeated inquiries some masterpiece of reply couched in the cautious conditional, while the hands of the clock with a humorous air survey the abandoned sight, till at length, without any obvious reason and with sudden stealth, the shame-stricken driver hurries his packed passengers off into the dark.'[7]

Those words were published in 1889. Worse was to come the following year when the Forth Bridge was opened, creating a new trunk route that poured in much increased traffic from Dundee and Aberdeen.[8] There was only one thing to be done. The line from Haymarket to Waverley had to be widened to four tracks, and Waverley station had to be reconstructed. The first of these measures raised a new storm of protest from the defenders of Princes Street Gardens. The second was a formidably complicated task, including the total reconstruction of the huge North Bridge; it was carried through

nobly under the engineers Blyth and Westland between 1892 and 1902. The whole station was rebuilt almost into its present form. It consisted mainly of one vast island platform, penetrated by bays for the traffic terminating there. It cost the immense sum of £1½ million.[9]

Waverley station is still not, in all respects, as good as it might be. Even British Rail has not managed to solve the problem of directing the 'bewildered crowds of tourists' clearly from one part of the great building to another, but it is an immeasurable improvement on the dismal caverns that Foxwell knew.

One last thing should be said about this line. It has seen an abnormally large number of accidents. Between 1845 and 1984 there were eleven fatal accidents to passenger trains on these 47 miles of railway, involving 124 deaths. The first of them was at Gogar in 1845, when a special train (consisting of one coach and a dilapidated little Bury four-wheeled engine), stumbling across from Glasgow to Edinburgh, was run into by another train following it. As a result William Paton, the locomotive engineer of the Edinburgh & Glasgow company, was charged with culpable homicide and sent to prison for a year. The worst accident was more recent: at Castlecary on 10 December 1937 one

Edinburgh (Waverley) station, viewed from the west end, 1956: in the background is the North Bridge on its rising slope, with the railway company's North British Hotel towering on the left.

Scot Rail push-and-pull Glasgow – Edinburgh express, 1985.

express ran into the rear of another which had pulled up in a snowstorm, and 35 people were killed. On 30 July 1984 an express push-and-pull train was derailed near Polmont after a collision with a cow that had strayed on to the track, and 13 passengers' lives were lost. On no other similar length of railway in Britain have there been so many accidents, causing so many fatalities, as on this one. Its closest competitor for this grim distinction would perhaps be the London – Brighton line, but that has always carried a much denser traffic.

Railway accidents usually *are* accidents: they occur haphazardly, from many causes, some of which are quite impossible to guard against. No generalisation can be made that covers them all, or that explains why this line – splendidly engineered, and difficult to work only at its two extremities – should have been so unfortunate.

Because the line is so level and straight, laid out for high speed, it might be thought that the trains on it have run exceptionally fast, and that this has been a cause of danger. No such thing: it was constantly pointed out that the Edinburgh & Glasgow company and its successors the North British and the London & North Eastern

in fact provided an unwarrantably slow service over the line, and the complaint was justified. In 1939 there were 14 up express trains on Mondays to Fridays and 11 down, running at an average speed of 44·4 mph. Today the number of trains has leapt from 25 to 63 and their speed to 61·6 mph.

The increased speed has been made possible by the introduction of lightweight push-and-pull trains, with diesel locomotives that can be driven from either end. Here is a pattern for the kind of service that can be effectively provided over short distances; with both railway terminals near the city centres, it is strongly competitive with private cars on motorways. The traveller need not worry about having to find parking space, or suffer the fatigue of driving; he may read and work during the journey – the thing simply advertises itself. This is one of the best kinds of service the railway can offer today. If it succeeds and is introduced elsewhere in similar conditions, the Edinburgh & Glasgow line will have fulfilled the hopes of those who planned it more than a century ago, so carefully and at such great expense. It is a noble example of the engineer's art, and it seems now to have come into its own.

TO
GREAT WESTERN HOTEL
AND BEACH

...WESTERN RAILWAY
TOURIST

THE RAILWAYS OF BRITAIN

CHAPTER

7

RESULTS & COMPARISONS

Previous page: a stream of holiday-makers pours out of Newquay station on the Cornish coast in 1903. The Great Western Railway encouraged traffic on its extreme western lines by skilful marketing of Cornwall's potential as a resort. It invented the name 'Cornish Riviera', and kept the attraction firmly in the travelling public's mind by bestowing the same name on one of its passenger express trains out of Paddington.

This book has provided a sketch of the railways of Britain, their history, equipment and operation. It has dealt with them as things in and for themselves. But there is another way of looking at railway history. Instead of describing what the railways were, one can ask what they did. What were the results of their work? What changes did they bring, or at least offer, to the people of the island? And how may their achievements be compared, in any useful way, with that of railways in other countries?

These questions are surprisingly difficult to answer, partly because they have not yet been thoroughly investigated.[1] Some important aspects of the railways' operations have hardly been examined at all. But a number of striking facts can be picked out from the statistics that are available.

The literature of railways has always paid most attention to the passenger business. In economic terms, as the table on the right shows, passengers were the less valuable part of the railways' operations. For 120 years they generated a smaller revenue for the companies than the carriage of freight. But travelling by train affected the life of the nation in the most direct and dramatic way. Among the many interesting changes the statistics reveal, the rapid growth of railway travel is one of the most impressive. In 1841 nearly 12 million passenger journeys were made. Over the next ten years the number increased tenfold, and by 1871 it had reached almost 360 million, virtually doubling to more than 600 million by 1881.

The new mobility was conferred on the whole people of Britain: on commercial men busy in the conduct of their business; on clerks and labourers travelling daily from suburbs into and out of the centres of great towns; on men dissatisfied with their work, or without any, searching for better opportunities elsewhere; on the millions who, as the Victorian age

NEWCASTLE & CARLISLE RAILWAY.

MONDAY THE 13th INSTANT,
BEING
HEXHAM HIRING DAY,

EXTRA TRAINS WILL START FROM

NEWCASTLE STATION at 7 o'Clock Morning for HEXHAM.
HAYDON BRIDGE - at 9 o'Clock Ditto - for DITTO.
HEXHAM - - - - at 5 o'Clock Afternoon for NEWCASTLE.
DITTO - - - - - at 8 o'Clock Evening for HAYDON BRIDGE.

By Order,

JOHN ADAMSON,

Railway Offices, Forth, Newcastle, May 9, 1844.   Clerk to the Company.

Newcastle-upon-Tyne : Printed at the Journal Office, 19, Grey-Street, by John Hernaman.

A Newcastle & Carlisle Railway poster advertises extra trains to take labourers to the Hexham hiring fair in May 1844. Railways settled down very quickly to playing their part in the ancient routines of country life, among them annual hiring fairs for the engagement of servants, shepherds and other agricultural workers.

TRAFFIC ON THE RAILWAYS OF GREAT BRITAIN, 1841-1981

Year	Miles of line open	No. of passenger journeys		Journeys per mile open	Population in thousands	Journeys per head of population	Receipts from passenger traffic,† in £ thousands	Receipts from freight traffic,† in £ thousands
		(a) exc. season-ticket holders in thousands	(b) inc. season-ticket holders					
1841	1,775*	11,962		6,740	18,534	0.65	2,601	866
1851	6,666	79,740		11,963	20,816	3.8	7,197	6,859
1861	9,442	163,042		17,268	23,128	7.1	10,967	14,699
1871	13,388	359,673		26,866	26,072	13.8	17,146	25,514
1881	15,734	605,404		38,478	29,710	20.4	22,760	35,270
1891	17,328	823,262		47,511	33,029	24.9	28,548	41,768
1901	18,853	1,145,543		60,762	37,000	31	44,623	51,235
1911	19,998	1,295,502		64,782	40,841	31.7	51,671	61,088
1921	20,299		1,786,671	88,018	42,769	41.8	105,853	109,552
1931	20,437		1,606,201	78,593	44,795	35.9	78,125	90,451
1941	No census taken							
1951	19,385		1,001,308	51,654	48,854	20.5	140,074	227,858
1961	18,240		999,525	54,799	51,284	19.5	213,831	236,842
1971	11,655		815,513	69,971	53,979	15.1	260,990	258,895
1981	10,831		718,500	66,338	54,284	13.2	1,022,800	623,100

No allowance has been made for changes in the value of money.

*Mileage opened since 1825. H. G. Lewin, *Early British Railways* (1925), p. 186.

†Excluding mails and parcels.

Sources: for the 19th century *Railway returns* (published annually in *Parliamentary Papers*); for the 20th century, D. L. Munby, *Inland Transport Statistics: Great Brtain, 1900-70*, (1978); for 1971-81, British Rail Reports, *Annual Reports,* 1971, 1981.

This table charts in summary form the expansion and contraction of the railways' business, analysed at ten-yearly intervals from 1841 to 1981 – the years when the national population censuses were taken. (No census was taken in 1941, during the war.)

The statistics available have been much criticised, and with justice. Those for 1841 (the first such figures ever to be collected in Britain) are manifestly very imperfect. In later years the basis for the returns made to the government was changed several times: in 1871 and 1913; in 1921 to meet the requirements of the grouping Act, and again at nationalisation in 1947.

Nevertheless, the figures do provide some sort of scale and means of comparison. One important change may be seen at the outset. In 1841 the companies' total revenue from passengers was about three times that from freight. Though passenger business increased rapidly in the following years, freight traffic grew more rapidly still. In 1852 freight traffic became the larger component in the companies' business, and it remained so for more than a century. In the later Victorian age, freight receipts usually exceeded passenger receipts by 20 to 25 per cent. It was the same after 1900 (except in the years 1919 and 1926, when freight traffic was much reduced by strikes), although the differential was less. Not until 1971 did passenger revenue again take the lead; it has kept it ever since.

The figures for passengers show an unbroken increase in the number of journeys up to 1921; then a decline, just reversed in 1961, but continuing again afterwards. Those for the Victorian age, however, exclude all passengers who travelled with season and workmen's tickets; these classes of ticket were not collected at the end of a journey and could not therefore be counted. Detailed censuses, in which every traveller was counted, were scarcely ever taken before 1900, and very seldom afterwards. A rough-and-ready formula for reckoning the number of season ticket holders first began to be used in 1913.

Great North of Scotland Railway

Manchester Sheffield & Lincolnshire Railway

Burry Port & Gwendreath Valley Railway

Railway tickets are not just collectors' pieces; they are also indicators of the purposes for which journeys were made. Five of the tickets shown here relate to journeys of special kinds: Scottish fisherfolk taking the train from Portessie on the coast down to Aberdeen; an Irish labourer coming over to work in England; a Welsh collier going to the pit. On the opposite page, there is a visitor to the British Empire Exhibition at Wembley in 1924; a traveller arriving off a ship at Plymouth; and a penny-a-mile Parliamentary passenger. This ticket was issued by the Bishop's Castle Railway in Shropshire: bankrupt within a year of its opening and for all the remaining 69 years of its life.

advanced, came to take annual holidays of a day or a week or more, at a distance from their homes. Above all it was conferred on the poorer classes. Even as early as 1851 more than half of those who travelled did so at the lowest rates – third class or 'Parliamentary'. By 1881 that proportion was more than four fifths; in the 20th century it has always been well over nine tenths.

A new freedom of movement had already begun to appear before the railways arrived. It was offered by horse-drawn buses in and around large towns, and by steamboats on some river estuaries – the Clyde, Mersey, Tyne and Thames.[2] But the railways outdistanced most of their competitors. A train could transport a far greater number of people in a single movement than any conveyance by road, and though crowded steamers could carry a large number of passengers they were crowded only in the summer – on many routes they did not run in the winter at all. The railways' superiority was maintained here, little challenged until their short-distance urban traffic began to be chipped away, first by horse-trams (another kind of railway) after 1870 and then, at the turn of the century, by electric trams and motor buses. Even then, their capacity to move people in large units remained unequalled. Four fifths of the commuters travelling into London today by public transport do so by train, and only one fifth by bus and private road vehicles taken together.

At first the poorest travellers on the railways were few, as they had been on the coaches. But some railway companies soon came to find it more profitable to convey a large number of passengers at the lowest fares than a small number at the highest, and they set themselves steadily – if not always graciously – to encourage third-class and Parliamentary travel. This policy gradually became accepted; and it was taken further on the British railways than on any of the other great systems in Europe. By 1914 third-class passengers were admitted to nearly all trains in Britain, whereas on the Continent they were barred completely from many of them or subjected to numerous restrictions and supplementary charges levied for travelling by express.

The British railway companies also did much more than any Continental administrations to promote travel at exceptionally low fares (much lower than those established in 1844) through excursion trains. These ran all over the country, not only in the summer or for special events but at other times in the year too.[3] Seaside towns came to depend on them. Some three million people were arriving at Blackpool by train every year at the opening of the 20th century; a quarter of them by special excursions and a great many more at reduced rates for a week's visit. Little Skegness, remote on the coast of Lincolnshire, received 750,000 visitors in 1913. Nearly all of them must have come by train in those days – from Nottingham, Leicester, Leeds and London, 80 to 130 miles away.[4]

The railways did not initiate large-scale movement for holiday-making – that had already begun, for example on the Thames, where steamers were plying from London to Margate in the 1820s. But the railways transformed it, in scale and in scope, so that it became a national amusement, enjoyed by people of all classes. The journeys made by these holiday-makers might be short or long: from Liverpool Street to Chingford, for Epping Forest, on a bank holiday; from Manchester to Bournemouth. The long-distance services did not convey any large excursion groups; they were used by families and individual people. Over short distances, on the other hand, the groups could be enormous. Bass, the brewers, made a practice of carrying their employees out on a marathon day-trip once a year to the seaside, requiring ten or more complete trains from Burton-on-Trent. The Great Western Railway offered its workpeople at Swindon the choice of a number of special trains, and in 1905 there were 22 of them, taking away half the population of the town in just over two hours.[5]

The details of the many millions of journeys made across a century and a half by excursionists and lone travellers, by suburban commuters and humbler people on the early morning workmen's trains are now mostly lost from both memory and records. Yet some of those individuals are not quite unknown to us. Sharp-eyed, articulate observers wrote accounts that enable us to relive episodes from the past. Here is Francis Kilvert on a long slow journey from Haverfordwest to Brecon in 1871, listening to the beautiful singing of the country people coming home from Neath market in the next compartment; Kipling letting off steam (no other expression will do) about the torpor of the railway on Sunday, a day of misery to British travellers in his time and ours; Hardy's convict on the station platform at Upwey, being played to by a little boy with his violin; Lord Curzon, off to an international conference, advancing to his Pullman car at Victoria 'majestically, as if he were carrying his own howdah', to be followed at the last minute by a temporary butler, unsteady with drink.[6]

We know of thousands more journeys, not described at all but recorded in a different way by means of the tickets issued for them. Some tickets were for journeys made for special purposes, or on special occasions – a visit to an exhibition, a trip by a repertory company on tour – and they remind us of the great range of facilities the railways offered throughout the community. These little pieces of pasteboard are part of the fabric of British railway history, as much as Acts of Parliament and directors' minutes, timetables, rules and regulations.

The journeys of those days were made at speeds unthinkable before railways arrived. Though the most remarkable advances in speed came at the outset, when the horse-drawn coach gave place to the train, the railways continued to increase the speed of their express trains (except during and after the two World Wars), and they have gone on doing so down to the present day. These advances are indicated in the table overleaf. It deals only with the fastest trains, not with the full railway service, which was quite often a different thing. Newcastle may have had two very fast trains from London in 1887, but they left close together in the morning and there were only four other expresses throughout the rest of the day, which were a great deal slower. Still, the impression given by the table is a fair one. The quickest trains showed what could be done in ordinary service. They set a standard, and it was usually only a matter of time before other trains were

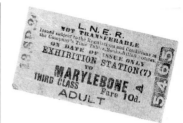

London & North Eastern Railway

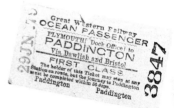

Great Western Railway

Bishop's Castle Railway

Employees of the Bass brewery, Burton-on-Trent, pile out of trains at Blackpool on their annual outing in 1911. Their dress displays a good mixture of social class, with almost as many women as men in the picture. Mammoth excursions such as this could be comfortably handled by the railways. The Bass outing was a famous one, taking the form of a day trip to a different holiday resort each year.

FASTEST TIMES TRAVELLING BY ROAD AND RAIL FROM LONDON TO TEN OTHER CITIES, 1836-1985

	1836 (by coach)	1852	1887	1914	1939	1961	1985
ABERDEEN	58 h 2 m	21 h 28 m	13 h 55 m	11 h 7 m	10 h 55 m	10 h 52 m	7 h
BRISTOL	12 h 15 m	2 h 45 m	2 h 36 m	2 h	1 h 45 m	1 h 45 m	1 h 30 m
CARDIFF	17 h 23 m	4 h 10 m	4 h 20 m	2 h 50 m	2 h 41 m	2 h 30 m	1 h 45 m
GLASGOW	42 h 30 m	12 h 20 m	9 h 45 m	8 h 15 m	6 h 30 m	7 h 28 m	5 h 10 m
LEEDS	21 h 22 m	4 h 50 m	3 h 55 m	3 h 42 m	2 h 43 m	3 h 39 m	2 h 13 m
MANCHESTER	18 h 30 m	5 h	4 h 15 m	3 h 30 m	3 h 15 m	3 h 57 m	2 h 33 m
NEWCASTLE	30 h 20 m	7 h 25 m	6 h 7 m	5 h 20 m	3 h 57 m	4 h 39 m	2 h 53 m
NORWICH	11 h	3 h 15 m	2 h 45 m	2 h 28 m	2 h 10 m	2 h 10 m	2 h 3 m
NOTTINGHAM	12 h 47 m	3 h 25 m	2 h 23 m	2 h 15 m	2 h 3 m	2 h	1 h 40 m
PLYMOUTH	21 h 35 m	7 h 5 m	5 h 10 m	4 h 7 m	4 h 5 m	4 h	3 h

Sources: 1836 – A. Bates, *Directory of Stage-Coach Services* (1969); 1852-1961 – *Bradshaw's Railway Guide*; 1985 – *British Rail Passenger Timetable*. The railway times given are those for the summer service.

accelerated to approach or equal their speed. In the country, however, away from large towns, it was different. The services on many rural branch lines, particularly on the borders of England with Wales and Scotland, remained much the same in 1939 as they had been in 1887.

Lively-minded Victorians, as they watched the increase in railway speed, speculated on its effects. Some thought they were harmful. Thomas Love Peacock, for instance, pointed in 1860 to the 'collisions and wrecks and every mode of disaster by land and by sea, resulting chiefly from the insanity for speed, in those who for the most part have nothing to do at the end of the race'.[7] Over the next 15 years the horrible frequency of accidents on railways – even though only a minority were caused by excessive speed – appeared to bear him out. But better management and the improvement of safety precautions reduced the number of accidents in the late 1870s. Speeds on British railways rose further and attracted the interest of observers abroad.[8]

In 1884 a most intelligent Englishman, Ernest Foxwell, thought it time to set out a comprehensive view of the social benefits that the fast trains of his country were conferring on its people. To him the express train had released a new power in human work: 'It is the invigoration put into men's energies *by the quick conversion of intention* into *deed* which is the most valuable effect of expresses. . . . High speed enables men to do more work and do it better, to come across a wider choice of facts and form surer decisions for dealing with them'. (Much the same is often said of air travel today.) Foxwell was trying to make his countrymen look at the revolution in transport that the railways had brought about and were continually taking further, and to urge them to consider its implications – implications that seemed to him almost wholly beneficent.[9]

The cost of railway travel is more difficult to evaluate than its speed. No accurate comparison can be made between coach and rail fares. Coach fares varied greatly. They were subject to no legislative control, whereas the railways' charges for the conveyance of both passengers and freight were governed by maximum rates laid down in their Acts of Parliament. Moreover, coach passengers were obliged to pay a number of supplements to their stated fares by way of 'vails' – tips to coachmen and guards – which

A flamboyant landmark of Liverpool's High Victorian architecture, the former North Western Hotel stands in front of the great glass-and-iron trainsheds of Lime Street station. Now used as offices, the building has hardly altered externally since it was built by Alfred Waterhouse in 1871 for the London & North Western Railway. The hotel boasted more than two hundred rooms as well as 37 water closets – a lavish provision at that time.

The stone and slate of Grange-over-Sands provide a perfect example of the attractive architecture of the best of the small stations. The Furness Railway built it in 1877, to designs by E. G. Paley. It replaced the earlier station which had become inadequate with the town's development as a seaside resort.

On the preserved Isle of Man Railway (far left), No. 4 Loch passes through a glen in Crogga Wood after leaving Port Soderick station on the way from Douglas to Port Erin. The railway, laid out to the 3ft gauge, was completed in 1874. This 2-4-0 tank engine, one of several still running on the island in the summer months, was built in 1874 by Beyer, Peacock of Manchester. Its maroon livery is very similar to that of the original company colour of madder brown.

A locomotive (left) on the only steam-worked rack-and-pinion railway in Britain pushes a solitary coach up Mount Snowdon in North Wales; its steam is just visible between the trees. The Snowdon Mountain Railway, laid out to a gauge of 2ft 7½in and only four and three quarter miles long, had a spectacular opening in 1896: the first of its Swiss-built engines from the locomotive works at Winterthur careered down the mountain and was destroyed. The engines are specially designed for mountain work, with angled boilers to counteract the 1 in 5½ gradient. The cost of running such a line is reflected in the high passenger fares; nonetheless, it does a very successful trade in the summer months, carrying visitors to the 3,560ft summit.

Preserved 0-4-4 tank locomotive No. 419, formerly of the Caledonian Railway, stands newly painted at Bo'ness station on the Firth of Forth. The overall trainshed in the background, which dates from 1842, was brought from Edinburgh's Haymarket station in 1983. The roof, the station, the engine and the line are now in the care of the Scottish Preservation Society.

One of the finest surviving large trainsheds in the country, James Carswell's iron-and-glass structure at Queen Street station, Glasgow, has a single span of 250ft and is 78ft high. Put up in the 1870s for the North British Railway, the station (recently remodelled) still provides excellent facilities, bringing travellers right into the centre of the city.

amounted on average to at least 15 per cent; there was nothing like that on the railways. Changes in the value of money have made it almost impossible to compare charges then and now. What does it mean when we say that in 1844 it was laid down that passengers should be allowed to travel by at least one train a day at 1d a mile? What useful and honest comparison can be made between a Victorian penny and our own? A further difficulty arises today, when the fares charged cannot be expressed as rates at all. British Rail has abandoned standard fares, fixed by distance and calculable on that basis by the traveller – whereas on the Continent the reckoning of fares in this way is still easy, as it surely ought to be everywhere, in fairness to the customer. The West German and Swiss railways, for example, state their tariff quite plainly in their timetables. British Rail now have no rates to quote in pence per mile; they do not even offer in their timetables any specimen rates for ordinary fares and 'savers' – from London to Manchester, for example, or from Bristol to Glasgow.

Despite all the difficulties of comparison, it is unquestionable that the railways not only speeded up long-distance travel very greatly but also cheapened it. For many travellers, in different ways, the saving of time represented an additional saving of cost. Dionysius Lardner made a calculation in 1850 of the total saving the railways had effected in the price of travel, compared with the price by stage coach, and he reached the conclusion that it amounted to 60 per cent.[10]

The British railways had been costly to build (costlier than almost any others in the world) and to equip. Usually, any improvement – in the materials and design of articles, in the facilities and amenities of life – involves a rise in price, at least when it is first introduced. To that general rule the railways provide a remarkable exception. The speed and comfort and service that they offered cost their customers not more than they had been paying before, but a good deal less.

Railways became a democratising force more completely in Britain than anywhere else in Europe. It is true that the railways in Belgium were quicker to encourage third-class travel than those in England (although not those in Scotland).[11] As early as 1836 more than half their revenue was derived from people travelling at the lowest rates; from 1844 to 1847, 62 per cent of all passengers were going third-class. But the trains in Belgium were slower than in Britain, the system there was extended more gradually, and the range of opportunities afforded by the railways was less attractive. By the early 1880s the number of railway passenger journeys made in the small island of Great Britain was *larger than in the whole of the rest of Europe combined.* Twenty-three journeys per head of the population were then being made in Britain every year; the next highest number was in Belgium (nine), while in the United States it was five.[12]

Foxwell's summary of this new mobility and its social consequences, written from the standpoint of a mid-Victorian Liberal, may look simplistic to us now, but it deserves to be read with respect: 'For fifty years people of every sort and variety have come across each other and been intimately mixed up in the affairs of life. This constant rubbing against one another has taught them more of the quality of the stuff of which they are all made ... and while it has in consequence created a wish to level everyone up to their best possibilities, the incessant contact of ideas has bred feasible plans for the wiser treatment of that stuff of which high and low are only variations. This is Democracy, and this is the work of railways.'[13]

But railways did not bring benefit only to those who had occasion to travel. They rendered services equally important to people who stayed where they were: to householders in their daily round, to every industry, large and small. The effects of some of these services on the national economy have been examined in a valuable book by G. R. Hawke, in respect of England and Wales from 1840 to 1870, leading him to conclude that railways 'could not have been sacrificed in 1865 without the need to compensate for a loss of the order of 10 per cent of the national income'.[14] And it was not only the quantity of goods and services that was affected, it was also their quality.

Railways helped to bring about great changes in diet and in public health. Both were affected by their conveyance of milk into large towns from country districts.[15] Before the arrival of the railways, most town-dwellers were supplied with the little milk they drank from cows kept in the towns. There were 20,000 of them in and around London in the 1850s, many of them tethered in back yards or confined in the cellars of houses. The hygienic consequences can easily be imagined. The railways first transported milk into Liverpool and Manchester. When they offered to do so into London their services were not welcomed, on the grounds that the milk would be damaged by their rough handling of it, whereas that produced on the spot was fresh and undisturbed. Presently, however, opinion changed. In 1864 George Barham successfully established his Express Country Milk Supply Company (later the Express Dairies), which brought up most of its milk by train from the pastures of Derbyshire, 130 miles away. Soon afterwards London milk production was disrupted by an outbreak of cattle disease. By 1870 the railways had captured more than half the business. Forty years later 96 per cent of the liquid milk brought into London came by rail, over distances of 300 miles and more. Much of it was carried in special express trains, running at speeds of 40-50 mph. The difference this made was considerable. In 1850 Londoners were reckoned to drink about 48 pints of milk a head in the year – less than a pint a week. By 1910 they were consuming half a pint a day. This was a great change in diet, and it was due in large measure to the railways.

Similar changes were brought about by the railways' transport of fish. In that business the provinces benefitted most, especially the large towns and industrial districts inland; the greater part of London's needs could be supplied by sea. As early as the 1840s, when fish came to be carried by railway from Hull, it was noted that the price in the market at Manchester fell to one eighth of what it had formerly been. At Nottingham forty years later, fish was nearly the largest business handled by the Midland Railway at its goods station. Special vehicles were needed for this traffic; and it is worth noting that the railway company owning the largest number of them was the Lancashire & Yorkshire, which did not go to London at all. Its services did much to help the growth of Fleetwood as a fishing port after 1896.[16]

The commodity the railways were most accustomed to handling was coal. When their system was extended after 1830, a great opportunity seemed to lie before them: to take coal to London, by far the largest of the chief cities of Britain, and the only one that lay far from a coalfield. But the market did not at first increase rapidly. A tight hold on it was exercised by the colliers sailing down the coast from Northumberland and Durham.[17] It was not until 1867 that the railways brought more coal into London than the coastal steamers, and that victory was not permanent. By the end of the 19th century the railways and the coasters were taking almost equal shares in the traffic. So the railways did not by any means knock out their old-established rival. But they enjoyed three superiorities in the competition.

This London Midland & Scottish tank wagon conveyed milk in bulk, not in separate cans as had been the general practice in the 19th century. Most long-distance milk traffic was carried by rail at least until the Second World War.

The Lancashire & Yorkshire Railway provided special vans, such as this one, for the fish traffic from Fleetwood to the northern industrial districts. Fleetwood Dock was opened in 1877, built with capital raised by the railway company. Fishing was already well established there, but it did not become a major industry until the 1890s. More than 1,000 tons of fish were moved out of the port in 1896 (the figure includes the weight of the packaging and the ice) and Fleetwood soon became the leading fishing port in north-west England.

First, they could ensure a much more regular supply than the ships, which were often held up by storms and fog in winter. The railways had to contend with fog too, but with their sophisticated safety precautions they could keep their trains moving.

Second, they controlled their own highways. By 1889 London was consuming 12 million tons of coal a year, 61 per cent of it brought in by rail. If that huge quantity had all come by sea and then been distributed throughout Greater London by carts, as in the past, the Thames would have been impassable with shipping and a new road system would have been required. The railways took their part of the coal directly from the colliery, first to marshalling yards in the coalfields, such as those at Toton and Colwick in Nottinghamshire, then up to other yards on the outskirts of London. From there the rail wagons could be hauled by a variety of routes around the great city to the coal depots and the goods yards attached to many suburban stations. Only there did the merchants and their carts take over, delivering to each consumer one by one.

On his 1929 billhead a coal
and coke merchant in
Harrow, north-west
London, graphically
advertises his varied
services, which include the
transport of building
materials and the removal of
furniture. His train of coal
wagons is hauled by one of
the large, eight-coupled
freight locomotives of the
London & North Western
Railway that were
constructed in substantial
numbers from 1912 onwards.
Dealing in coal, which was
brought from the mines by
railway to local goods yards,
often became the foundation
on which much other
business was built. A.
Wooster & Sons still thrive
today at the same address.

Lastly, the railways handled the produce of every coalfield in Britain, whereas most of what was brought into London by coastal shipping came only from north-eastern England. Many different types of coal were available; each had different properties, and was sold at a different price. The railways offered a far wider choice of them than the coastal steamers ever could. An additional benefit was that the competition between the two types of transport brought the general level of prices down from the 1880s onwards.

Coal was at that time an essential ingredient in the production of almost every kind of power. It was needed for the lighting of main streets. Every industry made use of it, most depending on it entirely. Though much coal went on being conveyed by water to factories and works that lay on canals or navigable rivers, the railways were great carriers of industrial coal too, whether in competition or in places where they had the business to themselves. Luton, which had no water transport, could never have started manufacturing motor cars, as it did in 1905, if it had not been for the services of the Midland Railway, which brought up both the coal the Vauxhall company needed, and also iron and steel from Yorkshire.[18]

The railways also created industries of their own to manufacture the machines and equipment they needed to operate their system. The manufacture of locomotives, rolling stock and other machinery was carried on much more extensively by the railways in Britain than anywhere else. In other countries it was more usual for railways to buy their equipment from commercial manufacturers. Both systems existed side by side on a great scale in Britain, generating employment and new urban development. Some towns, such as Shildon, Crewe and Eastleigh, were created almost from nothing by the railways; older towns like Derby, Swindon and Doncaster expanded greatly when railway works were established in them. Other cities grew to meet the needs of commercial manufacturers. Manchester was one of the biggest centres of locomotive production in the Victorian age. Glasgow became easily the biggest centre in Europe when the North British Locomotive Company was formed by amalgamation in 1903. The new company employed almost 8,000 men in addition to those already in the railway companies' own works at St Rollox and Cowlairs.

The British railways were concerned with much more than land transport. They owned between them the largest aggregation of docks in Europe, a shipping fleet (68,000 tons of it in 1913) for their busy services to Ireland and the Continent, and a chain of 92 hotels. They also went, at one time or another, into a great range of industrial activities, from coal-mining to brick-making and printing. The London & North Western company played an important part in the technically difficult launching of Bessemer steel. The London & South Western owned a big quarry at Meldon in Devonshire, from which it drew the ballast it used on its track; British Rail still keeps that quarry open today, for the same purpose. Some of these ancillary services made only a small profit, or none, and the nationalised railways have now had to shed most of them in order to concentrate exclusively on their own business, narrowly defined. But that does not condemn these enterprises in retrospect. Most of them were legitimate extensions of the companies' work, which was conceived in broader terms before 1914 than it has been since. They were rich corporations, and they had capital available for new development on a very large scale.

The London & South Western company, for example, totally re-invigorated the port of Southampton after it purchased the docks there in 1892, at a time when it was plain that no other capital would be forthcoming on anything like the same scale for the extension and improvement that were urgently required. The effect on the town's languishing economy was soon apparent. The total number of men and boys employed there in transport – rail, sea, river and docks – was 3,200 in 1891; twenty years later it was 8,800, almost one in five of the town's occupied male population. By 1907 Southampton was beginning to eclipse Liverpool in the handling of passenger traffic across the Atlantic. In 1893 the North Eastern company made a similar purchase of the Hull Dock Company, very much for the betterment of that port too. The Caledonian Railway greatly enlarged Grangemouth from 1897 to 1906, to make it the biggest industrial port on the east coast of Scotland. These undertakings brought in, at least for a time, a handsome revenue to the companies and their shareholders. But they had a much wider importance. They served and profited whole communities at the same time.

What they did for them they did, on a much greater scale, for Great Britain as a whole. They gave the country a unity it had never known before, drawing it tightly together by their rails, the telegraphs that went with them, the postal services they carried at unprecedented speed (with a

In a still from the famous 1936 Post Office film Night Mail *(below left), workers on the night shift sort bags of mail. The efficient and reliable transport of mail was one of the most socially beneficial tasks undertaken by the railways. Apparatus allowing mail to be collected and delivered by trains passing at speed was developed in stages from the 1840s onwards. In the photograph (below), a railwayman waits by the line to supervise collection. The heavy leather pouch was picked up automatically by an arm that extended from the mail van. The capacious net just behind him is for receiving the incoming mail that will be thrown out of the train as it passes.*

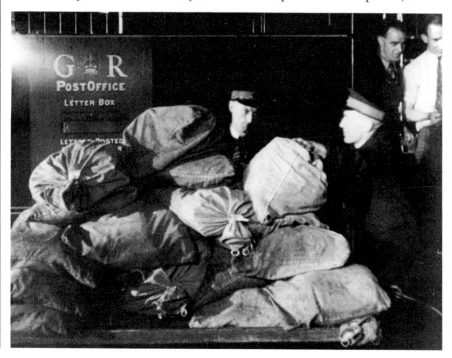

regularity and frequency that are vanished now), the newspapers they disseminated from Fleet Street every morning. The most illustrious newspaper and postal trains ran from Euston: the 5.15am newspaper express, with connections to remote parts of Wales and Scotland;[19] the West Coast Postal, running through to Aberdeen overnight, carrying never more than a handful of passengers, who were much less important than the postbags; and the Irish Mail, which welcomed travellers between London and Dublin and provided sleeping accommodation for them. These trains could be said to form an anatomy of the old United Kingdom. The Irish Mail continued to run under that name until 1985, sixty years after the kingdom, in its constitutional form, had gone.

The railways did more than any other single force to turn the centralisation of government from an ideal in the minds of politicians and administrators into a reality. Before the railways appeared, days or even weeks would go by before the government in London could know if the orders it had issued on a matter, say, in Cornwall or Argyll had been obeyed, and with what result. Now, anything it ordained could be effected almost instantly, backed up if required by police or soldiers dispatched by rail from the nearest military depot; with equal efficacy, it could quell Chartist demonstrations in Lancashire or ugly riots against the landing and dispatch of herring on Sundays in Wester Ross.[20]

This Victorian process of unification had one perfect symbol: the establishment of a single time throughout the island, determined at Greenwich. The railways were largely responsible for it. Until the 1840s all time in Britain was local, based on differences in longitude. At Glasgow it was 18 minutes behind Greenwich time, at Penzance 22; at Yarmouth it was eight minutes in advance.[21] When railways began to spread throughout the

Here is Greenwich Time, proclaimed in Edinburgh by the clock in the booking hall of Waverley station. Installed during reconstruction of the station in the 1890s, both the clock and its elaborate art nouveau ironwork were, most regrettably, removed when a face-lift was given to the station eighty years later.

country this diversity was evidently troublesome. The London & Birmingham began by attempting to adhere to the local variations; the Great Western, and presently the Caledonian, adopted Greenwich time from the outset, saying so in their timetables.[22] There was a general disposition to accept the railways' lead in this piece of standardisation. Manchester Town Council, for example, sensibly accepted the Lancashire & Yorkshire Railway's advice to adopt Greenwich time on all public clocks. Only the West Country hung back. Little struggles went on over the change – at Plymouth and Exeter, for example – but they were settled in favour of Greenwich time by 1852. As the railway system extended into remote places Greenwich time was transmitted down the line daily to each station.[23]

Not everybody liked this standardisation. Many people deplored the loss of the old ways and said so, sometimes with exaggerated over-emphasis. Baring-Gould remarked that railways had 'abolished every-where in Europe a local *cuisine*';[24] one wonders if he ever actually break-fasted in Scotland, lunched in Yorkshire or dined in Lyon. On the other hand, the standardisation of building materials in cities, towns and villages up and down the country that the railways undoubtedly did much to promote (p. 128) had aesthetic results that have been called, with justice, 'disastrous'.[25]

Even a glance at the effects wrought by the railways shows that there is much more to their history than an account of mechanical devices. They became vital elements in the whole life and work, the thinking and feeling, of the society they were built to serve, and still serve today.

A sketch by William McConnell of a Parliamentary train from Euston to the Midlands and Lancashire in 1859 captures the crowded scene which lay beyond the capacity of the early camera to record. There is nothing sentimental about this impression of the mixture of people that were conveyed in such trains, with some hints of the variety of their business. By no means all the passengers are of the working class. The man on the left reading his newspaper looks as if he could well have afforded to travel second class, but chose the Parliamentary train for economy, a practice much deplored and criticised by some railway managers who thought it deprived their companies of income.

NOTES

CHAPTER 1 THE MAKING OF THE RAILWAYS

1 C. E. Lee, *The Evolution of Railways* (2nd edn., 1943), p. 21. Lee, relying on Historical MSS. Commission, *Report on the MSS. of Lord Middleton* (1911), p. 169, gives the date of the first reference to this railway as 1598. This is a mistake for 1608; see R. S. Smith, *Renaissance and Modern Studies*, Vol. 1 (1957), pp. 120-21.

2 It is possible that a locomotive had been built at Coalbrookdale in 1802, but the evidence is insufficient to prove it. See E. A. Forward, *The Engineer*, 22 February 1952; A. Raistrick, *Dynasty of Iron Founders* (1953), pp. 161-67.

3 J. Clapham, *Economic History of Modern Britain* (1926-38), Vol. 1, p. 388.

4 *Dictionary of Commerce* (1832), p. 898; *Statistical Account of the British Empire* (1837), Vol. 2, p. 183.

5 See F. C. Mather, 'The railways, the electric telegraph, and public order during the Chartist period, 1837-48', *History*, Vol. 38 (1953), pp. 40-53.

6 J. Francis, *A History of the English Railway* (1851), Vol. 2, pp. 132-33.

7 For the emergence of this phrase, as early as 1825, see J. Simmons, *The Railway in England and Wales, 1830-1914* (1978), p. 24.

8 *Punch*, Vol. 10 (1846), p. 88.

9 *The Larchfield Diary* (1876), p. 70.

10 Earl Stanhope, *Notes of Conversations with the Duke of Wellington* (World's Classics edn.), p. 124.

11 The Stephensons' 4ft 8½in prevailed over most of Europe, though wider gauges were adopted in Russia (5ft) and Spain (5ft 6in). The USA showed a remarkable diversity of gauges, from 4ft 8½in to 6ft, and this diversity proved a serious handicap to its economic development. See G. R. Taylor and I. D. Neu, *The American Railroad Network, 1861-90* (1956) and, for a general survey, L. Day, *Broad Gauge* (1985).

12 The Eastern Counties Railway was converted from the 5ft to the 4ft 8½in gauge in 1844.

13 The only important exception to this statement is provided by the 'working union' between the South Eastern and London Chatham & Dover companies of 1899, which established a monopoly in Kent. See P. S. Bagwell, 'The rivalry and working union of the South Eastern and London Chatham & Dover Railways', *Journal of Transport History*, Vol. 2 (1955-56), pp. 65-79.

14 G. Findlay, *The Working and Management of an English Railway* (4th edn., 1891), p. 126.

15 See J. A. R. Pimlott, *The Englishman's Holiday* (1947), pp. 147-53.

16 The phrase is W. M. Acworth's: *The Railways of England* (1889), p. 412.

17 Cornwall Record Office, papers of A. P. Vivian of Bosahan, 12M/EC/19/10; E. T. MacDermot, *History of the Great Western Railway* (1964 edn.), Vol. 2, p. 223. The buses used by the Great Western company had been bought from Sir George Newnes, who had run them in association with the Lynton & Barnstaple Railway for a short time earlier in 1903. In Ireland the Belfast & Northern Counties Railway had begun to operate steam buses of its own in April 1902; see J. M. Cummings, *Railway Motor Buses* (1978-80), Vol. 1, p. 8; Vol. 2, p. 24.

18 *Passenger Transport in Glasgow and District* (British Transport Commission, 1951), p. 18.

19 See E. Davies, *The Case for Railway Nationalisation*, and E. A. Pratt, *The Case against Railway Nationalisation*, both published in 1913.

20 The damage from air raids is set out in E. A. Pratt's admirably informative *British Railways and the Great War* (1921), pp. 462-65.

21 It is true that the Great Northern had done something to overcome this disadvantage by the construction of the loop line from Wood Green to Stevenage, through Cuffley and Hertford. But this was an inadequate measure, as the company itself seemed to recognise by the tardiness with which it built the line. It secured the necessary powers in 1898 and opened the first part, as far as Cuffley, in 1910. The remaining section was opened, as a single line for goods traffic only, in 1918. It was not doubled and made available for passenger traffic until the London & North Eastern management had taken over, in 1924. The line has in fact never carried any very substantial traffic north of Hertford.

22 T. C. Barker and C. I. Savage, *An Economic History of Transport in Britain* (1974 edn.), p. 247. See also M. R. Bonavia, *The Four Great Railways* (1980), pp. 128-32.

23 R. Bell, *History of the British Railways during the War, 1939-45* (1946), pp. 57-58.

24 C. I. Savage, *History of the Second World War: Inland Transport* (1957), pp. 613, 647.

25 The quotations in this paragraph are taken from *Modernisation and Re-equipment of British Railways* (1955), pp. 5-7.

26 The line to Liverpool through Runcorn dates from 1869.

27 M. R. Bonavia, *British Rail: the First 25 Years* (1981), p. 43.

28 See K. M. Gwilliam, *Transport and Public Policy* (1964), pp. 175-76.

29 It is no accident that two of the ablest modern railway historians should lately have published books that are very gloomy indeed. Their titles speak for themselves: P. S. Bagwell, *End of the Line?* (1984), and M. R. Bonavia, *Twilight of the Railways* (1985).

30 See *Railway World*, Vol. 45 (1984), pp. 195-201.

JOURNEY 1

1 Much the best account of the station is that given by A. A. Jackson in *London's Termini* (2nd edn., 1985).

2 On a unique system, clearly explained in H. G. Lewin, *Early British Railways* [1925], p. 89.

3 H. D. Welch, *The London Tilbury & Southend Railway* (1951), pp. 4-5.

4 See T. B. Peacock, *P. L. A. Railways* (1952).

5 The early history of Tilbury Docks is conveniently summarised in J. Pudney, *London's Docks* (1975), chap. 11.

6 C. L. D. Duckworth and G. E. Langmuir, *Railway and Other Steamers* (2nd edn., 1968), p. 43.

7 For his life see H. Colvin, *Biographical Dictionary of British Architects, 1600-1840* (1978).

8 The only other one seems to be that on the Somersetshire Coal Canal, 66yd long, opened in 1910; see C. Hadfield, *Canals of Southern England* (1955), p. 276.

9 F. R. Conder, *The Men who Built Railways*, ed. J. Simmons (1983), chaps. 20, 21.

10 For an interesting account of this branch see E. Course, *Railways of Southern England: Secondary and Branch Lines* (1974), pp. 141-49.

11 The history of the Medway crossings is clearly recounted in *Railway Magazine*, Vol. 76 (1935), pp. 313-15. See also C. I. Savage, *History of the Second World War: Inland Transport* (1957), p. 259, and E. Course, *Railways of Southern England: Main Lines*, pp. 62-68.

CHAPTER 2
BUILDING THE SYSTEM

1 The story of the Cheltenham & Great Western Union company is told in E. T. MacDermot, *History of the Great Western Railway* (1964 edn.), Vol. 1, pp. 79-85.

2 H. Pollins in *Economica*, Vol. 19 (1952), p. 406.

3 For example, the landowners on the Slamannan Railway in Scotland and Sir John St Aubyn at Devonport; see F. Whishaw, *Railways of Great Britain and Ireland* (2nd edn., 1842), p. 400; *Journal of Transport History*, Vol. 4 (1959-60), p. 23.

4 Lincs. Record Office, STU 7/20 (89).

5 The Derby – Manchester line was described in some detail in previous editions of this book, pp. 209-22.

6 A useful list of those works undertaken in the Second World War is given in C. I. Savage, *Inland Transport* (1957), pp. 257-62.

7 J. K. Fowler, *Recollections of Old Country Life* (1894), p. 125.

8 T. R. Potter, *History and Antiquities of Charnwood Forest* (1842), p. 187.

9 *Murray's Handbook for Scotland* (6th edn., 1894), p. 408.

10 W. G. Hoskins, *The Making of the English Landscape* (1955), p. 207.

11 See J. Simmons, *The Railway in Town and Country* (1986), chap. 9.

12 *Journal of Transport History*, Vol. 1 (1953-54), p. 165; Tomlinson, *North Eastern Railway* [1915], pp. 101, 196 (henceforth abbreviated to Tomlinson).

13 *The Complete Works of John Ruskin*, ed. E. T. Cook and A. Wedderburn (1903-12), Vol. 19, p. 26.

14 See R. A. Lewis, 'Edwin Chadwick and the railway labourers', *Economic History Review*, Vol. 3 (1950-51), pp. 107-18; J. Simmons, 'The building of the Woodhead Tunnel', *Parish and Empire* (1952), pp. 155-65; G. Dow, *The Third Woodhead Tunnel* (1954).

15 Walker wrote a valuable account of the work: *The Severn Tunnel: its Construction and Difficulties* (1891).

16 The best accounts of these viaducts are by H. S. B. Whitley in *Railway Engineer*, Vol. 52 (1931), pp. 384-92, and by L. G. Booth in *The Works of Isambard Kingdom Brunel*, ed. Sir A. Pugsley (1980 edn.), pp. 114-35.

17 See P. S. A. Berridge, *The Girder Bridge* (1969), chaps. 9, 13.

18 H. N. Maynard, *Handbook to the Crumlin Viaduct* (1862), p. 30.

19 H. S. Smith, *The World's Great Bridges* (1953), pp. 85-86.

20 Bouch has not received the credit he deserves for his persistence, which was largely responsible, indirectly, for the final bridging of the Forth. In view of the subsequent history of the Tay Bridge, the speeches made at the laying of the foundation stone of his Forth Bridge have a pathos of their own; see *Railway Times*, Vol. 41 (1878), pp. 869-70.

21 See B. Morgan, *Civil Engineering: Railways* (1971), pp. 149-50.

22 See M. J. T. Lewis's splendid book, *Early Wooden Railways* (1970).

23 Other materials continued to be used for horse tramways. The Hay Tor Tramroad on Dartmoor, which was opened in 1820 and continued in use for over forty years, was built entirely of granite blocks.

24 Tomlinson, pp. 16, 405, 531.

25 *Transactions of the Leicestershire Archaeological Society*, Vol. 30 (1954), p. 96.

26 See the diagram in MacDermot, *History of the Great Western Railway* (1964 edn.; henceforth abbreviated to MacDermot), Vol. 1, p. 28.

27 Tomlinson, p. 530.

28 I am indebted for much information on the introduction of the steel rail to David Brooke.

29 Tomlinson, p. 648; MacDermot, Vol. 2, p. 266.

30 W. M. Acworth, *Railways of England* (5th edn., 1900), p. 69n; C. Baker, *The Metropolitan Railway* (1951), p. 18.

31 G. Findlay, *The Working and Management of an English Railway* (4th edn. 1891), p. 48.

JOURNEY 2

1 See *Railway Magazine*, Vol. 4 (1899); Vol. 33 (1913), p. 288.

2 J. Simmons, *The Railway in Town and Country* (1986), chap. 10.

3 *Ibid.*, chap. 9.

4 On this matter see *Ibid.*, chap. 1.

5 From this point onwards to Southampton the line is fully described by E. A. Course in his *Railways of Southern England: Main Lines* (1973), pp. 254-82. There are useful track plans on pp. 253, 254, but unhappily they have been misplaced, so that the second must be read before the first.

6 C. Hadfield, *Canals of Southern England* (1955), p. 269.

6 C. Hadfield, *Canals of Southern England* (1955), p. 269.

7 See A. Helps, *Life of Thomas Brassey* (1870), pp. 29-30, 161 (list of French contracts).

8 As for instance at Bradford-on-Avon, where the Wilts Somerset & Weymouth Railway agreed with J. H. Cotterell in 1847 that the embankment traversing his property should be 'planted by the company at the proper season next after their construction with ornamental shrubs or evergreens and protected and from time to time renewed': Bodleian Library, Oxford, MS. Top. Wilts. b.3, fol. 22v.

9 For example at Richmond (Surrey) in the same year, where the landlord was the Crown. It was stipulated that in crossing the Deer Park the railway must be planted to the satisfaction of the Commissioners of Woods and Forests: Local and Personal Act, 10 Vict. cap. 58, sec. 35.

10 For this process see A. Clifton-Taylor, *The Pattern of English Building* (1972 edn.), pp. 203-4.

11 Inspector's report: *Parliamentary Papers*, 1843, Vol. 47, p. 209.

12 See B. J. Turton, 'The railway towns of southern England', *Transport History*, Vol. 2 (1969), pp. 105-33; Simmons, *Railway in Town and Country*, chap 6. For the first purchase of land see PRO, RAIL 411/7, min. 1978, 411/8, mins. 106, 127.

13 E. A. Pratt, *British Railways and the Great War* (1921), pp. 1025-26; R. Bell, *History of the British Railways during the War of 1939-45* (1946), p. 210.

14 Course, *Railways of Southern England: Main Lines*, p. 265.

15 See A. T. Patterson, *History of Southampton*, Vol. 2 (1971), pp. 158-59, 167-69.

16 On this tunnel see Course, *Railways of Southern England: Main Lines*, pp. 277-79; Hadfield, *Canals of Southern England*, pp. 87-89; J. G. Cox, *Castleman's Corkscrew: the Southampton & Dorchester Railway* (1975), pp. 11-13, 18-21.

CHAPTER 3 ENGINEERING AND ARCHITECTURE

1 C. Baker, *The Metropolitan Railway* (1951), p. 39.

2 H. S. Goodhart-Rendel, *English Architecture since the Regency* (1953), p. 77.

3 An invaluable illustrated summary of railway buildings to be seen today is provided by *The Railway Heritage of Britain*, ed. G. Biddle and O. S. Nock (1983).

4 C. L. V. Meeks, *The Railway Station* (1957), p. 27.

5 *The Railway Heritage of Britain*, p. 162.

6 Professor Hitchcock was mistaken in stating that both roofs were replaced in 1869-70, 'when worn out by the smoke'; *Architecture: Nineteenth and Twentieth Centuries* (1958), p. 127. For the history of the station outlined above see C. H. Grinling, *History of the Great Northern Railway* (1898), pp. 114-15; *Illustrated London News*, Vol. 21 (1852), pp. 339-40, Vol. 22 (1853), pp. 427-28; G. Measom, *Official Illustrated Guide to the Great Northern Railway* (1857), p. 11; L.C.C., *Survey of London*, Vol. 24 (1952), pp. 115-16; A. A. Jackson, *London's Termini* (1985 edn.), chap. 4.

7 For the growth see J. Simmons, 'Suburban traffic at King's Cross, 1852-1914', *Journal of Transport History*, 3rd series, Vol. 6 (1985), pp. 71-78.

8 N. Pevsner, *The Buildings of England: London*, Vol. 2 (1952), p. 304.

9 See J. Simmons, *St Pancras Station* (1968).

10 Sir G. Scott, *Personal and Professional Recollections* (1879), p. 271.

11 J. Betjeman, *First and Last Loves* (1952), pp. 82-83.

12 [R. Thorne,] *Liverpool Street Station* (1978), pp. 27-32, 38-40.

13 This complicated story can be pieced together from MacDermot, *History of the Great Western Railway* (1964 edn.), Vol. 1, pp. 70-71, 107-

10, Vol. 2, pp. 76, 83; N. Pevsner, *The Buildings of England: North Somerset and Bristol* (1958), pp. 421-22; J. Latimer, *Annals of Bristol in the Nineteenth Century* (1887), pp. 291, 387-89, 420; J. Simmons, *The Railway in Town and Country* (1986), chap. 4. Latimer's book reflects the fierce hatred felt by many Bristolians for the Great Western Railway, and especially for the memory of Brunel.

14 *Parl. Papers* 1914-16, Vol. 60, pp. 719, 721, 794; PRO, RAIL 266/109, GWR statistics, 1913-20, sec. 7, p. 27.

15 In its early days it attracted an aristocratic clientele. The aged Lord John Russell had a family holiday at the Zetland Hotel in August 1870; see *The Amberley Papers*, ed. B. and P. Russell (1937), Vol. 2, pp. 370-72. For the early history of Saltburn see *Victoria History of Yorkshire, North Riding*, Vol. 2, p. 400, and J. Simmons, *The Railway in Town and Country* (1986), chap. 8.

16 C. J. Allen, *The Great Eastern Railway* (1955), p. 192; G. Measom, *Official Illustrated Guide to the Great Eastern Railway: Colchester Line* (1865), p. 184.

17 MacDermot, Vol. 1, pp. 75-76, Vol. 2, p. 213.

18 See, for example, J. Gloag and D. Bridgwater, *A History of Cast-Iron in Architecture* (1948), pp. 171-78; H. R. Hitchcock, *Early Victorian Architecture in Britain* (1954); C. L. V. Meeks, *The Railway Station: an Architectural History* (1957).

19 *British Transport Review*, Vol. 1 (1950-51), pp. 182-83. See also C. Barman's admirable *Introduction to Railway Architecture* (1950).

20 J. Bourne, *Drawings of the London to Birmingham Railway* (1839); D. Cole, 'Mocatta's stations for the Brighton Railway', *Journal of Transport History*, Vol. 3 (1957-58), pp. 148-57.

21 The payment of the early railway architects is an obscure and interesting subject, investigated for the first time by H. Parris in *Architectural History*, Vol. 2 (1959), pp. 56-61.

22 This attractive piece of mid-Victorian design is due to Charles

Liddell, engineer for this section of the Midland, and Driver & Webber, architects. Engravings of the details of Wellingborough and Kettering stations were published by Henry Laxton in 1858; there is a set in PRO, RAIL 491/753.

23 For a general account of these buildings see L. Menear, *London's Underground Stations* (1983), chaps. 3, 4.

24 That kind is now almost extinct, but an example can still be seen at Frome, Somerset.

CHAPTER 4
MOTIVE POWER

1 Calculation from C. F. D. Marshall, *A History of Railway Locomotives down to the End of the Year 1831* (1953).

2 No account is taken here of the fervent – and often acrimonious – controversies between the protagonists of one engineer and another, concerning the priority of inventions. Marc Seguin designed a locomotive with a multi-tubular boiler, which underwent its trials at Lyon at the same time as *Rocket*. But it seems that the two inventions were totally independent. The boilers, moreover, were widely different. Seguin placed his chimney at the back and produced the draught by great fans; whereas the boiler of *Rocket* was essentially like that in use today. See Marshall, *A History of Railway Locomotives*, pp. 150-52.

3 G. F. Westcott, *The British Railway Locomotive . . . 1803-53* (1958), p. 5.

4 E. L. Ahrons, *The British Steam Railway Locomotive, 1825-1925* (1927), p. 19.

5 The engine was preserved at Swindon Works until 1906, when the company, alas, broke it up. A replica of the engine in its original condition was built in 1925.

6 The last was No. 3219, completed at Swindon in 1948.

7 E. Foxwell and T. C. Farrer, *Express Trains: English and Foreign* (1889), p. 14. This book, with Acworth's *Railways of England* (5th edn., 1900) and Ahrons's *Locomotive and Train Working in the Latter Part of the Nineteenth Century* (6 vols., 1951-54), offers a vivid account of the running of late Victorian express trains.

8 Ahrons, *Locomotive and Train Working*, Vol. 2, pp. 37, 58-63; Acworth, pp. 353-54.

9 Ahrons, *Locomotive and Train Working*, Vol. 5, p. 58.

10 An apparatus designed to achieve economy through supplying steam to the cylinders 'dried' and therefore at a higher pressure than 'saturated' steam.

11 E. C. Poultney, *British Express Locomotive Development, 1896-1948* (1952), pp. 169-70. For an account of the rebuilding of these engines see *Railway Magazine*, Vol. 102 (1956), pp. 207-12.

12 On this matter see the evidence and the comments of the Inspecting Officer on the derailment at Milton, near Didcot, on 20 November 1955 (Report: HMSO 1956).

13 See R. M. Robbins, *190 in Persia* (1951).

14 See Brian Reed's excellent appraisal of the type in his *Locomotives in Profile* (1971-74), Vol. 4, pp. 193-216.

15 M. Robbins, *The North London Railway* (4th edn., 1953), p. 22.

16 C. L. Baker, *The Metropolitan Railway* (1951), p. 42; Ahrons, *The British Steam Railway Locomotive*, p. 156; Reed, *Locomotives in Profile*, Vol. 1, pp. 221-44.

17 The fullest account of this remarkable machine is by W. O. Skeat in *Transactions of the Newcomen Society*, Vol. 28 (1951-53), pp. 169-85, Vol. 29 (1953-55), pp. 263-64.

18 D. S. Barrie, *The Taff Vale Railway* (2nd edn., 1950), p. 35.

19 Royal Commission on Transport, *Final Report* (Cmd. 3751, 1931), p. 39.

20 *Electrification of the Manchester, Sheffield and Wath Lines* (1954), pp. 4, 28.

21 *Electrification of Railways* (British Transport Commission, 1951), p. 70.

22 For an account of these locomotives see *Railway Magazine*, Vol. 105 (1959), pp. 827-31, 864.

23 See H. Williams, *APT: a Promise Unfulfilled* (1985).

24 The best succinct account of the evolution of the heavy-oil-engined locomotive is in *Diesel Railway Traction*, Vol. 12 (1958), pp. 41-88. See also B. Reed, *Diesel Locomotives and Railcars* (2nd edn., 1939).

25 *Ibid.*, p. 14, Table VIII.

JOURNEY 3

1 The whole line is described, with useful maps and copious illustrations, in M. Bairstow, *The Manchester & Leeds Railway: the Calder Valley* (1983). For the history of its construction see J. Marshall, *The Lancashire & Yorkshire Railway* (1969), chaps. 3, 12.

2 M. Robbins, 'Thomas Longridge Gooch, 1808-82': *Transactions of the Newcomen Society* (forthcoming).

3 *Parliamentary Papers*, 1873, Vol. 57, p. 410.

4 See Marshall, Vol. 2, pp. 57-65, with useful plans.

5 For the Rochdale Canal see C. Hadfield and G. Biddle, *Canals of North-West England* (1970), pp. 263-72, 430-8.

6 Marshall, Vol. 1, pp. 41-43; F. Whishaw, *Railways of Great Britain and Ireland* (1842 edn.), pp. 317-18; S. Smiles, *Life of George Stephenson* (5th edn. 1858), pp. 370-72; A. F. Tait, *Views on the Manchester & Leeds Railway* (1845) – the most informative set of contemporary prints of a railway, apart from John Bourne's.

7 There is a fine contract drawing of this structure in PRO, RAIL 343/598.

8 Whishaw, p. 320.

9 As suggested in Robbins's paper on Gooch.

10 Their oddities are admirably indicated, one by one, in G. Biddle, *Victorian Stations* (1973), pp. 116-17.

11 Descriptions and pictures in *The Railway Heritage of Britain*, ed. G. Biddle and O. S. Nock (1983), pp. 34, 36.

12 D. Joy, *Regional History of the Railways of Great Britain: South and West Yorkshire* (1975), p. 129.

13 For the Lockwood viaduct see Marshall, Vol. 1, pp. 228-29; for 'snecking', A. Clifton-Taylor, *English Stone Building* (1983), pp. 81, 103.

14 *Murray's Handbook for Yorkshire* (3rd edn., 1882), p. 484. The account of the works given here is excellent.

15 For a plan of the railways in and around Bradford see Joy, p. 79.

16 E. L. Ahrons, *Locomotive and Train Working in the Latter Part of the Nineteenth Century* (1951-54), Vol. 2, pp. 42, 53-54.

CHAPTER 5
ROLLING STOCK

1 They took the name of the light open road vehicles that were called after the Hon. and Rev. Fitzroy Stanhope (1787-1864), for whom they were first made.

2 *The Glasgow & South Western Railway, 1850-1923* (Stephenson Locomotive Society, 1950), p. 5.

3 G. Dow, *Great Central* (1959), Vol. 1, p. 109.

4 J. D. Marshall, *Lancashire & Yorkshire Railway* (1969-72), Vol. 3, p. 103.

5 *The Builder*, Vol. 3 (1845), p. 167.

6 D. K. Clark, *Railway Machinery* (1855), Vol. 1, p. 264.

7 'Mugby Junction', chap. 3; *Christmas Stories*, Oxford Illustrated Edition, p. 522.

8 C. E. Lee, *Passenger Class Distinctions* (1946), p. 37; Midland handbill in bar of Crown & Mitre Hotel, Carlisle; G. P. Neele, *Railway Reminiscences* (1904), p. 214.

9 Scotland had been ahead of England in this matter; see W. M. Acworth, *The Railways of Scotland* (1890), pp. 178-79.

10 Ahrons, *Locomotive and Train Working*, Vol. 5 (1953), pp. 4-5.

11 See, however, A. G. Atkins and others, *History of GWR Goods Wagons* (1975-76); R. J. Essery, *Illustrated History of Midland Wagons* (1980); K. Montague, *Private Owner Wagons from the Gloucester Railway Carriage & Wagon Co. Ltd.* (1981).

12 Tomlinson, *North Eastern Railway*, p. 657. Three chaldron wagons are preserved at York.

13 MacDermot, *History of the Great Western Railway* (1964 edn.), Vol. 1, p. 450.

14 F. Whishaw, *Railways of Great Britain and Ireland* (2nd edn., 1842), pp. 9, 78, 111, 345; *Transactions of the Leicestershire Archaeological Society*, Vol. 30 (1954), pp. 89-90.

15 R. Essery, *Midland Wagons*, Vol. 1, pp. 5-6.

16 D. K. Clark, *Railway Machinery*, Vol. 1, p. 265.

17 *The Glasgow & South Western Railway, 1850-1923*, p. 43; *The Highland Railway, 1855-1955*, p. 52.

18 *Caledonian Railway Centenary* (1947), p. 55; MacDermot, Vol. 2, pp. 305-6; Atkins, *GW Wagons*, Vol. 2, pp. 51-61; Tomlinson, pp. 727-28.

19 E. Foxwell and T. C. Farrer, *Express Trains English and Foreign* (1889), p. 30.

CHAPTER 6
RUNNING THE SYSTEM

1 Explanations of the operation of signalling devices will be found in such books as M. J. Tweedie and T. S. Lascelles, *Modern Railway Signalling* (1925), and J. R. Day and B. K. Cooper, *Railway Signalling Systems* (1958).

2 Quoted in [T. S. Lascelles,] *A Centenary of Signalling* (Westinghouse Brake & Signal Co., 1956), p. 5.

3 On these early installations see G. Hubbard, *Cooke and Wheatstone* (1965), chaps. 6, 8, 9.

4 Quoted in Hamilton Ellis's useful analysis of this accident, *British Railway History*, Vol. 1, p. 233.

5 H. W. Parris, *Government and the Railways in Nineteenth-Century Britain* (1965), p. 197.

6 L. T. C. Rolt, *Red for Danger* (1955), p. 163.

7 Acworth, *The Railways of Scotland* (1890), pp. 163-66.

8 A joint line was one owned by two or more larger companies, like the Great Northern & Great Eastern joint line from Spalding to Lincoln, opened in 1882. Among the other *systems* that were jointly owned may be mentioned the Cheshire Lines and the Portpatrick & Wigtownshire.

9 E. Foxwell and T. C. Farrer, *Express Trains English and Foreign* (1889), p. 56; E. L. Ahrons, *Locomotive and Train Working in the Latter Part of the Nineteenth Century*, Vol. 1, p. 143.

10 J. C. Loudon, *Encyclopaedia of Cottage, Farm and Villa Architecture* (1863 edn.), p. 1169.

11 *The Builder*, Vol. 19 (1861), p. 341.

12 Acworth, *Railways of England* (1889), p. 306; O. S. Nock, *Scottish Railways* (1950), p. 109; G. F. Allen, *British Railways Today and Tomorrow* (1959), p. 171.

13 Samuel Smiles's *Lives of the Engineers* (1857-68) was the first attempt at collective biography in this field. Among his recent successors are O. S. Nock, *The Railway Engineers* (1955); H. Ellis, *Twenty Locomotive Men* (1958), and J. Marshall, *Biographical Dictionary of Railway Engineers* (1978).

14 A moving little autobiography of a railway navvy, out of work in 1849, is to be found in Henry Mayhew's *London Labour and the London Poor* (1861-62), Vol. 3, pp. 410-11.

15 *General Report on Accidents on Railways in 1870* (C. 294, 1871), p. 34.

16 *Victoria History of Wiltshire*, Vol. 4, p. 211.

17 D. S. Barrie, *The Taff Vale Railway* (2nd edn., 1950), pp. 36-37.

18 H. J. Hanham, *Elections and Party Management: Politics in the Time of Disraeli and Gladstone* (1959), pp. 87-89.

19 PRO, RAIL 1021/43/30 (Henry Pease to Thomas MacNay, 22 July 1868); R. Christiansen and R. W. Miller, *North Staffordshire Railway* (1971), p. 130.

20 M. Robbins, *The North London Railway* (4th edn., 1953), p. 28.

21 Acworth, *Railways of England* (1889), pp. 309-15.

22 *British Transport Review*, Vol. 3 (1954-55), pp. 244-51.

23 Ahrons, *Locomotive and Train Working*, Vol. 1, pp. 58-59.

24 *Ibid.*, Vol. 4, p. 105.

25 N. Crump, *By Rail to Victory* (1947), pp. 3-4.

JOURNEY 4

1 C. J. A. Robertson, *Origins of the Scottish Railway System* (1983), p. 119.

2 Scottish Record Office, Edinburgh: BR/FCN 1/2, fol. 182, 3 July 1771.

3 *Lizars' Guide to the Edinburgh & Glasgow . . . Railway* [1847], p. 23.

4 A. Robertson, *The Antonine Wall*, pp. 59-61.

5 *The Railway Heritage of Britain*, p. 146.

6 D. Robertson, *The Princes Street Proprietors* (1935), pp. 37-46.

7 E. Foxwell and T. C. Farrer, *Express Trains English and Foreign* (1889), p. 60.

8 John Thomas gave a graphic account of the new chaos this produced on the opening day in *Regional History*, Vol. 6, p. 247.

9 For a contemporary account of the work see *Railway Magazine*, Vol. 6 (1900), pp. 117-25. See also G. Dow, *The First Railway across the Border* (1946), pp. 19-22, and plan in Appendix B.

CHAPTER 7 RESULTS AND COMPARISONS

1 Some of the difficulties are discussed in J. Simmons, *The Railway in Town and Country* (1986), chap. 1.

2 Estimates of the numbers of passengers conveyed by all these services in London can be made from T. C. Barker and M. Robbins, *History of London Transport* (1975-76 edn.), Vol. 1, pp. 4, 26, 42-43.

3 For the sparing provision of them in France, Belgium, Germany, Austria and Italy, see the reports of British official investigators into the working of railways in those countries: *Parliamentary Papers* 1909, Vol. 77, pp. 394-95; 1910, Vol. 57, pp. 211, 265, 313-14, 416.

4 J. K. Walton, *The Blackpool Landlady* (1978), pp. 28-29; G. H. J. Dutton, *Ancient and Modern Skegness* (1922), p. 58.

5 Acworth, *Railways of England* (5th edn., 1900), p. 50; A. S. Peck, *The Great Western Railway at Swindon Works* (1983), p. 158.

6 *Kilvert's Diary*, ed. W. Plomer, Vol. 2 (1939), pp. 70-71; Kipling, 'My Sunday at Home', *The Day's Work* (1898); Hardy, 'At the Railway Station, Upwey', *Collected Poems* (4th edn., 1930), p. 575; H. Nicolson, 'Arketall', *Some People* (1927).

7 Thomas Love Peacock, *Gryll Grange*, chap. 19 (ed. R. Garnett, 1948, p. 877; see also pp. 932-34).

8 For example by R. S. Minot in his excellent paper *Railway Travel in Europe and America* (1882). The superiority in speed of British passenger trains, of all kinds, compared with French, is shown in P. Lefèvre and G. Cerbelaud, *Les Chemins de Fer* (1888), p. 225.

9 E. Foxwell, *Two Papers on Express Trains* (1884), p. 5. Foxwell was also co-author, with T. C. Farrer, of the much better-known *Express Trains English and Foreign* (1889).

10 D. Lardner, *Railway Economy* (1850), pp. 180-81.

11 C. J. A. Robertson, *The Origins of the Scottish Railway System* (1983), p. 237.

12 *Journal of the Statistical Society*, Vol. 1 (1838), pp. 114-15; Lardner, *Railway Economy*, pp. 423, 434; J. S. Jeans, *Railway Problems* (1887), p. 232.

13 Foxwell, *Two Papers*, p. 38.

14 G. R. Hawke, *Railways and Economic Growth in England and Wales, 1840-70* (1970), pp. 404-05.

15 The account given here is based largely on P. J. Atkins, 'The growth of London's railway milk trade, c.1845-1914', *Journal of Transport History*, n.s. Vol. 4 (1977-78), pp. 108-26. See also his articles on the Barhams in the *Dictionary of Business Biography*.

16 J. Morrison, *Influence of Railway Legislation* (1848), p. 137; F. S. Williams, *Our Iron Roads* (1888 edn.), p. 416; R. J. Essery and others, *British Goods Wagons* (1970), p. 84; J. Marshall, *Lancashire & Yorkshire Railway*, Vol. 1 (1969), p. 93.

17 For this coastal trade see R. Smith, *Sea Coal for London* (1961); for the railways' part in the business, see J. Simmons, *The Railway in Town and Country* (1986), chap. 2.

18 *Ibid.*, chap. 9.

19 Acworth, *Railways of England*, pp. 87-89.

20 F. C. Mather, 'The railways, the electric telegraph and public order during the Chartist period, 1837-48', *History*, Vol. 38 (1953), pp. 40-53; J. Thomas, *The Skye Railway* (1977), pp. 84-89.

21 See map reproduced in D. Howse, *Greenwich Time* (1980), p. 110.

22 MacDermot, *History of the Great Western Railway*, Vol. 1, p. 337; *London & Birmingham Railway: Table of Fares and Rates* [1838], copy in British Library, T 968*(4); Caledonian Railway timetable, Vol. 1, December 1847 (copy in Scottish Record Office, Edinburgh).

23 J. R. Kellett, *Impact of Railways on Victorian Cities* (1969), pp. 173-74; Howse, *Greenwich Time*, pp. 109, 112-13; Thomas, *Skye Railway*, p. 51.

24 S. Baring-Gould, *Old Country Life* (1913 edn.), p. 152.

25 A. Clifton-Taylor, *The Pattern of English Building* (1972 edn.), pp. 42, 229.

SOURCES OF KNOWLEDGE

Records

The principal collection of records relating to the railways of England and Wales is in the charge of the Public Record Office at Kew, near London. For the railways of Scotland they are in the Scottish Record Office, West Register House, Charlotte Square, Edinburgh. The nucleus of each was formed by the records of the old railway companies before nationalisation, transferred under the Transport Act of 1968. The Parliamentary records are in the House of Lords Record Office, London SW1.

Introductory accounts of these collections, indicating the kinds of record they contain, were published in the *Journal of Transport History* between 1953 and 1962. L. C. Johnson described the making of the British Transport Commission's archive in two articles in Vols. 1 and 5. D. B. Wardle surveyed the records relating to railways at the Public Record Office before the companies' records were taken to Kew, in Vol. 2. I gave a general account of the Scottish records of the Commission in Vol. 3. For the records at the House of Lords see M. Bond, 'Materials for transport history among the records of Parliament' (Vol. 4).

A large number of records, some of them important, are now in local record offices. I offered a general introduction to them in 'Railway history in English local records' (*Journal of Transport History*, Vol. 1, 1953-54); but since then many more such records have been taken into the custody of these offices, particularly the papers of landowning families who dealt with railway companies. For an illustration of the value of such documents see J. T. Ward, 'West Riding landowners and the railways' (*Journal of Transport History*, Vol. 4, 1959-60). *Record Repositories in Great Britain* (HMSO, 6th edn., 1979) provides a list of addresses of these offices. A postal inquiry, enclosing a stamped addressed envelope and indicating clearly the kind of information sought, will generally elicit a helpful answer.

Printed literature

In 1965 George Ottley produced his *Bibliography of British Railway History*, a work of reference that lists nearly all the books and pamphlets issued

before that date. It has now made its way into general circulation and has already had to be re-issued, in 1983. A supplement is now in the press, adding the publications down to 1980. The work is readily accessible in reference libraries. With this excellent key to the literature available in books (it is well arranged and thoroughly indexed), there is no need for any long list of them here. Some of the principal works may however be mentioned, and occasionally discussed.

The history of railways forms part of the general history of transport. W. T. Jackman, *Development of Transportation in Modern England* (1916), is full and learned, but unfortunately stops at 1850. Three shorter but valuable recent works may also be mentioned: H. J. Dyos and D. H. Aldcroft, *British Transport* (1969); T. C. Barker and C. I. Savage, *An Economic History of Transport in Britain* (1974); and P. S. Bagwell, *The Transport Revolution from 1770* (1974).

The fullest general history of British railways down to 1947 is by H. Ellis: *British Railway History* (1954-59). Readable throughout, it is well informed on technical matters but sketchy elsewhere. H. Pollins, *Britain's Railways: an Industrial History* (1971), supplies what its title promises. M. Robbins, *The Railway Age* (1962), and H. Perkin, *The Age of the Railway* (1970), are two excellent introductions to the subject. I have described the Victorian system and the ways in which it was worked in *The Railway in England and Wales, 1830-1914* (1978) and surveyed some of the services provided to Victorian local communities in *The Railway in Town and Country* (1986).

H. G. Lewin treated the early period in two books: *Early British Railways . . . 1801-44* [1925] and *The Railway Mania and its Aftermath, 1845-52* (1936; reprinted, with some corrections, 1968). C. J. A. Robertson, *The Origins of the Scottish Railway System, 1722-1844* (1983), is outstandingly good. Among the older, contemporary observers of railways, W. M. Acworth is particularly distinguished, with his *Railways of England* (1889; 5th edn., enlarged, 1900) and *Railways of Scotland* (1890). The work of the railways during the two world wars is chronicled in E. A. Pratt, *British Railways in the Great War*

(1921); R. Bell, *History of the British Railways during the War, 1939-45* (1946); and C. I. Savage, *Inland Transport (History of the Second World War: United Kingdom Civil Series)* (1957). Two useful studies of the history of railways since nationalisation have been produced by M. R. Bonavia: *The Birth of British Rail* (1979) and *British Rail: The First 25 Years* (1981).

Some admirable books have been published in recent years on the part played by railways in the economic and political life of Britain: for example, J. R. Kellett, *The Impact of Railways on Victorian Cities* (1969); G. R. Hawke, *Railways and Economic Growth in England and Wales, 1840-70* (1970); M. C. Reed, *Investment in Railways in Britain, 1820-44* (1975); P. S. Bagwell, *The Railway Clearing House in the British Economy, 1842-1922* (1968); H. Parris, *Government and the Railways in Nineteenth-Century Britain* (1965); G. Alderman, *The Railway Interest* (1973).

It is often useful to approach railway history by way of a study of localities. *A Regional History of the Railways of Great Britain*, edited by D. St J. Thomas and J. A. Patmore, is an invaluable aid to that study, covering the whole island south of the Forth – Clyde line in 14 volumes, written by various authors (1960-83). The *Victoria History of the Counties of England* has treated the railways of certain counties, for example Cambridgeshire, Leicestershire, Staffordshire, Warwickshire and Wiltshire. Other regional studies of value include F. G. Cockman, *The Railway Age in Bedfordshire* (1974); M. Robbins, *The Isle of Wight Railways* (1953); and W. J. Ward, *The Tanat Valley: its Railways and Industrial Archaeology* (1968). E. Course, *The Railways of Southern England* (1973-76), describes the system from Kent to Hampshire in great detail. Greater London is treated in the exemplary *History of London Transport* by T. C. Barker and M. Robbins (revised edn., 1975-76) and in A. A. Jackson, *London's Local Railways* (1978).

British railway history has chiefly been written in terms of the companies that owned and, for most purposes, controlled the system until nationalisation in 1947. The number of these studies is large, and they vary greatly in value. Those produced down to 1964 can easily be found in Ottley's *Bibliography*. I add here a selection of those published since, in alphabetical order of companies: R. Christiansen and R. W. Miller, *The Cambrian Railways* (1967-n.d.); P. E. Baughan, *The Chester & Holyhead Railway* (1972); J. Wrottesley, *The Great Northern Railway* (1979-81); *The Hull & Barnsley Railway*, ed. K. Hoole and B. Hinchliffe (1972-80); J. Marshall, *The Lancashire & Yorkshire Railway* (1969-72); R. H. G. Thomas, *The Liverpool & Manchester Railway* (1980), and *London's First Railway – The London & Greenwich* (1972); R. A. Williams, *The London & South Western Railway* (1968-73); J. H. Turner, *The London Brighton & South Coast Railway* (1977-79); J. Wrottesley, *The Midland & Great Northern Joint Railway* (1970); C. G. Maggs, *The Midland & South Western Junction Railway* (1967); J. Thomas, *The North British Railway* (1969-75); R. J. Irving, *The North Eastern Railway Company, 1870-1914* (1976) – one of the few historical studies of a British railway *company*, in terms of its organisation and management, that has yet been written; R. Christiansen and R. W. Miller, *The North Staffordshire Railway* (1971); J. Thomas, *The Skye Railway* (1977) and *The West Highland Railway* (1965).

M. R. Bonavia, *The Four Great Railways* (1980), is the best general account yet produced of the history of the companies created in 1921.

Much labour and energy have been put into the writing of railway company histories over the past hundred years. But even now two of the most important British companies, the London & North Western and the Midland, lack histories that can be called adequate.

The railway preservation movement will soon be important enough to merit a comprehensive study. A good preliminary survey, *Railways Revived*, was produced by F. J. C. Ransom in 1973. The same author's *Archaeology of Railways* (1981) is also valuable. F. G. Cockman, *Discovering Lost Railways* (4th edn., 1985), is a workmanlike guide to walking over certain disused lines.

There is no full work on the civil engineering of railways in Britain. A useful short introduction is B. Morgan, *Railways: Civil Engineering* (1971). Some of the big Victorian books, produced chiefly for the profession, are good, notably F. W. Simms, *Public Works of Great Britain* (1846), and W. Humber, *Record of the Progress of Modern Engineering, 1863-66* (1870). Another, much lighter, contemporary book is F. R. Conder, *Personal Recollections of English Engineers* (1868), reprinted as *The Men who Built Railways* (1983). An excellent set of essays devoted to one great engineer is provided in *The Works of Isambard Kingdom Brunel*, ed. Sir A. Pugsley (1980).

Perhaps the best introduction to the science and art of railway tunnelling is that given in *The Severn Tunnel: its Construction and Difficulties* (1888) by T. A. Walker, the contractor responsible for building it. For bridges see D. Walters, *British Railway Bridges* [1963] – brief, but good; and P. S. A. Berridge, *The Girder Bridge* (1969).

M. J. T. Lewis, *Early Wooden Railways* (1970), is a work of scholarship outstanding in British railway history. A clear, simple account of the emergence of the metal rail is to be found in C. E. Lee, *The Evolution of Railways* (2nd edn., 1943).

C. Barman, *Introduction to Railway Architecture* (1950), was a perceptive pioneering study. *Railway Architecture*, ed. M. Binney and D. Pearce (1979), covers a wide field and is well illustrated. *The Railway Heritage of Britain*, by G. Biddle, O. S. Nock, and others (1983), treats the heritage in terms both of civil engineering and of architecture. It is much the fullest and most important book yet devoted to those two subjects in combination. Among general works on stations perhaps the best books are C. L. V. Meeks, *The Railway Station: an Architectural History* (1957); G. Biddle, *Victorian Stations* (1973); and *All Stations*, the catalogue of a remarkable exhibition called *Le Temps des Gares*, first mounted at the Centre Georges Pompidou in Paris and subsequently shown in London. This presents stations in the context of the societies they serve. L. Menear, *London's Underground Stations* (1983), is a lively study of one of the most interesting groups of railway stations in the world. London main-line stations have been very well studied by A. A. Jackson in *London's Termini* (3rd edn., 1985). Two have been discussed individually in J. Simmons, *St Pancras Station* (1968), and [R. Thorne,] *Liverpool Street Station* (1978).

W. A. Tuplin, *The Steam Locomotive: its Form and Function* (1974), supplies a clear, brief account of the working of the steam locomotive. Its standard history is still E. L. Ahrons, *The British Steam Railway Locomotive, 1825-1925* [1927], continued by O. S. Nock in *The British Steam Railway Locomotive, 1925-65* (1966). *Locomotives in Profile*, ed. B. Reed (1971-74), is a work of exceptional interest, in which 36 types of steam engine are carefully and critically discussed; 17 of them are British. Most histories of railway companies treat their locomotives at some length. Full accounts have been published of three of the companies' chief works: J. B. Radford, *Derby Works and Midland Locomotives* (1971); B. Reed, *Crewe Locomotive Works and its Men* (1983) – see also W. H. Chaloner, *Social and Economic Development of Crewe* (1950); and A. S. Peck, *The Great Western at Swindon Works* (1983; admirably illustrated). For the history of locomotive construction see J. W. Lowe, *British Steam Locomotive Builders* (1975). The best history of a locomotive manufacturing firm is R. L. Hills and D. Patrick, *Beyer Peacock* (1982).

Other forms of traction are treated in C. Hadfield, *Atmospheric Railways* (2nd edn., 1985); F. J. G. Haut, *History of the Electric Locomotive* (1969); D. W. and M. Hinde, *Electric and Diesel Electric Locomotives* (1948); B. Reed, *Diesel Locomotives and Railcars* (2nd edn., 1939); B. Webb, *British Internal Combustion Locomotives, 1894-1940* (1973), and W. J. K. Davies, *Diesel Rail Traction* (1973).

The history of the railways' rolling-stock has, until recently, been little attended to. Hamilton Ellis was the pioneer in this branch of study, and his *Railway Carriages in the British Isles from 1870 to 1914* (1965) remains the standard general work. But a number of books – lavishly illustrated, mainly from official photographs – have now been published that deal with the passenger rolling-stock of some individual companies: for example, J. H. Russell, *Pictorial Record of Great Western Coaches* (1972-73); D. Jenkinson, *An Illustrated History of LNWR Coaches* (1978); D. Jenkinson and R. Essery, *Midland Carriages* (1984). The history of freight vehicles has been similarly investigated, for example by A. G. Atkins and others in *A History of GWR Goods Wagons* (1975-76) and by R. J. Essery in *A History of Midland Wagons* (1980). The private owner's wagon has been well treated in K. Montague, *Private Owner Wagons from the Gloucester Carriage and Wagon Co. Ltd.* (1981).

Nearly all these books concerned with locomotives and rolling-stock deal only with their technology and construction. If one wishes to know what they cost, for example, one turns in vain to all of them except those of Radford and Reed and the history of Beyer Peacock.

A good history of the railways' safety precautions, explaining their success and failure in simple language, is greatly needed. On signalling [T. S. Lascelles,] *A Centenary of Signalling* (1965), is perhaps the most useful general history. See also M. Tweedie and T. S. Lascelles, *Modern Railway Signalling* (1925); O. S. Nock, *Fifty Years of Railway Signalling* (1962); G. M. Kichenside and A. Williams, *British Railway Signalling* (1963), a useful short manual. R. D. Foster, *A Pictorial Record of LNWR Signalling* (1982) is much more than its title suggests: it is a careful history of the signalling devices, of all kinds, used by one great railway company.

The failure of safety precautions is reflected in accidents, on which a great deal has been written. The best general account is in L. T. C. Rolt, *Red for Danger* (4th edn., 1982). A. Trevena and K. Hoole, *Trains in Trouble* (1980-82), presents a series of photographs of accidents, carefully described. C. H. Hewison, *Locomotive Boiler Explosions* (1983), analyses some 140 accidents of that type occurring between 1815 and 1962.

The lives of the men who built and worked the railways, whether as individuals or in groups, have been studied a good deal, but there is still much more to be learnt about them. The leading men have, as we should expect, been treated most fully. A few figure in the *Dictionary of National Biography*. F. Boase, *Modern English Biography* (1892-1921), deals very briefly with many more. Some are treated in the *Dictionary of Business Biography*, now in course of publication. J. Marshall, *Biographical Dictionary of Railway Engineers* (1978), is useful but not always accurate.

The pioneer of full-length biography in this field was Samuel Smiles, with his *Life of George Stephenson* (5th edn. the best, 1858), extended to include George's son Robert in *Lives of the Engineers*, Vol. 3 (1862). Father and son have been well dealt with more recently by L. T. C. Rolt (1960) and M. Robbins (1966). On Brunel see lives by I. Brunel (1870) and L. T. C. Rolt (1957). There are also biographies of Locke, by N. W. Webster (1971); Vignoles, by K. H. Vignoles (1982), and Bidder, by E. F. Clark (1983). Daniel Gooch lacks a

biography; so does Hawkshaw, and T. E. Harrison of the North Eastern. Among the contractors only two have been adequately treated: Brassey (by A. Helps, 1870) and Firbank (by F. MacDermott, 1887). Railway managers have fared little better. There is a thorough study of Huish by T. R. Gourvish (1972). C. F. Klapper, *Sir Herbert Walker's Southern Railway* (1973) is also useful. A few wrote interesting accounts of their work themselves: Sir D. Gooch, *Memoirs and Diary*, ed. R. B. Wilson (1972); Sir G. Findlay, *The Working and Management of an English Railway* (6th edn., 1899), and G. P. Neele, *Railway Reminiscences* (1904) – both these dealing with the London & North Western Railway; E. S. Cox, *Locomotive Panorama* (1965-66); Sir John Elliot, *On and Off the Rails* (1982). But where are the studies that we need of Allport and Watkin, Gibb and Lord Ashfield?

There are not many accounts of the lives of railway men less eminent than these. D. Brooke, *The Railway Navvies* (1983), is admirable. Michael Reynolds wrote his *Engine-Driving Life* (1877) from first-hand knowledge. [H. A. Simmons,] *Ernest Struggles* (1879-80), is a serio-comic account of the career of a Great Western stationmaster. A. Williams, *Life in a Railway Factory* (1915), gives a realistic and unflattering account of employment in Swindon Works. Some sidelights on railway life and practices are thrown by W. Vincent, who sold newspapers at station bookstalls, in *Seen from the Railway Platform* (1919). N. Marlow, *Footplate and Signal Cabin* (1956), is valuable for its description of a signalman's work.

A good deal has now been published about labour relations on the railways. P. W. Kingsford, *Victorian Railwaymen* (1970), discusses them as far as 1870. The history of the chief trade unions has been written: of ASLEF by N. McKillop in *The Lighted Flame* (1950); of the NUR by P. S. Bagwell in *The Railwaymen* (1963-82), one of the longest and most careful studies yet devoted to any aspect of British railway history. F. McKenna, *The Railway Workers* (1980), presents a highly critical picture of railway employment. K. Hudson, *Working to Rule* (1970), deals interestingly with the codes of rules in Victorian railway workshops.

A vast quantity of material for the study of railway history is to be found in Acts of Parliament and in what are known as the *Parliamentary Papers*.

The *Index to Local and Personal Acts . . . 1801-1947* (1949) devotes over 150 pages to railways. There are copious indexes to the *Parliamentary Papers*; the British Library's set is the one most generally convenient for consultation.

Of the periodicals dealing with railways, many of the most valuable are now defunct: notably the *Railway Engineer*, the *Locomotive* and *Modern Transport*. Among the current monthlies the *Railway Magazine* has appeared continuously since 1897; *Railway World* and *Modern Railways* are newer. The *Transactions* and *Proceedings* of the Institutions of Civil and Mechanical Engineers, both extending over more than a century, are valuable – especially, to the student of history, for their obituaries. Of the surviving academic periodicals, the *Transactions of the Newcomen Society* (1920 onwards), the *Journal* of the Railway & Canal Historical Society (1955 onwards), and the *Journal of Transport History* (1953 onwards) may be mentioned.

Annuals include the *Railway Year Book*, issued from 1898 to 1932, when it was merged with the *Universal Directory of Railway Officials*. The *Railway Shareholders' Guides* and *Manuals* issued by Henry Tuck (1845-48) and George Bradshaw (1850-1922) furnish lists of directors and officers, together with statistical information. They are not always accurate, however, and must be used with some caution.

The published timetables are the only record we have of the passenger service that was afforded, or at least offered, to the traveller. *Bradshaw's Railway Guide* is the most important of them. It first appeared in a rudimentary form in 1839, and was then published monthly down to 1961. For its complex early history see C. E. Lee, *The Centenary of 'Bradshaw'* (1940). The *ABC Railway Guide* (published monthly since 1853) is valuable in showing the fares from London to provincial stations. The full working of a railway, including goods as well as passenger traffic, can be studied only in the companies' working timetables, which were never sold to the public and are therefore not held by the copyright libraries. The largest collections of them are at the Public Record Office and the Scottish Record Office; those for the English and Welsh railways are woefully incomplete.

Maps

Two kinds of maps are constantly needed for the study of railways: general topographical maps and specialised railway maps, such as those published by the Railway Clearing House.

General maps are valuable precisely because they are not devoted primarily to railways, treating them as one element in the topography of the country as a whole. They show, by means of shading or contours, the hills and valleys the railways had to scale or avoid. They indicate the physical size of communities and the rival means of transport – roads, rivers, canals, airfields. The most useful of these maps are those issued by the Ordnance Survey to the scale of one inch to the mile, first published from 1805 to 1873. The 97 sheets covering England and Wales were reproduced from later printings in 1968-70, with valuable accompanying notes by J. B. Harley. The 'Landranger' series issued by the Ordnance Survey today (scale 1:50,000) is still derived from these maps, with continual modernisation.

Among specialist railway maps those of Zachary Macaulay and John Airey are the most valuable – the latter coming to be published by the Railway Clearing House; see D. Garnett's article on them in the Railway & Canal Historical Society's *Journal*, Vol. 5 (1959). The Railway Clearing House also issued its *Junction Diagrams*, which show the ownership of railways at their complicated meeting-points. The edition of 1915 has been reprinted. For gradient profiles of lines see *Gradients of the British Main-Line Railways* (1947).

Two atlases currently available are useful: *British Railways Pre-Grouping Atlas and Gazetteer* (revised edn., 1976) and S. K. Baker, *Rail Atlas of Great Britain and Ireland* (4th edn., 1984), a well-designed presentation of the system as it is today.

J. B. Harley offers a general account of railway maps in his *Maps for the Local Historian* (1972), pp. 48-50.

Museums

Museums present another useful source of knowledge for railways, immensely enlarged in the course of the last 25 years. Before 1961 there were only three in Britain displaying any considerable collections of railway material: the Science Museum in South Kensington, London; the Royal Scottish Museum at Edinburgh, and the Railway Museum at York, established by the London & North Eastern Railway, and opened to the public in 1928. The British Transport Commission set up a Museum of British Transport at Clapham in London in 1961, followed by the Great Western Railway Museum at Swindon in 1962. The railway collection in the museum at Clapham, which formed the largest part of it, was later removed to York. This, with the collection in the York Museum of 1928, formed the basis of the National Railway Museum, opened in 1975: a richer and more wide-ranging railway museum than any other in the world. The Glasgow Museum of Transport is, in some respects, a national collection for Scotland.

The other railway museums in Britain, large and small, are far too numerous to be given here. They are listed in two annual publications: *Railways Restored* (Ian Allan) and *Museums and Art Galleries in Great Britain and Ireland* (British Leisure Publications).

For a general comparative survey of some of these museums see my *Transport Museums in Britain and Western Europe* (1970).

Collections of photographs are held by many museums, as well as some libraries and record offices. A considerable number relating to railways are to be found in institutions not specifically devoted to the subject: at Leicester, Whitby, Glasgow and Aberdeen, for example. See J. Wall, *Directory of British Photographic Collections* (1977).

ACKNOWLEDGEMENTS AND PICTURE CREDITS

The author and editors are indebted to Kevin Baverstock, for the maps on pp. 21, 58, 64-65, 105, 163, 212-13; to Valerie Chandler, B.A., A.L.A.A., for the Index; also to Mike Brown, Kathy Eason, Franky Eynon, Karin B. Hills and Lindsey Russell. The source for the map on p. 21 is R. S. Lambert, *The Railway King* (1934), p. 238, used by kind permission of George Allen & Unwin Ltd. The source for the gradient chart on p. 164 is J. Marshall, *The Lancashire & Yorkshire Railway*, Vol. 1 (David & Charles, 1969) and for that on p. 214 it is *Gradients of the British Mainline Railways* (Railway Publishing Co., 1947).

Sources for pictures in this book are listed in order from the top left corner to the bottom right corner of every page.

Jacket designed by Bob Hook and Ivor Claydon. Front cover painting – Peter Owen Jones. Back cover photographs (anti-clockwise from top centre) – Millbrook House; Sheldrake Press; Millbrook House; Anthony Lambert; Peter E. Baughan collection; Millbrook House. First endpaper – Aerofilms Limited. Last endpaper – Anthony Brown. Title page – R. C. Riley. 4-5 – courtesy of the National Railway Museum, York. 7 – © the National Railway Museum, York, courtesy of R. C. Riley; Leicestershire Museums, Art Galleries and Records Service.

8-9 – H. G. W. Household. 10, 11 – Trustees of the Science Museum. 12 – courtesy of the National Railway Museum, York. 13 – Ironbridge Gorge Museum Trust: Elton Collection. 15 – courtesy of the National Railway Museum, York. 16 – courtesy of the National Railway Museum, York; Ironbridge Gorge Museum Trust: Elton Collection. 17 – Young and Co.'s Brewery, Wandsworth; Julia Elton and Frank Newby Collection. 18 – Julia Elton and Frank Newby Collection; Darlington Borough Council. 19 – Trustees of the Science Museum. 23 – all *House of Commons Paper No 419*, 1845. 25 – Francis Whishaw *The Railways of Great Britain and Ireland*, 1842; H. G. W. Household collection. 28 – John R. Hume collection. 29 – R. Anderson, British Rail. 30 – Royal Institution of Cornwall, Truro. 31 – National Museum of Wales. 32 – Leicestershire Museums, Art Galleries and Records Services: Newton Collection. 33 – courtesy of the National Railway Museum, York. 34 – Peter E. Baughan; V. Cummings, by courtesy of Philip J. Kelley. 35 – both London Regional Transport. 36 – R. C. Riley collection. 37 – T. A. Barry collection, courtesy of Peter E.

Baughan. 38 – Peter E. Baughan. 39 – both R. C. Riley collection. 40 – courtesy of the National Railway Museum. 41 – courtesy of the National Railway Museum, York. 42 – courtesy of the National Railway Museum, York. 43 – Imperial War Museum. 45 – R. C. Riley. 47 – National Union of Railwaymen. 48 – R. C. Riley collection. 49 – courtesy of the National Railway Museum, York; National Maritime Museum, London. 50 – C. C. B. Herbert, R. C. Riley collection. 51 – National Museum of Wales. 52 – both London Regional Transport. 54 – Gordon Buck. 56 – R. C. Riley. 60 – M. Pope. 61 – Peter E. Baughan. 62 – Tyne and Wear Transport. 63 – M. Pope.

64 – Philip J. Kelley; Peter E. Baughan. 66 – H. G. W. Household; Peter E. Baughan. 67, 68, 69, 70, 71 – all Peter E. Baughan.

72-73 – Leicestershire Museums, Art Galleries and Records Service. 76 – Trustees of the Science Museum. 77 – D. W. Winkworth. 78 – courtesy of the National Railway Museum, York. 79 – R. A. Read collection, courtesy of J. L. Stevenson. 80 – Leicestershire Museums, Art Galleries and Records Service: Newton Collection; R. C. Riley. 82 – H. B. Oliver collection, National Railway Museum, York, courtesy of R. C. Riley. 83 – courtesy of the National Railway Museum, York. 84 – Newcastle-upon-Tyne City Libraries; W. Humber, *Record of the Progress of Modern Engineering*, 1864. 85 – Leicestershire Museums, Art Galleries and Records Service: Newton Collection. 87 – National Museum of Wales; Leicestershire Museums, Art Galleries and Records Service. 88, 90 – courtesy of the National Railway Museum, York. 91 – by permission of the Curator of the Museum of Welsh Antiquities, University College of North Wales, Bangor. 92 – Illustrated London News Picture Library; British Rail. 93 – Glasgow Museums and Art Galleries; Ironbridge Gorge Museum Trust: Elton Collection. 94-95 – Ironbridge Gorge Museum Trust: Elton Collection; Anon., *The South Devon Atmospheric Railway from the working plans and sections with sketches on either side of the line*, 1846, reproduced by kind permission of the Institution of Civil Engineers, photograph by David Trace. 96 – H. G. W. Household collection. 98 – Illustrated London News Picture Library. 99 – courtesy of the National Railway Museum, York; Philip J. Kelley. 100 – Gordon Buck; Francis Whishaw, *The Railways of Great Britain and Ireland*, 1842. 101 – Leicestershire Museums, Art Galleries and Records Service; E. T. MacDermot, *History of the Great Western Railway*, 1927-31. 103 – both British Rail.

104 – M. Pope. 106 – Mortimer Local History Society; George Measom, *The Official Illustrated Guide to the London and South-Western Railway*. 107, 108 – Peter E. Baughan. 109 – Peter E. Baughan; R. C. Riley. 110 – © the National Railway Museum, York; R. C. Riley. 111 – both British Rail. 112-113 – R. C. Riley. 113 – F. E. Box collection, the National Railway Museum, York, courtesy of R. C. Riley.

114-15 – courtesy of the National Railway Museum, York. 117 – Trustees of the British Museum. 118 – Peter E. Baughan. 120 – British Rail. 121 – British Architectural Library, R.I.B.A., London. 122 – E. T. MacDermot, *History of the Great Western Railway*, 1927-31. 123, 124 – courtesy of the National Railway Museum, York. 125 – Ronald A. Chapman. 126 – courtesy of the National Railway Museum, York. 128 – John R. Hume; courtesy of the National Railway Museum, York. 130 – Leicestershire Museums, Art Galleries and Records Service: Newton Collection; London Regional Transport. 131 – courtesy of the National Railway Museum, York; British Rail.

132-33 – Ivo Peters, courtesy of R. C. Riley. 135 – F. W. Simms, *Public Works of Great Britain*, 1846, reproduced by courtesy of the Institution of Civil Engineers Library, photograph by David Trace. 136 – Trustees of the Science Museum; © the National Railway Museum, York. 139 – courtesy of the National Railway Museum, York, © the National Railway Museum, York. 141 – courtesy of the National Railway Museum, York. 142 – both M. Pope. 144 – courtesy of the National Railway Museum, York, photograph by J. Russell-Smith. 145 – Peter E. Baughan; M. Pope. 146 – H. G. W. Household; Peter E. Baughan. 147 – both R. C. Riley. 148, 150 – M. Pope. 151 – R. C. Riley collection. 153 – National Museum of Wales. 154 – Philip J. Kelley. 156 – Glasgow Museums and Art Galleries. 159 – R. C. Riley collection; B. Watkins. 161 – Peter E. Baughan.

162, 164 – R. Anderson, British Rail. 165 – Ironbridge Gorge Museum Trust: Elton Collection. 166, 167 – all R. Anderson, British Rail. 168 – © the National Railway Museum, York; courtesy of the National Railway Museum, York. 169, 170 – Gordon Biddle. 171 – West Yorkshire Passenger Transport; R. Anderson, British Rail.

172-73 – courtesy of the National Railway Museum, York. 175 – © the National Railway Museum, York. 176 – The Royal Commission on the Ancient and Historical Monuments of England, courtesy of R. C. Riley. 177 – courtesy of the National Railway Museum, York. 178 – *Cumberland News*; © the National Railway Museum, York. 179 – © the National Railway Museum, York. 181 – R. C. Riley collection. 183 – Dr I. A. Glen. 185 – Beamish North of England Open Air Museum. 186 – Trustees of the Science Museum. 187 – D. K. Clark, *Railway Machinery*, 1855, reproduced by kind permission of the Institution of Civil Engineers Library; J. B. Hodgson. 188 – British Rail. 189 – R. C. Riley; British Rail.

190-91 – courtesy of the National Railway Museum, York. 192 – Francis Whishaw, *The Railways of Great Britain and Ireland*, 1842. 193, 194 – courtesy of the National Railway Museum, York. 195 – courtesy of *Punch*. 197 – Gordon Biddle. 198 – Philip J. Kelley. 199, 201 – Peter E. Baughan. 202, 203 – Gordon Biddle. 204 – Gordon Buck; © the National Railway Museum, York. 206 – courtesy of the National Railway Museum, York; British Rail. 208 – courtesy of the National Railway Museum, York. 209 – G. P. Neele, *Railway Reminiscences*, 1904. 210 – Illustrated London News Picture Library; © the National Railway Museum, York.

213 – British Rail. 214 – both John R. Hume collection. 215 – D. W. Winkworth; Graham Collection, Mitchell Library, Glasgow, courtesy of John R. Hume. 216 – W. S. Sellar; T. H. Noble. 217 – both T. H. Noble. 218 – J. L. Stevenson. 219 – J. T. Ormiston; W. S. Sellar. 220 – J. L. Stevenson. 221 – British Rail.

222-23 – R. C. Riley collection. 224 – © the National Railway Museum, York. 226 – all tickets © the National Railway Museum, York. 227 – Bass Museum of Brewing, Burton-on-Trent; all tickets © the National Railway Museum, York. 229 – Gordon Biddle. 230 – M. Pope. 231 – R. C. Riley. 232 – J. T. Ormiston; British Rail. 235 – R. C. Riley; © the National Railway Museum, York. 236 – Wooster & Sons, Harrow. 237 – Post Office © reserved; Sheldrake Press. 238 – The Royal Commission on the Ancient and Historical Monuments of Scotland. 239 – G. A. Sala, *Twice Round the Clock*.

INDEX